"I am grateful that Jerry Bridges and B.. .... invested them-selves in considering the substitutionary atonement of Christ, for as they have shown, the cross brings a timely and unparalleled message of costly love and forgiveness. Their work is a thorough examination of this rich truth in the Scriptures, and you will be richer for their biblical insights."

—Ravi Zacharias, author and speaker

"The next time I am asked for my top-ten reading list, this will be included! Clear and comprehensive, it leaves the reader in no doubt that this 'great exchange' is not only the heart of biblical theology but also the pivotal event of human history."

—Alistair Begg, senior pastor, Parkside Church, Cleveland, Ohio

"In this timely book, men who have taught us so much about God's transforming grace now marshal their resources to defend and define the glorious blessings of Christ's atonement that exchanges our sin for his righteousness. No truth is more important; no book more needed."

—Bryan Chapell, president, Covenant Theological Seminary

"The gospel announces a great exchange: the innocent God-Man assum-ing our debt as we inherit his righteousness. Those who love to hear that story will love to read this book and will be filled with fresh enthusiasm to share it with others."

—Michael Horton, J. G. Machen professor of theology,
Westminster Seminary California

"All who read this book will be blessed and better informed."

—Alan Andrews, president, U.S. Navigators

"I commend this volume to everyone who wants to understand more fully the nature of the atonement as taught by the apostles."

—Timothy George, founding dean, Beeson Divinity School;
senior editor, *Christianity Today*

"All too often in our contemporary culture and, sadly, even in our con-temporary church, we walk by the cross and offer only a passing glance. There is nourishment for the mind and the heart in the pages of *The Great Exchange*, because the subject is so profound and our need is so great for a long look and a deep drink."

—Stephen B. Kellough, chaplain, Wheaton College

The Great
Exchange

The Great Exchange

My Sin for His Righteousness

An Exposition of the Atonement of Jesus Christ
Patterned after *The Apostles' Doctrine of the Atonement*
by George Smeaton

Jerry Bridges
and Bob Bevington

CROSSWAY BOOKS

WHEATON, ILLINOIS

The Great Exchange: My Sin for His Righteousness
Copyright © 2007 by Jerry Bridges and Robert C. Bevington
Published by Crossway Books
    a publishing ministry of Good News Publishers
    1300 Crescent Street
    Wheaton, Illinois 60187

Cover design: Josh Dennis
First printing 2007
Printed in the United States of America

Library of Congress Cataloging-in-Publication Data

Bridges, Jerry.
    The Great Exchange: My Sin for His Righteousness / Jerry Bridges and Robert C. Bevington.
        p. cm.
    Includes bibliographical references and index.
    ISBN 978-1-58134-927-6 (tpb)
       1. Atonement—Biblical teaching. 2. Bible. N.T.—Theology. I. Bevington, Bob, 1956- II. Title.

BS2545.A8B75 2007
232'.3—dc22

                            2007002653

DP		17	16	15	14	13	12	11	10	09	08	07
15	14	13	12	11	10	9	8	7	6	5	4	3	2	1

The Cross—where the God-man,
Jesus Christ, traded places with the sinners he redeemed,
exchanging his perfect righteousness
for their sin, condemnation, and death.

"For our sake he made him to be sin who knew no sin,
so that in him we might become
the righteousness of God."
—2 Corinthians 5:21

Contents

Foreword

It is a great privilege and pleasure to have the opportunity to introduce and commend this important book. It is written by two authors who have something of the spirit of the men of Issachar in Old Testament days, who "had understanding of the times, to know what . . . to do" (1 Chron. 12:32), for *The Great Exchange* addresses one of the greatest weaknesses of the contemporary evangelical church—a failure to be centered on the center of the gospel.

Perhaps a little history will help clarify what I mean.

Sometime on October 31, 1517, in Wittenberg, Germany, a thirty-three-year-old monk of the Augustinian Order took a small mallet from his cassock, found a nail, and hammered into place some sheets of paper on which he had written, in as legible Latin as he could write, almost one hundred statements about the Christian gospel. It was his way of provoking discussion on topics he was prepared to discuss and, if need be, to debate in public. He could have had no expectation that these sheets of paper would almost overnight shake sixteenth-century Europe to its foundations and impact the structures of Western society for centuries to come. But he himself was in the process of discovering the power of the gospel to save and transform people's lives, and he understood that at the heart of the gospel message stood the cross.

The monk's name was, of course, Martin Luther. The sheets of paper he posted came to be known publicly as the Ninety-five Theses. Among the last of them were these two statements:

> Away, then, with all those prophets who say to the people of Christ, "Peace, peace," and there is no peace! (Thesis 92)
> Blessed be all those prophets who say to the people of Christ, "Cross, cross," and there is no cross! (Thesis 93)

Luther meant that any gospel that does not focus on the death of Christ and its true significance, and any teaching on Christianity that does not emphasize a life of cross bearing cannot be the biblical gospel nor produce a Christ-honoring life. But when the cross is preached, and when a cross-centered life is lived, true joy and peace are known. At the heart of this gospel, Luther believed, lies the great and wonderful exchange that Christ has made for us on the cross. There Christ exchanged his righteousness for our sin, so that through faith we might exchange our sin for his righteousness (2 Cor. 5:21). Luther understood what Paul meant when he said that of first importance in the message of the gospel is this: "Christ died for our sins in accordance with the Scriptures" (1 Cor. 15:3). Ever since, evangelical Christians—gospel people—have believed, taught, preached, lived, died—and, yes, written books—in this conviction.

The world into which Luther spoke was in many ways different from ours. We have come far since then in science, in technology, in medicine, and a in thousand other things. But in the Western world at least, in one sphere we are in danger—perhaps surprisingly—of readopting patterns of life that bear an uncanny resemblance to those which Luther addressed. That sphere is to be found in the Christian church.

How so? The church of the Middle Ages was marked by several obvious characteristics. There was a strong emphasis on influence and power. One index of this was the way in which church leaders sought—and gained—social and political leverage and enjoyed having a voice at the table of the affairs of this world. Another was the rise of what we call "megachurches" (which they called "cathedrals"). Here well-known and influential pastors (whom they called "bishops") exercised great influence in their society. The model to which young ministers were encouraged to aspire was not faithfulness to the gospel, but success. In these churches the "quality of worship" was thought to be outstanding (stunning acoustics, magnificent musical performance beyond the ordinary). It was also a world where the image dominated the Word, where people—so it was thought—would not listen to preaching, and so drama became the order of the day, whether in the colorful liturgy of the services or in the famed medieval mystery plays. And, to some degree, if one wanted health, wealth, and (especially eternal) happiness, these, too, the church could provide, for it had men who possessed charismatic gifts. Indeed, from the extraordinary power in their hands one could receive forgiveness, and from them, or at least from objects they possessed, one could seek even physical healing.

But something was sadly absent from all this, as Luther, who was once part of the whole system well knew. The true message of the cross was lacking, and its true meaning obscured. Of course, the church would have argued that it was there—after all, even the buildings were shaped in the form of a cross, not to mention the crosses that were worn or carried by its ministers. But the cross was not the message that was being preached; the way of the cross—a cross-centered and cross-driven life—was not seen as the very epicenter of Christianity.

It is difficult to avoid seeing some unnerving parallels to the evangelical church in our own society: megachurches, desire for political influence, ministers as gurus, charismatic gift-givers, an emphasis on worship as performance, drama as necessary for a nonverbal culture, and one other thing—a relative silence about the cross and its true meaning.

A moment's reflection is likely to confirm that this is true. What have been the themes of the seminars, conferences, books, sermons, classes, DVDs, CDs, and songs that we have attended, heard, seen, read, and talked about recently? How many—what percentage of

them—have been cross-centered? Of the titles of Christian books you
have read, or of which you know, how many highlight the cross?

The answer to that question should probably alarm us.

More than thirty years ago in his landmark book *Knowing God*,
J. I. Packer noted, "If you want to judge how well a person understands Christianity, find out how much he makes of the thought
of being God's child, and having God as his Father."[1] I would add
today: "If you want to judge how well a person understands the
gospel, ask him what he makes of the death of Christ, and what the
message of the cross is." The real Christian answers that while the
message of the cross is foolishness to some and a stumbling block
to others, to Christians it is the saving wisdom and power of God
(1 Cor. 1:18–24). The confession of the real Christian is, "Far be
it from me to boast except in the cross of our Lord Jesus Christ,
by which the world has been crucified to me, and I to the world"
(Gal. 6:14).

We need to understand that the cross stands at the center and
heart of the gospel. Without it there is no gospel. That is why the
message of this book is potentially so important for us and for our
Christian living, and for the shape, style, and ethos of our church
life. It is a book about what Jesus Christ accomplished on the cross.
It takes us to the heart of the gospel.

I noted that this book has two authors. Perhaps it would be
better to say that it is a book with two builders and one architect.
For behind it, as a kind of architectural design, lies the work of a
wonderful, but now-little-known, nineteenth-century Scottish author
and theologian, George Smeaton. In 1868 and 1870 he published
two magnificent volumes, totaling almost one thousand pages, in
which he carefully expounded all of the New Testament passages on
the atonement. They bore the titles *Christ's Doctrine of the Atonement* and *The Apostles' Doctrine of the Atonement*.[2]

Smeaton was an outstanding scholar with a brilliant mind and
a deep love for Christ. My own conviction is that these two great
volumes should regularly be in the hands of every person who
teaches and preaches the gospel of Christ. They are treasure troves.

But they are also lengthy. Now, out of a shared deep appreciation for the good that Smeaton's exposition has done for them personally, Jerry Bridges and Bob Bevington have taken the architectural design he employed for the second of these volumes, *The Apostles' Doctrine of the Atonement*, and have built their exposition of the gospel from the same biblical materials Smeaton first used.

The Great Exchange is the wonderful result. It meets the standard set by Lord Bacon's famous essay "Of Studies": "Some books are to be tasted, others to be swallowed, and some few to be chewed and digested." Here is spiritual food to be chewed and digested. It will do you good. And it may well make you sing,

> Bearing shame and scoffing rude,
> In my place, condemned he stood;
> Sealed my pardon with his blood:
> Hallelujah! What a Savior![3]

I, for one, hope it does.

Sinclair B. Ferguson
First Presbyterian Church
Columbia, South Carolina

Preface

This book is first and foremost about the gospel, the good news that Jesus Christ is the sinless sin bearer of all who are united to him by faith. But this raises two questions: (1) What does it mean that Jesus is our sinless sin bearer? And (2) What does it mean to become united to him by faith? Our purpose in this book is to answer these all-important questions by unpacking the key verse of our book—"For our sake he made him to be sin who knew no sin, so that in him we might become the righteousness of God" (2 Cor. 5:21)—within the context of the rest of Scripture.

The Great Exchange, in which God caused our sin to be traded for Christ's righteousness, is crystallized and summed up in 2 Corinthians 5:21. The Great Exchange and the related expression *substitutionary atonement* represent the banners under which we will examine many passages of Scripture. These two banners will lead us deep into the historical gospel as the sole source and substance of the Christian faith.

Why write a book on this subject? Why now? The gospel is a timeless message and therefore extremely relevant for our day and age. But it is not only relevant; it is essential, because it is the only solution ever offered by God for the perpetual sin dilemma of mankind. Throughout history, the message of the Bible has not changed. The original languages are still the original languages, and the ancient manuscripts still declare this same message.

14

Yet, in recent times it has become apparent that some in the church have drifted away from the historical gospel and ventured to redefine sin and redemption and even the meaning of the cross. Some have done this in a sincere attempt to make the gospel message more acceptable to today's culture. Others have attempted to usher in an age of greater authenticity and depth of commitment. But regardless of sincerity, no attempt to reform the church can succeed if it departs in any way from the centrality of the message that our sinless Christ actually died on a real cross as the sin bearer for those who are united to Christ by faith in his substitutionary sacrifice and righteousness.

The message of the cross—the historical gospel of the God-man, Jesus Christ, who personally visited the earth, which was created through him, with the mission of redeeming his own people with his own infinitely precious, bloody, substitutionary death—has been and must remain the solitary basis and the singular foundation of the Christian faith and worldview.

This gospel—that Christ died for our sins according to the Scriptures—is rooted in pre-creation, revealed in ancient prophecy, and fulfilled in real, time-space, dimensional history. It is a message that is alive, and it is the only message that imparts life. It is a message that simply will not budge in order to morph into the paradigms of seekers or culture. It consists of its own unchangeable paradigm. Yes, it is absolutist; if there is one thing in the universe that deserves to be, it is the gospel. Its immutability is woven into the fabric of authentic Christianity.

We do recognize, however, that the gospel is like an infinitely precious diamond in which there are multiple facets reflecting and refracting the brilliance of the message in various ways. But all facets of the gospel are necessarily connected to the substance of the gospel—the message of substitutionary atonement. The substance of the gospel and all its facets emanate from and draw attention to the cross, the site of the Great Exchange, where the light of the knowledge of the glory of God is seen by redeemed sinners in the face of Christ crucified (2 Cor. 4:6; 1 Cor. 2:2). The facets, while never ceasing to be connected to the substance, supply wonderful truths that help us more fully apply the meaning of Christ's great atonement. Here are a few:

1) In the gospel, our worldview is radically changed. We refer to this facet as the gospel of the kingdom. It means that our definitions of health, wealth, security, comfort, and prosperity are turned upside down compared to the world's view. It means we embrace the paradoxes of Christ's teachings—to live is to die, to be great is to be a servant of all, and to be rich is to give sacrificially. All our values change, as do our views on community, poverty, gender, racism, orphans and widows, and the sick and the weak. But none of this can happen authentically apart from the cross, where our sin was exchanged for his righteousness.

2) In the gospel, Jesus provides us with the perfect example of how to live. When we need insight and direction, we can ask, "What would Jesus do?" We search the Scriptures to see how he handled situations. We look for the attitudes he conveyed and the way he communicated. But all of his doing and saying was connected to his mission in which he set his face like a flint to provide a perfect, sinless sacrifice. And were it not for the fact that his mission was successfully completed at the cross, we would never have the ability to apply the example of Jesus to our lives.

3) In the gospel, Satan was dethroned, and we were set free from his dominion. Sin and Satan and death no longer reign over us. We are free for the process of renewal, to be transformed into the image of the Son. But our freedom is not a stand-alone feature of the gospel; it is linked to the cross, where we are united into Christ in his obedient life, death to sin, and glorious resurrection. And the outward evidence of our transformation should primarily serve to deflect the eyes of observers to the cross that made our freedom possible.

4) In the gospel, we are provided with the Holy Spirit who empowers us to grow, to be transformed, and to preach and serve. The Holy Spirit provides gifts of inward and outward fruit bearing. The gospel would not be complete without the role of the Holy Spirit, but the Holy Spirit is not the complete gospel. The Holy Spirit came because Christ died for our sins as our substitute.

So we conclude that our goal is to declare the whole counsel of God in the gospel and to show how every aspect can be traced back to its substance in the substitutionary atonement. Our book is not about us; it is not our story. We aim to disappear now and display Christ and him crucified as the treasure of all time. We pray that you, too, will become self-forgetful as you turn these pages, because what you see here is God in Christ doing something that is truly larger than life, namely, providing an all-sufficient substitutionary atonement for us by his perfect, obedient life in the flesh and his perfect sacrificial death in the flesh. Herein you will find the meaning of the Great Exchange, the monumental reality that in the gospel: "For our sake [God] made [Christ] to be sin who knew no sin, so that in [Christ] we might become the righteousness of God" (2 Cor. 5:21).

This book is patterned after a nineteenth-century classic, *The Apostles' Doctrine of the Atonement*,[1] written by Scottish theologian George Smeaton. While our book is neither an abridgment nor a modernization, it is nevertheless designed to make the brilliance and depth of Smeaton's work accessible to mainstream readers while faithfully and accurately representing the intent of his original exposition. We acknowledge that we stand on the shoulders of others in addition to George Smeaton. We especially acknowledge our indebtedness to John Piper. Readers of Dr. Piper will recognize some of his well-known expressions and concepts in our text.

We also want to thank Greg Plitt for his invaluable assistance with the earlier drafts of the manuscript. Thanks also to Allan Fisher, senior vice president of book publishing at Crossway, and to Lydia Brownback for her outstanding editorial work. And also thanks to the number of friends who read portions of the original draft for their encouragement and suggestions. Finally, we invite you to visit **www.thegreatexchangebook.com,** where you will find a free study guide and other tools for deepening your personal or your group's appreciation of the wondrous cross.

Introduction

When the apostle Paul wanted to remind the Corinthian church of the gospel, he wrote, "For I delivered to you as of first importance what I also received: that Christ died for our sins in accordance with the Scriptures" (1 Cor. 15:3).

Christ died for our sins. The gospel is the solution to our sin problem. So, before we can understand and appreciate the gospel, we need to understand the doctrine of sin. The basis for this understanding takes us back to the garden of Eden, where, from the moment Adam ate of the forbidden fruit (Gen. 3:6), sin became humanity's overarching problem. Adam, by God's appointment, stood as the representative of the entire human race so that his guilt became our guilt, and his resulting sinful nature was passed on to all of us. Paul speaks of this representative nature of Adam's sin and its consequences when he states:

> Therefore, just as sin came into the world through one man, and death through sin, and so death spread to all men because all sinned. . . . Therefore, as one trespass led to condemnation for all men, so one act of righteousness leads to justification and life for all men. For as by the one man's disobedience the many were made sinners, so by the one man's obedience the many will be made righteous. (Rom. 5:12, 18–19)

Thus, we were born sinners. In fact, David wrote that we were sinners even from the time of conception in our mother's womb

(Ps. 51:5). And because we were born sinners, committing our own personal sins serves to compound our condition on a daily basis.

What is sin? It is often described as "missing the mark"—that is, failure to live up to the rigorous standard of God's holy law. But the Bible makes it clear that it is much more than that. In Leviticus 16:21, sin is described as *transgression*; literally, as rebellion against authority. In the prophet Nathan's confrontation of David over his sins of adultery and murder, Nathan describes sin as a *despising* of both God's Word and God himself (2 Sam. 12:9–10). And in Numbers 15:30–31, Moses characterizes sinners as acting "with a high hand," meaning defiantly. Therefore, we can conclude that sin is a rebellion against God's sovereign authority, a despising of his Word and his person, and even a defiance of God himself. It is no wonder Paul wrote that because of our sin, we were by nature objects of God's wrath (Eph. 2:3).

We would like to think that, as believers, such descriptions of sin no longer apply to us. We look at the gross and obvious sins of society around us, and we tend to define sin in terms of those actions. We fail to see that our anxiety, our discontentment, our ingratitude toward God, our pride and selfishness, our critical and judgmental attitudes toward others, our gossip, our unkind words to or about others, our preoccupation with the things of this life, and a whole host of other subtle sins are an expression of rebellion against God and a despising of his Word and person.

The truth is that even the most mature believers continue to sin in thought, word, deed, and especially in motive. We continually experience the inward spiritual guerilla warfare Paul describes when he states, "For the desires of the flesh are against the Spirit, and the desires of the Spirit are against the flesh, for these are opposed to each other, to keep you from doing the things you want to do" (Gal. 5:17). That is why it was necessary for the apostle Peter to exhort us to "abstain from the passions of the flesh, which wage war against your soul" (1 Pet. 2:11).

This, then, is the doctrine of sin. Because of Adam's sin as representative of the entire human race, we are born with a sinful nature and as objects of God's wrath. We then aggravate our condition before God with our personal sins, whether they be the gross, obvious sins, or the subtle sins we too often tolerate in ourselves and in our Christian circles. And it is in view of this truth of the doctrine of sin that we should understand Paul's words, "Christ died for our sins." It is with this understanding of the nature and reality of sin that we should understand the words of the angel to Joseph, "You shall call his name Jesus, for he will save his people from their sins" (Matt. 1:21).

Christ died for our sins. This phrase suggests two ideas—substitution and sacrifice. Christ died in our place as our substitute and representative. Just as God appointed Adam to act as representative of all humanity, so he appointed Jesus Christ to act on behalf of all who trust in him. There is no better Scripture to see the idea of substitution than this one:

> Surely *he* has borne *our* griefs
>   and carried *our* sorrows;
> yet we esteemed him stricken,
>   smitten by God, and afflicted.
> But *he* was wounded for *our* transgressions;
>   *he* was crushed for *our* iniquities;
> upon *him* was the chastisement that brought *us* peace,
>   and with *his* stripes *we* are healed.
> All we like sheep have gone astray;
>   we have turned every one to his own way;
> and the LORD has laid on *him*
>   the iniquity of *us* all. (Isa. 53:4–6)

Note the repeated contrast which the Spirit-inspired prophet draws between the words *he* and *our*, or *him* and *us*. Surely any unbiased reader cannot fail to see in the passage the idea that Jesus suffered as our substitute, bearing the punishment for sin that we deserve.

The second idea, sacrifice, is foreshadowed in the sacrificial system of the Old Testament era, especially in the sacrifices required on the annual Day of Atonement as described in Leviticus 16. On that day, the high priest would cast lots over two goats, one of which was to be killed, its blood carried into the Holy Place to be sprinkled over and in front of the mercy seat, thus symbolizing the propitiation of the wrath of God.

After performing this ritual, the high priest would emerge from the holy place and place his hands on the live goat and confess over it all the sins of the people, symbolically putting those sins on the head of the goat. Then the goat would be led away into the wilderness, signifying the removal of the people's sins from the presence of both God and the people. The result of Christ's death was foreshadowed by both goats. The sprinkled blood of the first goat pictured the death of Christ as propitiating or exhausting the cup of the wrath of God toward us because of our sin (Matt. 26:39; John 18:11). The sending away of the second goat pictured the result of Christ's death in removing our sins from us. As Psalm 103:12 says, "As far as the east is from the west, so far does he remove our transgressions from us."

Psalm 103:12, as well as other Old Testament word pictures such as "blotting out our transgressions" and "remembering sins no more" (Isa. 43:25) and casting "all our sins into the depths of the sea" (Mic. 7:19) speak of the forgiveness of our sins. This message of forgiveness of sin through the death of Christ was central to apostolic preaching. See, for example, Acts 2:38; 10:43; and 13:38, as well as Paul's words in Romans 4:7–8; Ephesians 1:7; and Colossians 2:13. And as the writer of Hebrews wrote, "Without the shedding of blood there is no forgiveness of sins" (Heb. 9:22). (In fact, for those who want to pursue further the nature and purpose of Christ's sacrifice, Hebrews 9 is a good place to start).

But forgiveness of our sins is not the ultimate purpose of Christ's death. As Paul says in Titus 2:14, "[Jesus Christ] gave himself for us to redeem us from all lawlessness and to purify for himself a people for his own possession who are zealous for good works." It was never God's intent that Jesus should die to pay the penalty for our sins so that we might continue to live in them. He died so that all who believe in him might become new creations (2 Cor. 5:17).

But that could not occur until after the sin that separated us from God had been dealt with through the substitutionary sacrifice of Christ on the cross.

The key word in Leviticus 16 is the word *atonement*. Animals were sacrificed to make atonement for sins. This, of course, was only a picture of the one great sacrifice of atonement that Christ would make, once for all time, to put away the sin of all who would ever trust in him. Atonement is defined as: "The satisfactory compensation made for an offense or injury, in which a price is paid on behalf of the offending party, resulting in their discharge from the obligation to pay the due penalty." Atonement allows for restoration of the previously disrupted relationship. Simply stated, atonement is the price paid to reconcile enemies.

In the biblical context, we have the following:

- *The offended party* is God—the holy and omnipotent sovereign.
- *The offense* is sin of any kind, as defined by the Bible.
- *The offending party* consists of sinners, that is, all humanity.
- *The penalty* is the full force of God's inconceivable eternal wrath.
- *The price paid* on behalf of sinners is the atoning death of Christ.

Because Christ made atonement for our sins by suffering in our place as our substitute, we speak of the *substitutionary atonement* of Christ. A similar expression used to sum up the work of Christ is *penal substitution*, meaning that as our substitute, Christ paid the penalty for our sins. These two terms have, to some degree, fallen out of fashion in today's evangelical world. But they are basic to our understanding of the gospel and so need to be restated and reaffirmed for twenty-first century readers. That is what we are seeking to do in this book.

Although *atonement* rarely appears as a stand-alone word in the New Testament, the concept of Christ's atonement and its application comprise the primary themes of the entire Bible—Old and New Testament alike. The passages included in this study contain synonyms of the word *atonement* or concepts related to atonement, such as: *the death of Christ, the blood of Christ, the cross, sacrifice, ransom, propitiation, redemption, mediator,* and *reconciliation.*

There are two features of Smeaton's book *The Apostles' Doctrine of the Atonement* that make it relevant and important to us today. First, he examines and expounds every passage of Scripture from Acts through Revelation that deals with the atonement. Because of Smeaton's design to address every passage dealing with the subject, the book is redundant in a wonderfully effectual manner—the reader keeps getting the same message from slightly different perspectives so as to enhance, embellish, and deepen his or her understanding of the gospel. And with that comes passion for the person of Christ and gratitude for his finished work on the cross.

Second, Smeaton provides excellent description and emphasis on the believer's union with Christ as the basis for our ability to enjoy the benefits of Christ's atoning work. Today, for example, some people ask how it can be just for God to punish an innocent man, Jesus, for the sins of other people. The answer, which is clearly taught in Scripture, is found in the believer's legal union with Christ; that is, because Christ was our representative in his life and death, it was just of God to punish him for our sins. As the prophet Isaiah said, "The LORD has laid on him the iniquity of us all" (Isa. 53:6).

Before Christ died for our sins, however, he lived a perfectly obedient life. He fully obeyed the moral will of God every second of his life. And just as our sins were charged to him so that he justly paid their penalty, so Christ's perfect obedience, which culminated in his obedience unto death on the cross, is credited to all who trust in him—once again because of our legal union with him. And it is Smeaton's grasp of this truth and his continual emphasis of it that makes his book so exciting. For example, he writes in this vein: "When Christ lived a perfect life, we believers lived a perfect life. And when Christ died on the cross, we believers died on the cross."

In other words, Christ didn't just live and die for us. Rather, we are so united to him by faith that God sees his perfect life as our life and his death as our death.

It is often said that the life of Jesus is to be imitated by his followers. This, of course, is the idea behind the popular question "What would Jesus do?" That we are to follow the example of Christ is indeed taught in the Scriptures (for example, see John 13:13–15 and 1 Pet. 2:21). The reality, though, is that our very best efforts at following his example are always imperfect and defiled by our sinful nature. By contrast, his obedience was always perfect and complete and never defiled. Therefore, we should always look first at what Jesus did *as our representative* before looking at him *as our example*. All our efforts toward spiritual growth should flow out of the realization of what he has already done to secure for us our perfect standing before God.

George Smeaton also authored a companion volume to *The Apostles' Doctrine of the Atonement* entitled *Christ's Doctrine of the Atonement*,[1] which examines similar Bible texts in the Gospels of Matthew, Mark, Luke, and John, and in which Christ personally explains the scope, nature, and outcome of his upcoming death on behalf of sinners. Smeaton examines how Jesus explains his death and resurrection as the guarantee that God indeed forgives those sinners who trust in his substitutionary death for the resolution of their personal sin dilemma. In these gospel accounts, Jesus offered insight into the *divine view* of the cross.

Whereas Christ spoke of his upcoming suffering and death for sin, the apostles offered the *completed view* of Christ's work of atonement since they spoke and wrote of it after the fact. The apostles refer to it as an eternally valid, historical, and central fact bursting with blood-bought blessings that abide now and forever. In their inspired works, they explore Old Testament Scriptures and relate them to the life and death of Christ to explain how his great atonement covers, colors, and shapes the lives of those who receive it and are thereby saved by it. In this book, we will focus on the apostles' view of the atonement.

This book, then, is about Christ's glorious work of atonement culminating at the cross. There are no stories inserted to illustrate points. There are no anecdotes added to entertain the reader. None of this is needed, because a rightly understood view of the cross as the treasure of all time can never be boring, trivial, or lacking in excitement. Our goal is to assist the reader in exulting in the unfathomable riches of Christ's atonement as contained in God's Word.

This book is for every Christian, regardless of one's level of spiritual maturity. Many believers view the gospel only as a message to be shared with unbelievers but not personally applicable to themselves anymore. We have learned from personal experience, as well as from the writings of some of the great writers of previous centuries, that we need the gospel as well. We need it to remind ourselves that our day-to-day standing with God is based on Christ's righteousness, not our performance. We need the gospel to motivate us to strive in our daily experience to be what we are in our standing before God. We need it to produce joy in our lives when we encounter the inevitable trials of living in a fallen and sin-cursed world.

It is our prayer, then, that God will be pleased to use this book to help many believers think afresh and more deeply of the gospel so that they may rejoice in the good news of the gospel of Christ's great atonement, and that, above all, Christ may be glorified.

Part One

CHRIST'S ATONEMENT: OVERVIEW AND CONTEXT

CHAPTER 1

The Unique Qualifications
of the Apostles

The word *apostle* means "representative," in the sense of one who is sent with the full authority of the sender. After Christ accomplished the great atonement on the cross, a radical transformation took place in the lives of the apostles. Prior to the resurrection, John and Peter shunned the idea of Christ's death whereas Paul looked on and applauded it (Acts 8:1). But once the eyes of these men were opened by Christ himself to the fact and meaning of the completed transaction and its saving effect, they were truly ready to live, suffer, and die for the message of the atonement, the gospel of Jesus Christ. But still, why should we listen to them?

We should listen because, made apostles by God, these men were uniquely qualified as divinely appointed messengers of the atonement in three ways: first, as eyewitnesses of the atoning events and personal instruction in the Scriptures given by the risen Lord; second, in their supernatural empowerment by the Holy Spirit; and third, in their unique and personal commissioning by the Lord himself.

For these reasons, the testimony of the apostles is of supreme value and worthy of our careful time and attention.

The Apostles: Eyewitnesses

That which was from the beginning, which we have heard, which we have seen with our eyes, which we looked upon and have touched with our hands, concerning the word of life—the life was made manifest, and we have seen it, and testify to it and proclaim to you the eternal life, which was with the Father and was made manifest to us—that which we have seen and heard we proclaim also to you, so that you too may have fellowship with us; and indeed our fellowship is with the Father and with his Son Jesus Christ. (1 John 1:1–3)

The apostles were eyewitnesses to Jesus alive, then dead, then alive again. As they followed Christ for three years on earth, they often heard his teaching on the atonement; it foreshadowed the sacrifice that was to come, but at the time they understood little of this message. After the resurrection of Christ, however, they saw *prophesied* atonement become *fulfilled* atonement; they saw promise become fact, anticipation become reality, and Old Testament give birth to New Testament. Where they had previously "regarded Christ according to the flesh" (2 Cor. 5:16), after the resurrection they gained a revolutionary new understanding of who Christ is and the purpose of his atoning work, based on their direct experience with him.

The lips of the resurrected Christ imparted fresh oral instruction to the apostles, uniquely equipping them for their mission. Christ took pains to explain everything necessary for them to possess the most accurate knowledge of the atonement—especially by revealing how the Old Testament Scriptures described and pointed to himself and to his atoning work. This is clearly seen in this important passage at the end of the Gospel of Luke:

"These are my words that I spoke to you while I was still with you, that *everything written about me in the Law of Moses and the Prophets and the Psalms must be fulfilled.*" Then he opened their minds to understand the Scriptures, and said to them, "Thus it is written, that the Christ should suffer and on the third day rise

from the dead, and that repentance and forgiveness of sins should
be proclaimed in his name to all nations, beginning from Jerusalem.
You are witnesses of these things." (Luke 24:44–48)

Notice the extent of Jesus' exposition: "The Law of Moses and
the Prophets and the Psalms." Jesus supplied the apostles with the
keys for understanding his atoning death from three major divisions
of Old Testament Scripture. The Law of Moses calls to mind the
animal sacrifices for sin and the institution of priests—both symbolic of Christ's atoning role as sacrifice and priest. The Prophets,
from Isaiah through Malachi, contain hundreds of prophecies of
the coming Messiah, which were fulfilled in the life, death, and
resurrection of Jesus Christ. The Psalms recall the phrases Christ
uttered as the suffering Messiah. The direct interpretation of these
passages by the risen Christ formed the basis and authority for the
apostles' interpretation. It provided the foundation for all that the
apostles subsequently taught and wrote.

With regard to the apostle Paul, even though Jesus did not personally instruct him prior to the cross as he had done with the other
apostles, Paul nevertheless learned the gospel directly from the risen
Christ. We can see this clearly in Galatians 1:12, where he states,
"For I did not receive it [instruction] from any man, nor was I taught
it, but I received it through a revelation of Jesus Christ."

Furthermore, Paul's personal encounter with the resurrected
Lord on the road to Damascus (Acts 9:3–9) and his experience of
being "caught up to the third heaven" (2 Cor. 12:1–13) constitute
firsthand experiences that qualify him to be counted among the
apostolic eyewitnesses.

The Apostles: Supernaturally Empowered by the Holy Spirit

Prior to his death, Jesus promised to send the great "remembrancer,"
the Holy Spirit, to give the apostles special empowerment to enable them to accurately recall all the Lord did and taught. This is
evident in John 14:26, where Jesus said, "But the Helper, the Holy
Spirit, whom the Father will send in my name, he will teach you

all things and bring to your *remembrance* all that I have said to you." The Gospel of John quotes Jesus a few chapters later declaring, "When the Spirit of truth comes, he will guide you into all the truth" (John 16:13a).

After his resurrection Jesus again assured the apostles that this promise of divine power would be fulfilled, saying "Behold, I am sending the promise of my Father upon you. But stay in the city until you are clothed with power from on high" (Luke 24:49). The Holy Spirit, with his infinite power capable of flawlessly evoking the past from the cache of human memory, resuscitated all the words and deeds of Jesus necessary to display his person and explain his atoning work. Furthermore, the Holy Spirit exerted supernatural influence on the human authors of the Bible so that they composed and recorded God's message to mankind without error. He fixed the words in the apostles' minds, mouths, and pens with precision and clarity for our benefit (2 Pet. 1:21). Therefore, we are not listening to the words of mere men, but to the words of God. It would behoove us to listen.

Uniquely and Personally Commissioned by Christ

Not only were the apostles eyewitnesses to the resurrection and later supernaturally empowered by the Holy Spirit, but they also were personally sanctioned by Jesus, who had said, "Whoever receives you receives me, and whoever receives me receives him who sent me" (Matt. 10:40). Clearly, the importance and authority of the apostles' writings as canonized in New Testament Scripture cannot be overstated. All they declared and wrote is divine revelation and no less true than if it had been personally spoken by Christ himself. To disregard apostolic writing is unthinkable and unwise, since Jesus personally and emphatically commissioned them.

Following the completion of the redemptive work of Christ, the apostles, in their teaching, preaching, and writing, put the great atonement in its proper place as the central article of Christianity. They proclaimed the work of the atonement finished for all time, never to require repetition (Heb. 7:27). It was left to the apostles, under the divine guidance of the Holy Spirit, to interpret, apply, and further develop Christ's teaching on all points, including the great doctrine of the atonement. Their role extended to defending the doctrine against the heresies that arose in many of the early churches, as well as those appearing right up to the present day.

Some have argued that in order to restore Christianity to its original simplicity, one should abide exclusively by the "red letter" words of Jesus. Others maintain that the apostles altered the truth of Christ's message. The church must be vigilant to mark and oppose such false teachings, because to disregard the apostles is, without a doubt, to disregard not only them, but also the one who chose, taught, commissioned, and sanctioned them. As Jesus said, "The one who hears you hears me, and the one who rejects you rejects me, and the one who rejects me rejects him who sent me" (Luke 10:16).

Thus, direct experience with Jesus combined with the supernatural empowerment of the Holy Spirit and the apostles' personal commissioning by Christ provide a threefold assurance of a full conformity between the teaching of Christ and the God-breathed writings of the apostles. The writings of the apostles can therefore be trusted as infallible and inerrant witnesses to the truth of Christ's great atonement; they should be regarded as equal in reliability and importance to the teachings of Christ.

It must have been that Jesus became increasingly more glorious to the Apostles as the reality of who He really was became more fully understood by them . . It is somewhat like this in our journey of faith as we grow in our understanding of the richness + depth of the Gospel, Christ becomes more glorious to us!

CHAPTER 2

Christ's Atonement:
The Apostles' Summary

Coming face-to-face with the resurrected Christ in the aftermath of the crucifixion, the apostles finally and clearly understood Jesus to be God incarnate, that is, God in the flesh. Jesus no doubt intended to impact these men with this truth when he declared to Thomas, "'Put your finger here, and see my hands; and put out your hand, and place it in my side. Do not disbelieve, but believe.' Thomas answered him, 'My Lord and my God!'" (John 20:27–28).

This new understanding—Jesus is God—filled the apostles with wonder and delight. It became one of the foundations for their testimony to the atoning work of Christ. Later in their inspired writings where they describe the Lord's work of redemption, the apostles always directly or implicitly ascribe to him a divine nature. For example, they speak of the Jews killing the Author of life (Acts 3:15) and of them crucifying the Lord of glory (1 Cor. 2:8). The writer of the book of Hebrews describes the Son who made purification for sins as "the radiance of the glory of God and the exact imprint of his nature" and showed that "he upholds the universe by the word of his power" (Heb. 1:3).

The deity of Christ in his atoning work is of paramount importance in understanding the gospel. In order for Jesus Christ to qualify as the atonement for the sins of the redeemed, he must be personally *perfect*—that is, holy, having lived a sinless life. In order to be perfect, Christ must be more than a mere man—he must be divine. God's chosen mediator, Jesus Christ, is himself fully God (John 1:1, 18) and thus uniquely qualified to complete the work of redemption.

However, because man sinned, man must bear the penalty of sin, so in addition to being fully God, the mediator must also be fully man in order to bear the sin of man as their representative. Also, the mediator must be a man since the mediating act of atoning for sin requires a sacrificial death (Lev. 17:11; Heb. 9:22), and it is impossible for God to die. The apostles affirm that the eternal Son of God, who exists outside of the realm of time and who created the universe (Heb. 1:2b; John 1:1–3), allowed, accepted, and welcomed an infinite reduction in stature in order to become the incarnate Son of Man. Perhaps this can be seen most clearly where Paul states:

> [Jesus Christ] who, though he was in the form of God, did not count equality with God a thing to be grasped, but made himself nothing, taking the form of a servant, being born in the likeness of men. And being found in human form, he humbled himself by becoming obedient to the point of death, even death on a cross. (Phil. 2:6–8)

Furthermore, the apostles explicitly assert that the incarnation took place in a single, historic person who became the *representative head* of the redeemed multitude who find their righteousness, justification, and sanctification in Christ as the Last Adam (Rom. 5:18–19). Paul writes, "Thus it is written, 'The first man Adam became a living being'; the last Adam became a life-giving spirit. . . . The first man was from the earth, a man of dust; the second man is from heaven'" (1 Cor. 15:45, 47). Both the first Adam and the Last Adam were men. But the Last Adam is a man who came from heaven. His incarnation, sinless life, and substitutionary death on the cross were inseparable steps toward accomplishing his unified purpose: conquering death and giving eternal life to those who are united to him by faith.

Jesus Christ is the God-man. He was "born of woman . . . to redeem man" (Gal. 4:4–5). He took on flesh and blood that "through death he might destroy the one who has the power of death, that is, the devil" (Heb. 2:14b). He "appeared . . . to destroy the works of the devil" (1 John 3:8b). And he "came into the world to save sinners" (1 Tim. 1:15b). Much more than merely a sinless man, the Son of God, Jesus Christ, embodies the union of the two natures, possessing all-sufficient value and validity. Jesus Christ, the God-man, was, therefore, the perfect sacrifice.

The Legal Aspects of Christ's Atonement

The apostles placed the death of Christ in a judicial context: God is the supreme judge of his creation, and his judicial actions always reflect his holiness and perfection. God is a God of justice—absolute justice. Therefore, he must by his very nature condemn and punish sin. He never deals with the due penalty of sin by sweeping it under the rug of the universe. With regard to sin, he never lowers the bar or turns a blind eye. If he did, he would become unjust and defiled—something that is unthinkable. In order to remain holy he must hold court, declare sinners guilty, and execute the sentence due, which is eternal condemnation and death for all mankind (Rom. 3:10–18).

But is this God of perfect justice not also a God of perfect love? Aren't these two attributes of his in conflict? To deal with this judicial dilemma, God devised, initiated, and executed the perfect plan of judicial redemption. It is a plan that required atonement, a judiciously paid penalty. It is a plan that involved the cross:

> And you, who were dead in your trespasses . . . God made alive together with him, having forgiven us all our trespasses, by canceling the record of debt that stood against us with its legal demands. This he set aside, nailing it to the cross. (Col. 2:13–14)

[handwritten margin note: IS THIS A CORRECT WAY TO VIEW IT?]

At the cross, forgiveness was achieved by canceling the record of debt that stood against us with its legal demands. What are these demands? They are the demands that the lawful penalty be actually and fully executed. What is the penalty? The penalty is the punishment that sinners rightly deserve—death. This penalty must be executed by a holy God. Yet, "God shows his love for us in that while we were still sinners, Christ died for us" (Rom. 5:8). While we were still sinners, God nailed the record of our legal debt to the cross of Christ's death.

Man's sin was not a mere paper debt. It was not a hypothetical debt. It was an actual legal debt. It was Christ's own flesh that was nailed to the cross, as he was made sin on our behalf (2 Cor. 5:21). Paying our legal debt cost Christ agonizing pain and separation from his Father as he bore the full force of God's wrath against the offense of sin.

At the cross, Christ extinguished the wrath of God toward believing sinners by his own bloody death, thereby paying the full legal debt due by sinners. The result: with the penalty paid, the justice of God was forever satisfied, and sinners united to Christ have been justly forgiven (declared not guilty), and justified (declared righteous). In God's plan of redemption, he remains just in forgiving sinners, since a qualified person actually paid the legal penalty required by the law. At the infinite cost of his Son's life, God constructed the judicial solution in such a way that does not cause God to be defiled or believing sinners to be eternally condemned. Biblically speaking:

> God put forward [Christ Jesus] as a propitiation by his blood, to be received by faith. This was to show God's righteousness, because in his divine forbearance he had passed over former sins. It was to show his righteousness at the present time, so that he might be just and the justifier of the one who has faith in Jesus. (Rom. 3:25–26)

The death of Christ is the basis for the believer's exemption from condemnation, the courtroom equivalent of acquittal, pardon, and forgiveness. As Paul said, "Who is to condemn? Christ Jesus is the one who died . . ." (Rom. 8:34).

Numerous other passages in the Bible describe God's forgiveness, all of which presuppose atonement. One example of this is found in Ephesians where the apostle Paul argued, "In [Jesus] we have redemption through his blood, the forgiveness of our trespasses, according to the riches of his grace" (Eph. 1:7). Here, Paul shows redemption and forgiveness to be a direct, objective benefit of the blood (death) of Christ.

In another example we are told, "[God] will remember their sins and their lawless deeds no more" (Heb. 10:17). As can be seen in the context of Hebrews 10, the Judge chooses to remember sins no longer for a very specific reason—the sacrifice of Christ (vv. 10, 12, 14, 18–22). Because of Christ's great atonement, our sin record is completely expunged forever!

It must be noted that the death of Christ bought more than a strictly legal settlement. The phrase *in Christ*, which appears seventy-three times in the New Testament, refers to a union with Christ in which the redeemed have one life with him, as truly as the head and the members of the same body have one life. This is a great, sacred, and glorious mystery, one to be further explored in chapter 7. But for now, let it suffice to say that none of this is possible apart from the atoning work of Jesus Christ, the perfect sacrifice.

Sadly, not everyone understands this requisite necessity for God to be just. Many picture him exclusively as absolute and unconditional *love*, thinking he will dismiss the legal demands that result from mankind's sin on that basis alone. This approach is offensive to God because it demeans two of the other essential facets of his unfathomable nature—holiness and justice. In addition, to see God solely as *love* is to overlook the beauty and the purpose of the cross. For at the cross, the perfect holiness of God meets his perfect love in action. Worse, it is to belittle the costly price of Christ's sacrifice. Neglecting the holiness of God and misunderstanding the vital significance of the cross is more than simply a theological error—it may have damning consequences, since apart from appropriating

Christ's great atonement, sinners must eternally bear the judicial penalty for their own sin.

The Cross: The Perfect Place for Curse Bearing

Today the cross has been romanticized and mythologized. In order for us to understand its significance, it must be placed back into its original, horrific context. History records that crucifixion incorporated a method resulting in the deepest possible humiliation and disgrace. It was the most scandalous and shameful of punishments, inflicted only on slaves. Free men could not be crucified until first being degraded into the category of a slave by the public application of servile stripes known as scourging, such as was done to Christ prior to nailing him to the cross.

Romans and Jews alike considered those executed by crucifixion to be cursed. To the Jews, a person suspended on a wooden cross had a special significance: it was a form of being hung on a tree, synonymous with being cursed by God for sin. This is clearly seen in the Old Testament:

> If a man has committed a crime punishable by death and he is put to death, and you hang him on a tree, his body shall not remain all night on the tree, but you shall bury him the same day, for a hanged man is cursed by God. (Deut. 21:22–23a)

To get a context for that passage, we must travel all the way back to the garden of Eden. In Genesis 3, the Bible reveals that sin originally entered the world by Adam's willful violation of God's commandment regarding the Tree of the Knowledge of Good and Evil in the garden. As a result, mankind was placed under a trifold curse: separation from God (spiritual death), physical death, and pain in labor (in obtaining provision and in childbearing). Furthermore, all of Adam's descendents inherited both the penal consequences of his sin and a predisposition to sin personally, and, thus, these curses were diffused over the entire human race. Paul states this succinctly when he writes, "Therefore, just as sin came into the world through one man, and death through sin, and so death spread to all men because all sinned" (Rom. 5:12).

The original sin and its resulting curse are associated with a tree, and so it is no coincidence that God's plan for redeeming us from sin and curse would also involve a tree, the wooden cross. Could there ever be a more appropriate place for the sin-bearing and curse-bearing work of the atonement to take place? As Peter states in his epistle, "He himself bore our sins in his body on the tree" (1 Peter 2:24a). There, on that tree, Christ bore our curse.

Christ became a curse, not because of the cross, but because God "made him to be sin" for our sake (2 Cor. 5:21). Thus, the cause of the curse was the sin with which he was charged. Hanging on the tree was simply the public display of the fact that he *became a curse*. Paul said it like this to the Galatians: "Christ redeemed us from the curse of the law by becoming a curse for us—for it is written, 'Cursed is everyone who is hanged on a tree'" (Gal. 3:13).

The punishment of God was just and fitting: the public and cursed death of a cursed man hung on a tree.

The Great Exchange: Trading Places with Christ

> In Christ God was reconciling the world to himself, not counting their trespasses against them. (2 Cor. 5:19)

The reconciliation of the relationship between God and sinners is a result of forgiveness and is seen in this verse as vitally connected with his *not counting*, or not imputing, Christians' sins against them. The non-charging of sin to the believer, by charging, or imputing, it to Christ instead, demonstrates the first part of the Great Exchange. Paul develops this thought in the first part of 2 Corinthians 5:21, where he declares, "for our sake [God] made [Christ] to be sin who knew no sin." God did this. And he did it for our sake out of his infinite love. The sinless Christ was made to be sin, a demonstration of the very essence of imputation. Since Christ had no sin of his own, the only place from which sin could have originated was man. Christ, in essence, assumed the sinner's identity; he became the Christian's sin substitute.

We see the second part of the Great Exchange in the latter half of the verse: "so that in [Christ] we might become the righteousness of God" (2 Cor. 5:21b). Once they are *in* Christ, sinners *become* the righteousness of God, because God credits (imputes) Christ's perfect righteousness to them. In the eyes of God, these sinners have fulfilled the requirement of the law because the Sinless One fulfilled the law on their behalf by his perfect life and obedient death on the cross; they are, in effect, clothed in Christ's righteousness (see the foreshadow of this in Isa. 61:10). In an overwhelming miracle of grace, in God's eyes these sinners have taken on Christ's identity—they are equally as righteous as Christ himself.

Thus, the Great Exchange that results from the death of the perfect sacrifice is a twofold substitution: the charging of the believer's sin to Christ results in God's forgiveness, and the crediting of Christ's righteousness to the believer results in his justification. More than being declared not guilty, in Christ believers are actually declared righteous. Redeemed sinners and their Christ have traded places.

This is a glorious transaction. If this is not the best news of all time, what is? Paul proclaims in Colossians, "You, who once were alienated and hostile in mind, doing evil deeds, he has now reconciled in his body of flesh by his death, in order to present you holy and blameless and above reproach before [God]" (Col. 1:21–22). "Holy," "blameless," and "above reproach" are words that describe Christ's own righteousness—a righteousness in which the Christian is presented before God because of Christ's great atonement. As a result, God and redeemed sinners can enjoy each other in perfect unity.

The Centrality of the Cross

Once Christ illuminated the apostles as to the meaning of his atoning death for their own sins, they promptly gained an understanding of its application to all people for all time—past, present, and future. From that point on, the message of Christ's atonement became preeminent in all their preaching, teaching, and writing, and the cross became emblematic of and synonymous with the atonement they taught.

The apostles triumphed and gloried in the cross; it became their confidence and their boast (Gal. 6:14). They could not live without it, and they were willing to die for it. The apostles were faithful to the message of the cross, and in so doing, they exposed themselves to hardships and danger, persecution and death. And yet they preached the cross, undeterred and undaunted, assured they were ordained to deliver this message, which was unspeakably dear to their souls.

The message of the atoning death of Christ for sin is the heart of their gospel and is forever to be the cornerstone of the Christian faith. Paul wrote:

> Now I would remind you, brothers, of the gospel I preached to you, which you received, in which you stand, and by which you are being saved, if you hold fast to the word I preached to you—unless you believed in vain. For I delivered to you as of first importance what I also received: that Christ died for our sins in accordance with the Scriptures, that he was buried, that he was raised on the third day in accordance with the Scriptures. (1 Cor. 15:1–4)

The apostles' teaching shows that Christ's work of atonement colors the entire range of Scripture, Old and New Testament alike. All doctrine and practical application is drawn from the grace and truth that flow from it, which, moreover, is the central message of the entire Bible, since it forms the sole basis for sinful man's relationship with a holy God. The apostles exalt this message of the cross above all human wisdom as the central fact in all of the entire history of the world. It is the chief topic and essential truth from which they always start and to which they always return.

Furthermore, and of extreme significance to us, almost without exception the apostles address their New Testament writings to specific churches or groups of believers. We can conclude that the message of the atonement is for all believers, not just unbelievers or new believers. As Christians, we do not meet the Savior at the cross and then move past it or outgrow our need of it. The blessing of a restored relationship with God does not become something we merit apart from the cross as we grow. All our blessings were Key blood bought. And the only hope of avoiding false doctrine and heresy, such as legalism (inadequate grace) or license to sin (abused grace), is to continually treasure the cross and the tremendous price of Christ's atonement.

In view of this, the church should beware whenever the moral code taught by Jesus, or the example of Jesus, is declared the essential Christian message. In such cases, the true central message of the Bible, the atoning death of Christ, may become diminished or even lost. While following the moral code may lead to outward obedience, it will never lead to true forgiveness of sin or a transformed life. It inevitably results in a shallow spirituality or worse—legalism, spiritual pride, and eventually burnout under the weight of law keeping and shipwreck of one's faith.

The Apostle Paul: Adamant about Christ's Atonement

> [Christ Jesus] gave himself as a ransom for all, which is the testimony given at the proper time. For this I was appointed a preacher and an apostle. (1 Tim. 2:6–7)

Here the apostle Paul declares the purpose of his preaching and apostleship—to testify to the world that Christ gave himself as a ransom. Elsewhere he summed up his preaching as "the word of the cross" (1 Cor. 1:18) and "Christ crucified" (1 Cor. 1:23a). Later in the same letter, he emphatically displays the epicenter of his message when he declares, "I decided to know nothing among you except Jesus Christ and him crucified" (1 Cor. 2:2).

In the epistle to the Galatians, the apostle Paul contends that the gospel is no gospel unless the full significance of the cross is kept central. He condemns the Judaizers, teachers who did not present the cross as the sole ground of acceptance before God but instead constrained the Galatians to observe the Law of Moses as a requirement for acceptance with God. In effect, they attempted to supplement the cross with circumcision and obedience to Mosaic law and

Jewish customs. The apostle vehemently attacked any suggestion that the basis of man's acceptance by God could ever be anything other than, or in addition to, the cross. He wrote:

> I am astonished that you are so quickly deserting him who called you in the grace of Christ and are turning to a different gospel—not that there is another one, but there are some who trouble you and want to distort the gospel of Christ. But even if we or an angel from heaven should preach to you a gospel contrary to the one we preached to you, let him be accursed. As we have said before, so now I say again: If anyone is preaching to you a gospel contrary to the one you received, let him be accursed. (Gal. 1:6–9)

Paul pronounces, with seriousness and repetition, a curse on anyone, including himself or any angelic being, who would attempt to distort or undermine the true gospel in which the atonement is the sole basis of redeemed sinners' position of acceptance before God.

Paul flatly rejects all semblances of legalism—the rites, the ceremonies, and the legal observances—on which these legalists based their pride and confidence. In the epistle to the Philippians, he denounces them with the remarkable words: "[They] walk as enemies of the cross of Christ" (Phil. 3:18b). They were enemies of the cross of Christ in the sense that they denied that salvation is available only by the bloody, substitutionary death of the sinless sin bearer. In addition, they were enemies of the cross in the sense that they devalue the atoning obedience of the Savior and instead exalted their own works as if those works had saving merit.

Furthermore, Paul repeatedly declares that the cross is his sole source of glory. He states, "Far be it from me to boast except in the cross of our Lord Jesus Christ, by which the world has been crucified to me, and I to the world" (Gal. 6:14). And so it is clear that Paul personally and profoundly identifies with Christ's crucifixion. Furthermore, he reveals that a response of gratitude for Christ's love, as demonstrated at the cross, is the compelling motive for a justified sinner's subsequent obedience:

For the love of Christ controls us, because we have concluded this: that one has died for all, therefore all have died; and he died for all, that those who live might no longer live for themselves but for him who for their sake died and was raised. (2 Cor. 5:14–15)

These words do not mean that the believer suddenly ceases sinning the moment his legal union to Christ by faith takes place. No justified sinner has ever immediately become experientially sin-free. The cross is not a mere first step toward spiritual development; it is the all-encompassing foundation for Christian growth. The cross does not mystically infuse spiritual life or experiential sinlessness. Instead, it first provides complete forgiveness of past, present, and future sins, and then it becomes a means of the deliverance by which we are freed from bondage to sin. As Paul affirms, "[Christ] gave himself for our sins to deliver us from the present evil age" (Gal. 1:4a).

By tying the transformation of the believer to the cross, Paul makes his point abundantly clear: everything we need for life and eternity is provided by virtue of Christ's great atonement. Furthermore, in everything God is for us; he is for us *in Christ* wisdom instead of ignorance, justification instead of condemnation, sanctification instead of sinfulness, and redemption instead of slavery. "[God] is the source of [our] life in Christ Jesus, whom God made our wisdom and our righteousness and sanctification and redemption" (1 Cor. 1:30). In view of this, it is no wonder Paul is adamant and unwavering regarding the centrality of the cross of Christ. The fulfillment of every hope we have is blood bought by the atoning work of Christ on the cross. And the work of Christ on the cross must remain our only hope.

The Cross: A Stumbling Block to Jews, Foolishness to Gentiles

As the apostles preached this message of the atonement after receiving the Holy Spirit, their good news of the cross was in perpetual collision with Jewish arrogance and legalism, as well as with Gentile pride and philosophical wisdom. The apostles preached "Christ crucified, a stumbling block to Jews and folly to Gentiles" (1 Cor. 1:23).

What was the essence of the Jewish stumbling? It was the fact of grace, righteousness gained by faith in the atoning work of Christ, not self-willed or self-meritorious law keeping. Paul states it like this:

> Israel who pursued a law that would lead to righteousness did not succeed in reaching that law. Why? Because they did not pursue it by faith, but as if it were based on works. They have stumbled over the stumbling stone, as it is written, "Behold, I am laying in Zion a stone of stumbling, and a rock of offense; and whoever believes in him will not be put to shame." (Rom. 9:31–33)

The cross required the Jews to acknowledge their personal sinfulness, helplessness, and need for reconciliation. It summoned them to reject their perceived personal merit and self-justification and to accept the righteousness of the suffering Messiah. This was humbling to the Jews; their pride became an obstacle to faith in Christ crucified and deterred them from participating in the Great Exchange.

To the Gentiles, on the other hand, the message of the cross was foolishness because it was devoid of man-centered, philosophical rhetoric. The gospel is so simple a child can understand it; there is no pride in understanding its message or articulating its complexities. No self-satisfaction can be gained from mastering its meaning. But the Gentiles prided themselves in their ability to invent schemes of reality. The gospel, presented as God's design, not man's, did not appeal to the natural inclinations of the ancient Gentile mind.

In all probability, the cross would not have been offensive to the Gentiles if the apostles had explained it as merely evidence of the *sincerity* of Jesus, demonstrating that he was willing to die for his beliefs. The Gentiles certainly would have perceived the cross as adding validity to Jesus' argument and to his teachings, as in the case of Socrates and other philosopher-martyrs. But this was not the apostles' message.

Amazingly enough, although Jewish and Gentile oppression was frequently severe, the apostles never lost confidence or felt shame.

Instead, they confidently boasted in the cross as the power of God and the wisdom of God, with its impact infinitely beyond all the resources of human law keeping or wisdom. Paul writes, "But we preach Christ crucified, a stumbling block to Jews and folly to Gentiles, but to those who are called, both Jews and Greeks, Christ the power of God and the wisdom of God" (1 Cor. 1:23–24).

The stumbling block of the cross cannot be removed by the notion that Jesus was a philosopher, an occupation in which sufferings incur no disgrace. Nor can it be removed by portraying him as the founder of a rational religion taking the place of a ritualistic one. The offense is removed when the personal presence of sin and its consequence is acknowledged; when the God-appointed Sin Bearer is believed and treasured, and when his atoning suffering and death on behalf of undeserving sinners is embraced, resulting in forgiveness, redemption, imputed righteousness, and reconciliation. Only then can the stumbling be removed. Then, and only then, will glorying in the cross begin. Then will we, the redeemed, boldly proclaim with the apostle, "For I am not ashamed of the gospel, for it is the power of God for salvation to everyone who believes, to the Jew first and also to the Greek" (Rom. 1:16).

CHAPTER 3

Atonement Foreshadowed:
The Old Testament Sacrifices

S ince he was writing to first-century Jewish believers, it is not surprising that the unnamed writer of Hebrews provides keen insight into the comparisons and contrasts between the old covenant and new covenant atonements. Addressed to those living at the historic point of transition between the two covenants, the epistle to the Hebrews is greatly beneficial today in gaining insight into the context of Christ's atoning work as the perfect sacrifice and Great High Priest.

Atonement by Animal Sacrifice: Its Origin, Method, and Purpose

> Abel also brought of the firstborn of his flock and of their fat portions. And the LORD had regard for Abel and his offering. (Gen. 4:4)

It is doubtful that the act of sacrificing was an invention of Adam, Cain, or Abel. The first garments of Adam and Eve were almost certainly the skins of animals offered in sacrifice by a method devised and instituted by God himself (Gen. 3:21). In the first mention of sacrifice, the Bible gives the impression that the offerers were given specific instructions by God to govern the form and method of making an acceptable offering. The Bible declares Abel's sacrifice acceptable to God, and more acceptable than Cain's because it was offered in faith:

> By faith Abel offered to God a more acceptable sacrifice than Cain, through which he was commended as righteous, God commending him by accepting his gifts. And through his faith, though he died, he still speaks. (Heb.11:4)

The suggestion that God was the originator of the sacrificial system becomes even more certain in the national organization of Israel as a covenant people. The God-given Law of Moses defined sin and its penalties and imposed a long series of commands and rules designed to expose the extent and flagrancy of their sin (Rom. 5:20). God also made their consciences alive to the guilt of their sin. Both the priests and the people were afraid of violating the rules or duties in the least degree since doing so subjected them to guilt, defilement, and danger. Sometimes a trespass was followed by immediate death at the hand of God (e.g., see Num. 16:31–35). At other times, the punishment included a prescribed period of separation from the congregation and disqualification from the privilege of approaching God in worship.

This system set God apart as uniquely holy. But at the same time, God saw fit to provide a mechanism for demonstrating his merciful love. He instituted an elaborate sacrificial system, which, along with the law, became the focal point of the Hebrew faith. An example of this can be seen in the Levitical law where it states, "Thus shall he do with the bull. As he did with the bull of the sin offering, so shall he do with this. And the priest shall make atonement for them, and they shall be forgiven" (Lev. 4:20).

Atonement by animal sacrifice was the method by which sinning Jewish believers, estranged from God and excluded from covenant standing, were forgiven and restored to relationship with the inflexibly holy and yet merciful God. The penalty for sin was separation and death; if a sin occurred, so must a separation and a death. No amount of remorse, regret, or improved behavior could remove the guilt. The offender was required to die without the possibility of restored fellowship to God—unless the God-ordained animal substitute was offered (separated) and killed (sacrificed) in the place of the sinner. The act of substitutionary death was the main point of the old covenant atonement for sin. In viewing the sacrificial process, defiled Israelites were reminded of what they would have endured if the sacrifice had not intervened.

It is important for us to note that this God-given system of animal sacrifices united three essential concepts: divine holiness, the consequences of sin, and the necessity of God's intervention to supply the means of forgiveness. The atoning animal-substitute deaths were intended to impress these truths on every heart.

The great symbolic truth shown here is that God will not forfeit his holiness to his love. God will not allow his mercy to violate the spotless integrity of his uncompromised justice. By establishing the principle of sacrifice and its symbolism, God revealed that a satisfaction of divine justice was the only path to reconciliation between himself, a holy God, and sinful man. He heralded the indispensable necessity of atonement by a substitutionary death.

These sacrifices were not made merely as acts of homage to an invisible king, or as renewal of allegiance, or as expressions of repentance; the purpose of the sacrifice was always atonement: compensation made for sin, forgiveness, and restored covenant favor with God. Without atonement, the sacrifice was meaningless, for "under the law almost everything is purified with blood, and without the shedding of blood there is no forgiveness of sins" (Heb. 9:22).

The apostles frequently refer to the old covenant animal sacrifices in explaining and elaborating on Christ's sacrificial death on the cross. They describe both the death of animals and the priestly service as foreshadowing the symbolic work of Christ's work. As seen through the eyes of the apostles, the purpose of the Old Testament law and sacrificial system was to cast light on the nature of God's prescribed method of dealing with sin: forgiveness by substitutionary punishment in the form of the consummate substitutionary sacrifice, Jesus Christ.

The apostles draw many comparisons between the foreshadows and the fulfillment. Paul asserts, "Christ, our Passover lamb, has been sacrificed" (1 Cor. 5:7b). Here, and in many other places, the symbolism of atonement by animal sacrifice furnishes a vocabulary to the New Testament church, providing words that believers can relate to on the subject of the atonement in order to understand it more deeply.

There is also another purpose for the old covenant sacrifices: as symbolic foreshadows, they furnished a *prophetic* expectation. As we will explore in the next chapter, Christ's great atonement fulfilled that expectation as the reality and final accomplishment of what the symbolic sacrifices had represented.

Atonement by Animal Sacrifice: Symbolic Shadows

There are priests who offer gifts according to the law. They serve a *copy and shadow* of the heavenly things. (Heb. 8:4b–5a)

The law has but a *shadow* of the good things to come instead of the true form of these realities. (Heb.10:1a)

The writer of Hebrews refers to the sacrificial system as a *copy* and *shadow*—terms indicating a similarity in form but lacking in substance. A copy, or shadow, is wholly dependent on the actual item and has no existence or reality apart from it. It is merely a symbol.

The old covenant animal sacrifices were symbolic on two levels. First, the physical actions involved in the process of substitutionary animal sacrificing were symbols of the way God provided the solution for Israel's sin dilemma under the old covenant. Second, the animal sacrifices were shadowy pictures of the substance and reality of Christ's great atonement in the new covenant.

In the light of these two levels of symbolism, it is helpful to examine the old covenant rites of making animal sacrifice for atonement of sins. We will briefly examine seven of these.

1) *The unblemished sacrifice*. The animal was to be free from defect, blemish, or disease. This symbolized the purity and innocence of the animal. It had no imperfection of its own for which it merited punishment or death. Jesus, likewise, had to be perfectly righteous in order to die for the unrighteous; he had to be innocent in order to die for the guilty. Atonement could only be made "with the precious blood of Christ, like that of a lamb without blemish or spot" (1 Pet. 1:19). His spotless holiness was a necessary and essential condition for the great atonement. Jesus Christ had to be a *perfect* sacrifice.

2) *The sinner's hand on the victim's head*. The next act of the ritual was the laying of the hand on the animal's head. This was to symbolize the transfer (imputation) of the sinner's guilt to the animal substitute. We can see many passages in the new covenant correlating to this concept, including where Paul states, "For our sake [God] made [Jesus] to be sin who knew no sin, so that in him we might become the righteousness of God" (2 Cor. 5:21).

3) *The death of the sacrifice is caused by the offender*. Sin and death stand related as cause and consequence. The animal must die by the hand of the one it will represent; it is his or her sin and death that are laid on the sacrifice. A clear correlation is obvious in the death of Christ: the cause of his death was the sin of those he represented in the new covenant; our sin was charged to him. Isaiah shows this clearly when he writes, "But he was wounded for our transgressions; he was crushed for our iniquities; upon him was the chastisement that brought us peace, and with his stripes we are healed" (Isa. 53:5). It was our sin, not his own, that killed Jesus.

4) *The priestly service*. The Old Testament priest, the God-appointed mediator, was responsible for transferring the sacrificial blood to the altar for appropriation as atonement for sin. This was symbolic of Jesus as priest and mediator between a holy God and sinful man.

> Therefore [Christ] is the mediator of a new covenant, so that those who are called may receive the promised eternal inheritance, since

a death has occurred that redeems them from the transgressions committed under the first covenant. (Heb. 9:15)

On the annual Day of Atonement, when sacrifice was made for the sins of the nation, the high priest received the flowing blood of the dying animal and took it within the veil into the Most Holy Place. There he sprinkled the mercy seat, symbolically covering the sins of the people. Finally, after hundreds of years of this symbolic practice, the Great High Priest, Jesus, came once and for all to atone for man's sin. At the moment of Christ's death, the veil of the temple was torn from top to bottom, and Jesus, the fulfillment of the foreshadow, entered with better blood—his own. The true sprinkling of the heavenly mercy seat took place, fully removing the wrath of God and resulting in forgiveness and restoration for all trusting in his eternally redemptive blood. And so, "[Jesus] entered once for all into the holy places, not by means of the blood of goats and calves but by means of his own blood, thus securing an eternal redemption" (Heb. 9:12).

5) *The return of the high priest from the holy place*. The Old Testament people of Israel waited anxiously while the high priest was within the veil. If God rejected their offering, the priest and the people could well be consumed. There was relief and rejoicing when the high priest reappeared, because it signified that God accepted the sprinkled blood as atonement, assuring his holy wrath had been set aside. The correlate in the great atonement was the bodily resurrection of Christ, proof that all was indeed finished, as he said with his dying breath (John 19:30). His resurrection is proof that satisfaction for sin was paid in full; divine wrath was exhausted, justice was fulfilled, forgiveness was granted, and relationship was restored. Then "after making purification for sins, [his Son] sat down at the right hand of the Majesty on high," (Heb. 1:3b) where he continues to function as our Great High Priest. "Since then we have a great high priest who has passed through the heavens, Jesus, the Son of God, let us hold fast our confession" (Heb 4:14).

6) *The burning of the sacrifice*. After the blood of the sacrifice was drained, the dead animal body was carried outside the camp

to be burned in a public place. There, fire, symbolic of the Holy
Spirit, consumed the sacrifice and produced an aroma pleasing
to God. While the sprinkled blood is symbolic of Christ's substitutionary death, the burning of the innocent sacrifice with its
pleasing aroma symbolizes Christ's substitutionary fulfilling of
the law. Christ's obedience in carrying out his redemptive work
on the cross is the sweet-smelling fulfillment of these shadows.
Paul writes, "Christ . . . gave himself up for us, a fragrant offering and sacrifice to God" (Eph. 5:2). The writer to the Hebrews
says it like this:

> For the bodies of those animals whose blood is brought into the holy
> places by the high priest as a sacrifice for sin are burned outside the
> camp. So Jesus also suffered outside the gate in order to sanctify the
> people through his own blood. (Heb. 13:11–12)

Christ's death as payment for sin, resulting in the removal of God's
wrath and in forgiveness, is the *negative* side of atonement. Christ's
sinless obedience resulting in the imputation of his own righteousness
to the believer is the *positive* side. These are two sides of the same
coin. The Bible clearly shows these two sides: "For our sake he made
him to be sin who knew no sin, so that in him we might become the
righteousness of God" (2 Cor. 5:21). The concept of imputed righteousness is so vital to our understanding of the atonement that we
devote an entire chapter to the subject (see chapter 6).

7) *Restoration of the offender*. The old covenant sacrifices were
the God-appointed means for restoring the relationship between
sinners and the Almighty. Correspondingly, for those whose sins
are covered by the blood of Christ's great atonement, though once
distant and separated from God they are now intimate: "But now
in Christ Jesus you who once were far off have been brought near
by the blood of Christ" (Eph. 2:13). When as condemned sinners
we were once timid before God, as redeemed believers we are now
confident: "Since then we have a great high priest who has passed
through the heavens, Jesus, the Son of God, let us hold fast our
confession. . . . Let us then with confidence draw near to the throne

of grace, that we may receive mercy and find grace to help in time of need" (Heb. 4:14, 16).

As foreshadows, these seven components involved in the system of old covenant animal sacrifices provide valuable insight into the depth of the meaning and purpose behind Christ's great atonement. Indeed, a glimpse into the depth of the wisdom and knowledge of God is obtainable by the careful study of the atonement in the Old Testament.

The Inadequacies of the Old Covenant Atonement

> For it is impossible for the blood of bulls and goats to take away sins. (Heb. 10:4)

It should be no surprise to discover that created elements of this world, like bulls and goats, cannot secure an all-inclusive, eternal atonement for sin. The writer of Hebrews begins to expose the limitations and insufficiencies of the old covenant animal sacrifices as compared to the superiority of Christ's great atonement when he writes, "But into the [Most Holy Place] only the high priest goes, and he but once a year, and not without taking blood, which he offers for himself and for the unintentional sins of the people" (Heb. 9:7). As we will see, articulated here are a number of inadequacies of the old covenant, three of which are briefly illuminated below, proving that this system was merely an inadequate foreshadow. It could not save!

1) *The Jewish high priest, a fellow offender, needed personal atonement for his own sin just like the rest of the people.* But in Christ's priestly service his blood is presented without blemish. As our representative, Christ was subjected to the same temptation to sin as we are, yet he remained sinless. The following three verses demonstrate these truths clearly:

> How much more will the blood of Christ, who through the eternal Spirit offered himself *without blemish* to God, purify our conscience from dead works to serve the living God. (Heb. 9:14)

For it was indeed fitting that we should have such a high priest, *holy, innocent, unstained, separated from sinners*, and exalted above the heavens. (Heb. 7:26)

For we do not have a high priest who is unable to sympathize with our weaknesses, but one who in every respect has been tempted as we are, *yet without sin*. (Heb. 4:15)

2) *The old covenant offerings provided atonement only for unintentional sins.* Unintentional sins were limited to three specific classes: trespasses of a ceremonial nature, sins of ignorance, and trespasses of the laws that separated Israel from other nations (e.g., bodily defilement related to menstruation or childbirth or resulting from the prohibition of touching a dead body). The old covenant provided sacrifices to restore the trespasser to ceremonial covenant relationship with God. But these sacrifices were powerless to remove the penalty and guilt of moral offences such as murder, adultery, stealing, lying, or idolatry. We read:

> By this the Holy Spirit indicates that the way into the holy places is not yet opened as long as the first section is still standing (which is symbolic for the present age). According to this arrangement, gifts and sacrifices are offered that cannot perfect the conscience of the worshiper, but deal only with food and drink and various washings, regulations for the body imposed until the time of reformation. (Heb. 9:8–10)

The "time of reformation" mentioned here refers to the inauguration of the new covenant, mediated by a perfect priest, built on better promises (Heb. 8:6), and able to atone for moral sin, including moral sins committed by believers who lived before the time of Christ's finished work on the cross. We see this finally revealed in the New Testament: "God put forward [Jesus] as a propitiation by his blood, to be received by faith. This was to show God's righteousness, because in his divine forbearance he had passed over former sins" (Rom. 3:25).

By his great atonement, all who are his (past, present, and future) have all their sins (past, present, and future) charged to him, and they receive forgiveness as a result because he bore their curse and exhausted their due wrath, and his perfect righteousness was credited to them. Aware that the all-sufficient price was paid in full, they enjoy a clean conscience and a permanently restored relationship with the infinitely holy God of justice and love.

3) *The old covenant system of atonement required repetition of sacrifices annually, as well as for repeated offenses.* Christ, on the other hand, by virtue of offering a better sacrifice (himself) and by virtue of performing a better priesthood (his own), has taken away the sins of redeemed sinners by a single act—his finished work on the cross. The Great High Priest, Jesus, "has no need, like those high priests, to offer sacrifices daily, first for his own sins and then for those of the people, since he did this *once for all* when he offered up himself" (Heb. 7:27). The high priest Jesus "has appeared *once for all* at the end of the ages to put away sin by the sacrifice of himself" (Heb. 9:26b).

The Jewish high priests continually stood, year after year, to offer more and more sacrifices; they had no permanent rest in their work. But when Christ completed his priestly work of atonement, he sat down at the right hand of the Father, his work forever finished. Jesus, "after making purification for sins . . . sat down at the right hand of the Majesty on high." (Heb. 1:3b)

There are other contrasts between the Old Testament shadows and the true atonement. Christ's atonement brings with it:

- *A better sanctuary*:

But when Christ appeared as a high priest of the good things that have come, then through the greater and more perfect tent (not made with hands, that is, not of this creation), . . . for Christ has entered, not into holy places made with hands, which are copies of the true things, but into heaven itself, now to appear in the presence of God on our behalf. (Heb. 9:11, 24)

- *A permanent priesthood*:

But [Jesus] was made a priest with an oath by the one who said to him:

"The Lord has sworn
and will not change his mind,
'You are a priest forever.'"

This makes Jesus the guarantor of a better covenant. The former priests were many in number, because they were prevented by death from continuing in office, but [Jesus] holds his priesthood permanently, because he continues forever. Consequently, he is able to save to the uttermost those who draw near to God through him, since he always lives to make intercession for them. (Heb. 7:21–25)

• *Sinners are made perfect*:

For since the law has but a shadow of the good things to come instead of the true form of these realities, it can never, by the same sacrifices that are continually offered every year, make perfect those who draw near. (Heb. 10:1b)

For by a single offering he has perfected for all time those who are being sanctified. (Heb. 10:14)

Christ the Fulfillment

Christ is the fulfillment and end of the old covenant shadow. The book of Hebrews teaches that once the fulfillment came, the symbolic ceased. With the prophetic symbolism of the old covenant atonement forever fulfilled in Christ, its system of sacrifice became ineffectual and pointless. The church was instructed to dispense with the old covenant sacrifices. Because the ultimate and infinite substance had arrived in Christ's great atonement, the mere *copies and shadows* were of no further use in dealing with sin. We are told:

On the one hand, a former commandment is set aside because of its weakness and uselessness (for the law made nothing perfect); but on the other hand, a better hope is introduced, through which we draw near to God. (Heb. 7:18–19)

The old covenant sacrifices were clearly inadequate, for if they were adequate, Jesus Christ would not have come to die for sins. As great high priest and perfect sacrifice, Christ's comprehensive, eternally sufficient atonement for all sins of the redeemed superseded and replaced the old system and with it brought a better hope and an unprecedented nearness to God.

CHAPTER 4

Atonement Expected:
The Old Testament Prophecies

As previously noted, the Old Testament sacrifices provide evidence of the necessity for punishment and sacrificial death for sin. They also provide a prophetic anticipation—the foreshadow must one day become a reality.

The Old Testament contains hundreds of prophecies designed to enable the nation of Israel to recognize their coming Messiah. These include a variety of highly specific identifiers such as his lineage (Gen. 22:18; Ps. 132:11), his birthplace (Mic. 5:2), and the virgin birth (Isa. 7:14).

The earliest prophecy of the atonement (Gen. 3:15) was somewhat general in character. But as time moved forward, increasingly clearer prophetic signals were given until, with the psalms, incredibly specific detail was revealed. This trend continued with the prophets, in particular the prophet Isaiah, who outlined the design and nature of the atonement and the sufferings of the Messiah so plainly that at times one may seem to be reading history. One example of this is found in Isaiah 7:14: "Therefore the Lord himself will give you a sign. Behold, the virgin shall conceive and bear a son, and shall call his name Immanuel."

Looking back on these prophesies not only affirms the authenticity of the person and ministry of Christ, but it also provides insight into the very nature of Christ's great atonement and offers some of Christianity's most cherished portraits of Christ's suffering and death for sin. Paul declared that the Old Testament prophecies supported everything he preached because they were fulfilled by Christ's suffering, death, and resurrection; that is to say, they were fulfilled by his atonement. He is quoted in Acts as saying, "To this day I have had the help that comes from God, and so I stand here testifying both to small and great, saying nothing but what the prophets and Moses said would come to pass: that the Christ must suffer and that, by being the first to rise from the dead, he would proclaim light both to our people and to the Gentiles" (Acts 26:22–23). These prophecies on the atonement were so explicit and clear that the apostles usually did little more than identify and apply them. They did not need to be developed further.

What follows in the remainder of this chapter are representative Old Testament passages that the apostles identify and apply as prophetic and applicable to the understanding of Christ's atoning sacrifice.

The Messianic Psalms

Messianic psalms contain prophetic elements that foreshadow the identity of the Messiah. The prophetic messages of many of these passages were veiled to those living before the time of Christ's fulfillment. However, it is now apparent that two meanings were intentionally conveyed, one applying to the psalmist in an actual sense, and the other applying to the Messiah in a prophetic sense.

In addition, we now have the great advantage of being able to identify a passage as prophetic by virtue of its interpretation in the New Testament. For example, it may not initially be clear to us whether this verse, "For you will not abandon my soul to Sheol, or let your holy one see corruption" (Ps. 16:10), was written about

David or about his great descendent, Jesus Christ. But the apostle Peter leaves no doubt as to this issue, proclaiming this passage prophetic with the resurrection of Christ as its fulfillment:

> Brothers, I may say to you with confidence about the patriarch David that he both died and was buried, and his tomb is with us to this day. Being therefore a prophet, and knowing that God had sworn with an oath to him that he would set one of his descendants on his throne, he foresaw and spoke about the resurrection of the Christ, that he was not abandoned to Hades, nor did his flesh see corruption. This Jesus God raised up, and of that we all are witnesses. (Acts 2:29–32)

Another example is Psalm 8:5, which declares, "Yet you have made him a little lower than the heavenly beings and crowned him with glory and honor." We read in Hebrews, "We see him who for a little while was made lower than the angels, namely Jesus, crowned with glory and honor because of the suffering of death, so that by the grace of God he might taste death for everyone" (Heb. 2:9).

Two messianic psalms shed particular light on the nature of the atonement, Psalm 40 and Psalm 110.

Psalm 40

The book of Hebrews reveals that the true subject of this passage is the Messiah in his role as the true sin offering. This would indicate that David, the author of Psalm 40, was writing not solely about himself but was prophesying about Christ's atonement. David writes:

> Sacrifice and offering you have not desired,
>   but you have given me an open ear.
> Burnt offering and sin offering
>   you have not required.
> Then I said, "Behold, I have come;
>   in the scroll of the book it is written of me:
> I desire to do your will, O my God;
>   your law is within my heart." (Ps. 40:6–8)

The writer of Hebrews prefaced his quotation from Psalm 40 with these words: "Consequently, when Christ came into the world, he said . . ." (Heb. 10:5a). He then adds further clarity about Christ's fulfillment of this prophecy:

> When he said above, "You have neither desired nor taken pleasure in sacrifices and offerings and burnt offerings and sin offerings" (these are offered according to the law), then he added, "Behold, I have come to do your will." He abolishes the first in order to establish the second. And by that will we have been sanctified through the offering of the body of Jesus Christ once for all. (Heb. 10:8–10)

Here the apostle contrasts the absolute insufficiency of the old covenant sacrifices with the Messiah's obedience and atoning work. Since animal sacrifices could not provide any real atonement for moral sin, they neither pleased God nor fulfilled the law of God. They were a mere foreshadow of what was to come—the Messiah, the true priest and perfect sacrifice.

The Bible makes it clear that God requires a personal and moral obedience and righteousness from all, yet no human has ever met the righteous requirements of the law (Rom. 3:10). Only Christ, as the holy and righteous law keeper, could offer a perfect sacrifice for sins, because he perfectly obeyed God's law. By his sinless life (his *active* obedience) and his substitutionary death (his *passive* obedience), God's requirement—that is, his will—was fulfilled on behalf of those whom Christ represents in the new covenant. When Christ said, "I desire to do your will, O my God," he in essence reveals that an agreement or pact between the Father and the Son existed before the actual incarnation. God's will denotes the infinitely loving will of God, which led him to plan our redemption. It is as if Jesus were saying, "I come to execute your requirement, as we agreed. Yes, I will carry out the work of the atonement."

Some may object that verse 12 applies to David and not to Christ. How could it apply to Christ when it states, "For evils have encompassed me beyond number; my iniquities have overtaken me, and I cannot see; they are more than the hairs of my head; my heart fails me" (Ps. 40:12)? Did Christ commit iniquity? Was Christ encompassed by evil. This apparent difficulty vanishes when the reader considers that the Messiah is speaking through David regarding imputed sins charged to himself as the substitutionary sin bearer for his people. He became sin for his people and therefore was overtaken by iniquity.

Psalm 110

Psalm 110 is another messianic prophesy. King David composed this coronation psalm in response to a vision of the Messiah's ascension to his throne. David wrote, "The LORD says to my Lord: 'Sit at my right hand, until I make your enemies your footstool'" (Ps. 110:1). Both Jesus and his apostles quote verse 1 as messianic prophecy (Matt. 22:44; Acts 2:34–35; Heb. 1:13; 5:5).

But here Christ is not merely king. David adds Christ's role of priest to his royal kingship: "You are a priest forever after the order of Melchizedek" (Ps. 110:4; see also Heb. 5:6; 7:17). This passage informed the Jewish nation that the Messiah would be *like* Melchizedek, a mysterious person who is mentioned briefly in Genesis 14:18–20. The Bible tells little about him, but what it does reveal is important because of the prophetic significance attached to him in Psalm 110 and in the epistle to the Hebrews. It is clear that he was a priest whose order was outside of the line of Aaron. Furthermore, Melchizedek simultaneously held both priestly and royal offices, a combination not permitted by the Levitical priesthood. Melchizedek was symbolic of the Messiah, who would be both Great High Priest and King of kings. Christ's priesthood was the foundation of his dominion; the cross was the basis of his throne.

Interestingly enough, while little is written about Melchizedek in the Old Testament, Hebrews reveals seven additional aspects of Christ's fulfillment of the Melchizedek prophecy. Like Melchizedek:

1) *Christ had a divine call to the priesthood.*

So also Christ did not exalt himself to be made a high priest,
but was appointed by him who said to him,

"You are my Son,
today I have begotten you";
as he says also in another place,

"You are a priest forever,
after the order of Melchizedek." (Heb. 5:5–6)

Jesus Christ was no self-proclaimed high priest, nor was he appointed by man. His priesthood was bestowed upon him by the
highest spiritual authority—God himself.

2) *Christ is both "king of righteousness" and "king of peace."*

And to him Abraham apportioned a tenth part of everything. He is
first, by translation of his name, *king of righteousness,* and then he
is also king of Salem, that is, *king of peace.* (Heb. 7:2)

As king of righteousness, Christ is both personally holy and the
source of imputed righteousness for all his own people. As king
of peace, Christ is the sin-bearing sacrifice that accomplished the
great atonement that brought us acceptance and therefore peace
with God. These two titles could be combined to render "king of
holy sacrifice."

3) *Christ, like Melchizedek, has a special, superior lineage.*

He is without father or mother or genealogy, having neither beginning
of days nor end of life, but resembling the Son of God he continues
a priest forever. (Heb. 7:3)

Melchizedek had no traceable family register; he came upon the scene
and passed away as if he had neither father nor mother, beginning
nor end, resembling the Son of God. This was symbolic of Christ,
who in his earthly nature had no father, and in his divine nature
had no mother. Christ is the true eternal Son of God.

4) *Christ's priesthood replaced the Levitical priesthood and law.*

Now if perfection had been attainable through the Levitical priesthood (for under it the people received the law), what further need
would there have been for another priest to arise after the order of
Melchizedek, rather than one named after the order of Aaron? For
when there is a change in the priesthood, there is necessarily a change
in the law as well. (Heb. 7:11–12)

The entire old covenant system of ceremonial law was based on the
Aaronic (Levitical) priesthood, so this change of priesthood would
necessarily result in a change of law as well. The first priesthood
was fundamentally defective, and so was the law; they made nothing perfect. The new priesthood introduces a superior covenant by
which a perfect, imputed righteousness is obtainable.

5) *Christ's priesthood is based on God's unchangeable oath.*

And it was not without an oath. For those who formerly
became priests were made such without an oath, but this one
was made a priest with an oath by the one who said to him:

"The Lord has sworn
    and will not change his mind,
'You are a priest forever.'"

This makes Jesus the guarantor of a better covenant. (Heb.
    7:20–22)

Appointed without an oath, the Levitical priesthood was changeable,
and its covenant was temporary and symbolic. The royal Melchizedek
priesthood of Christ ushered in a better covenant, permanent because it
is guaranteed by God's own oath. Nothing better can ever replace this
priesthood; otherwise God could not have sworn this binding oath.

6) *Christ's priesthood is superior because it is eternal.*

The former priests were many in number, because they were prevented
by death from continuing in office, but he holds his priesthood per-

manently, because he continues forever. Consequently, he is able to save to the uttermost those who draw near to God through him, since he always lives to make intercession for them. (Heb. 7:23–25)

Nothing can violate or replace the eternal priesthood of Christ. His interminable office enables him to save men perfectly and forever.

7) *Christ's priesthood is superior since it offers one sacrifice for all time.*

For it was indeed fitting that we should have such a high priest, holy, innocent, unstained, separated from sinners, and exalted above the heavens. He has no need, like those high priests, to offer sacrifices daily, first for his own sins and then for those of the people, since he did this once for all when he offered up himself. For the law appoints men in their weakness as high priests, but the word of the oath, which came later than the law, appoints a Son who has been made perfect forever. (Heb. 7:26–28)

Sealed with the Father's own oath, and superseding the law, Christ's superior priesthood and superior sacrifice are the basis of his superior atonement, the great atonement. In his Melchizedek priesthood, the sinless Jesus, as the ever-living high priest, offers a sacrifice so meritorious and complete that it requires no repetition. It results in a single atonement of unimaginable cost, infinite value, and inexhaustible validity. Never will a supplementary mediator or sacrifice be required. Christ's perfect sacrifice applies equally to every person in every decade of the history of man and the kingdom of God.

Isaiah 53

The prophet Isaiah is known as the Old Testament evangelist because of his vivid, prophetic descriptions of the Messiah's sufferings, atonement, and reward, especially as recorded in Isaiah 52:13–53:12. Written seven centuries before the crucifixion and death of Jesus, this passage unfolds the essential elements of the atonement as it describes the details of Christ's sufferings with astonishing precision. It sheds light on the deep purpose of his sufferings, as well as the fact that God himself pre-appointed every detail.

It is clear from an objective reading of this passage that in Isaiah's day, the prevailing viewpoint was that the Messiah was the subject of this prophecy. After the time of Christ's fulfillment, embarrassed by the constant appeals by Christians to this chapter, Jewish religious leaders took the position that the true Messiah was to be a military conqueror and, therefore, this passage was not messianic in nature. Today, some Jews assert instead that the subject of Isaiah 53 is the nation of Israel.

The New Testament confirms that the passage refers to the Messiah and was fulfilled by Christ in several clear references to the prophecy including Matthew 8:17, Acts 8:32, Romans 15:21, 1 Peter 2:22, and in 1 Peter 2:24b, which reads, "By his wounds you have been healed."

Isaiah provides valuable insights regarding Christ's future atonement, and the apostles declare, advance, and apply these insights in several ways. We will look briefly at five of these.

1) *The Messiah would be without personal guilt.*

. . . Although he had done no violence, and there was no deceit in his mouth. (Isa. 53:9b)

Peter renders this: "He committed no sin, neither was deceit found in his mouth" (1 Pet. 2:22), alluding to Christ's spotless purity in thought, word, and action.

2) *The Messiah would suffer as a direct result of the sin of his people.*

But he was wounded for our transgressions;
    he was crushed for our iniquities;
upon him was the chastisement that brought us peace,
    and with his stripes we are healed. (Isa. 53:5)

This verse reveals *why* he suffered. Bearing the penal consequences of our sin (transgressions, iniquities) would be the cause of his wounds, chastisement, and stripes. We see this repeatedly throughout this passage:

- "The LORD has laid on him the iniquity of us all" (v. 6).
- "He shall bear their iniquities" (v. 11).
- "Yet he bore the sin of many" (v. 12).

To *bear sin* is to endure the burden of its punishment, to provide satisfaction for the infinite justice of God by exhausting his wrath toward sin. The chastisement put upon him brought us peace with God. "He himself bore our sins in his body on the tree, that we might die to sin and live to righteousness. By his wounds you have been healed" (1 Pet. 2:24).

3) *The Messiah would suffer as the substitute for his people.*

The concept of vicarious substitution colors this entire passage. *Vicarious* means "performed or suffered by one person as a substitute for another and to the benefit or advantage of another." As the representative of his people, the Messiah would suffer directly as a result of taking on the obligation caused by their sin. The punishment due to them was at the moment of transfer charged (imputed) to his account. Since he had no sin of his own, he clearly acted vicariously when he endured the punishment required to atone for their collective sins. He could have no connection with sin except by substitution.

Isaiah also stated, "His soul makes an offering for sin . . ." (Isa. 53:10). As we discussed earlier, the Messiah was to become a sin offering, reminiscent of the old covenant animal sacrifices in which the sin of the offerer was symbolically and vicariously transferred to the head of the innocent sacrifice.

4) *God's own hand inflicted the Messiah's sufferings.*

> Yet it was the will of the LORD to crush him;
> he has put him to grief. (Isa. 53:10)

The Hebrew word rendered "will" in verse 10 may also be translated as "pleased" or "delighted." God not only willfully permitted the slaughter of Christ at the hand of man, but he had pleasure and delight in it because it manifested his glory. Therefore the suffering and crucifixion of Jesus Christ were not the direct result of the Jews or Romans; God crushed Jesus in the exercise of divine punitive justice against the sin Christ representatively bore. God himself caused the punishment to descend on the sin-bearing Christ (Acts 4:27–28). In this perfect act of wisdom, man's sin dilemma was perfectly solved, God's justice remained intact, and his perfect love was fully displayed. The redemption of elect sinners was based entirely on God's own predetermined plan of atonement, and he delighted to provide it, even at the infinite cost of his own Son. The apostles echo this theme frequently, as can be seen in Romans 8:32 where Paul writes, "He who did not spare his own Son but gave him up for us all, how will he not also with him graciously give us all things?"

5) *The Messiah's death would result in tremendous rewards for him and for us.*

Isaiah 53 lists several rewards to be bestowed on the Messiah as a result of his victorious obedience:

- "He shall see his offspring" (v. 10).
- "He shall prolong his days" (v. 10).
- "He shall divide the spoil with the strong" (v. 12).

In addition to the rewards received by Christ, verse 5 reveals two other rewards he would purchase on behalf of his redeemed people: he bought our peace and he bought our healing. For "upon him was the chastisement that brought us peace, and with his stripes we are healed" (Isa. 53:5b).

Here *peace* refers to our peace with God—that is, the believer's reconciliation with God. This peace would not be the result of absolute or unconditional love apart from any intervention. This peace required a price, an atonement. In short, the chastisement due us would be fully executed on the substitute.

The term "healing" denotes pardon, deliverance from sin, and growth in godliness. The stripes by which that healing would be purchased refer both to the effects of the scourging inflicted by man's hand and to the far worse yet invisible punishment inflicted by the hand of God. The visible strokes of punishment were merely the outward emblem of the invisible, incomprehensible ones.

Here we come to a paradox: how can wounds inflicted on one be the healing of another? The moment we recall the idea of substitution, or changing places, it becomes clear: by cause and effect, the wounds of the vicarious sufferer usher in true healing for every sin sickness. For "out of the anguish of his soul he shall see and be satisfied; by his knowledge shall the righteous one, my servant, make many to be accounted righteous, and he shall bear their iniquities" (Isa. 53:11).

This verse reveals yet another breathtaking reward earned by God's righteous servant—imputed righteousness for his people. The phrase *accounted righteous* means "credited with his righteousness," and as a result, from the moment one enters his kingdom by faith, he or she is justified, acquitted, and accepted by God. The phrase *by his knowledge* refers to the knowledge by which he is known, not the knowledge that he possesses. Men are justified by the knowledge of him, which is the same as to be justified by faith.

And so here again an Old Testament prophecy clearly and specifically reveals the essential elements of Christ's later atonement. Isaiah's words are clearly a foreshadowing of Christ's future glorious work of redemption for us on the cross.

Part Two

THE APOSTLE-AUTHORED SCRIPTURE ON CHRIST'S ATONEMENT

CHAPTER 5

The Acts of the Apostles

I n the book of Acts, Luke records several fragments of the apostles' evangelistic sermons interwoven with historical narrative. His record visibly demonstrates the centrality of the apostles' preaching on the atonement. Their preaching centered on the eternally valid reality of the death of Christ and his resurrection, not as mere historic facts, but in terms of their purpose as the great atonement for sin.

Luke's reporting of the apostles' discourses was not designed to provide a comprehensive explanation of the doctrine of the atonement, perhaps because the church was still in its infancy and not yet able to embrace many of the deeper interpretations and applications of it. But one thing is clear: the message of Christ crucified was their principal proclamation, and this message was presented to all in its causal connection with forgiveness of sins.

This was Peter's central message as he addressed the crowd, saying, "What God foretold by the mouth of all the prophets, that his Christ would suffer, he thus fulfilled. Repent therefore, and turn again, that your sins may be blotted out" (Acts 3:18–19). Peter's reference here to the atonement made by the Suffering Servant is brief. When later called to defend himself before the council, he added further insight to what he had said before: "There is salvation in no one else, for there is no other name under heaven given among men by which we must be saved" (Acts 4:12). Thus, salvation stands connected with the name of Jesus Christ to the exclusion of every other. He alone is the Messiah, the perfect sacrifice.

Although written by Luke, the apostles Peter and Paul are the principle speakers in the book of Acts. The following is a representative sampling of their explanation regarding the subject of the atonement.

Acts 2

As the early church assembled on the day of Pentecost, a display of God's supernatural power took place. This was no less extraordinary than when Moses received the Ten Commandments on Mount Sinai. In the narrative found in Acts 2, Peter provides the explanation of this event to his amazed, multi-national Jewish audience. He declares that both miracles (v. 22) and fulfilled prophecy (Joel 2:28–32; Ps. 16:8–11; 110:1) give testimony to Jesus, being the Messiah in whom the forgiveness of sins was to be found. He proclaims Jesus to be the Christ, which is the Greek translation of the Hebrew word for *Messiah* (vv. 31, 36, 38). He boldly proclaimed, "Let all the house of Israel therefore know for certain that God has made him both Lord and Christ, this Jesus whom you crucified" (Acts 2:36).

Without providing an exhaustive discourse on the doctrine of the atonement, Peter's sermon on the day of Pentecost nevertheless faithfully exhibits its key elements: Jesus Christ's finished work on the cross as the sinless sin bearer resulted in acceptance of sinners by the infinitely holy God. Peter presents Jesus as both a "man" (v. 22) and God's "Holy One" (v. 27). Peter also presents Jesus as one who walked on earth in uninterrupted fellowship with the Father. Through the inspiration of the Holy Spirit, Peter demonstrates this when he attributes the messianic prophesy of Psalm 16:8 to Christ: "For David says concerning him, 'I saw the Lord always before me, for he is at my right hand that I may not be shaken'" (Acts 2:25).

On the basis of his personal sinlessness, Jesus had absolute personal immunity from sin suffering of every kind. It was solely as our substitute that he bore the condemnation and wrath we deserved at the hand of God.

In verse 23a, Peter tells the Jews that Jesus was "delivered up according to the definite plan and foreknowledge of God." In this statement, Peter reveals a startling fact—even though Christ was "crucified and killed by the hands of lawless men" (v. 23b), it was God's design for Jesus to bear punishment and death. Though sinful men performed the execution, God himself, for his own good reasons, caused Jesus to suffer and die. The ransom price for sinners was acceptable only because God himself arranged the plan. The death of the Son had to happen; it was no mistake. It was God's will; he would not have had it any other way.

And yet Jesus demonstrated perfect willingness and obedience in voluntarily subjecting himself to the actions required by the preordained covenant with the Father. He would be delivered over for punishment on behalf of sinners; yet no man could lay a finger on him unless both God the Father and God the Son consented (John 10:18).

It is noteworthy that God chose to make his Son a sin offering at the hands of wicked men instead of by priestly hands or directly by the hand of God. This was fitting because it demonstrated the Great Exchange: God delivered the innocent Christ over, as a judge delivers a criminal to punishment, that the prisoners might go free instead. Christ was innocent—until our guilt was made his own. Christ took our sin and punishment; we took his innocence and vindication. The treason and blasphemy charged to Christ by the human tribunal was an emblem of our own treason and blasphemy against God for everything, from our apathy toward him, to thinking we can do God a favor by attending church, to the in-your-face rebellion that we deliberately commit at times.

It is important to note as well that Pontius Pilate, the human judge, in a most unprecedented way, declared Christ sinless (Luke 23:4) and yet sentenced him to the death penalty by crucifixion. In doing this,

Pilate paralleled God the judge, who regarded Christ in a similar way: personally sinless and yet the consummate sinner as our sin bearer. The human judge could only pass a sentence on Christ's body, but God's condemnation took effect upon both Christ's body and his soul; God applied his undiluted curse and wrath upon both.

The invisible hand of God executed, in infinite measure, punishments that were carried out by the hands of men: Christ's arrest, bonds, condemnation, mockery, scourging, desertion, nails and spear, blood and death. Surly men committed heinous sin in crucifying Christ, and yet their actions were both ordained and orchestrated by the very hand of God. The cross was planned from before the foundation of the world as the place where God would inflict his Son with the curse and wrath due redeemed sinners as their sin was charged to him. Behind the visible tribunal and the visible punishment was something infinitely more formidable and severe. What Christ suffered directly at the hand of God is beyond human imagination. Is it any wonder the God-man "cried out with a loud voice, saying, 'Eli, Eli, lema sabachthani?' that is, 'My God, my God, why have you forsaken me?'" (Matt. 27:46)?

Christ's atoning work on the cross fully satisfied God's requirement for recompense. Because Christ paid the penalty in full, those sinners that would become his own are forever acceptable before God's throne; they are declared *not guilty*. More than that, they are declared *righteous*.

Christ's body and soul had been made a sin offering, a sweet-smelling aroma to God. Since death could reign only where there was sin, once the price was paid in full Christ was released in glorious resurrection. A sinner whose guilt is not discharged may be held under death, but the Holy One of God could no longer be held under its power once payment was made on our behalf. As Peter says, "God raised him up, loosing the pangs of death, because it was not possible for him to be held by it. . . . 'For you will not abandon my soul to Hades, or let your Holy One see corruption'" (Acts 2:24, 27). Only Christ could fully atone for our sin and not be held by it forever.

Without a doubt, as a consequence of bearing sin's curse, the human soul of the Messiah *was* for a time in a state of separation from his body, but only temporarily. The pangs of death and separation of body and soul continued only until the perfect sacrifice satisfied divine justice. And then . . . resurrection. By this most glorious of all events, the Judge confirmed our acceptance secured, our inheritance restored, and our eternal life assured.

In essence, Christ said to the Judge through David's messianic psalm (Ps. 16:8–11 quoted by Peter in Acts 2:25–28): "You will permit me to spring forth from the disembodied state into which my soul entered and rise from the grave into which my body descended, because the guilt charged to my account has been deleted and the necessity of wrath removed by my vicarious death."

Acts 13:15–41

The second principal speaker in the book of Acts is the apostle Paul. His testimony to the atonement, full and explicit in his various epistles, is also apparent in the brief excerpts of his sermons recorded in Acts. The constant and common thread throughout Paul's words may be summed up in this: "For I decided to know nothing among you except Jesus Christ and him crucified" (1 Cor. 2:2).

In Acts 13, Paul delivers that message in the Jewish synagogue at Antioch. He leads his hearers to the cross as the essential point of his preaching in a manner similar to Peter's sermon on the day of Pentecost. He describes Jesus as the "Seed of David" (v. 23) and the "Son of God" (v. 33). He touches on the sinlessness of Jesus (v. 28). He even announces Jesus as Savior when he proclaims, "Of this man's offspring God has brought to Israel a Savior, Jesus, as he promised" (Acts 13:23).

Another way Paul testifies to the atonement in Acts is when he makes an appeal to the testimony of John the Baptist and points to the fulfillment of prophecy to show that Jesus the Christ died, was buried, and rose again from the dead, according to the Scriptures (Acts 13:24–37). He concludes with the triumphant statement, "Let it be known to you therefore, brothers, that through this man for-

giveness of sins is proclaimed to you, and by him everyone who
believes is freed from everything from which you could not be freed
by the law of Moses" (Acts 13:38–39).

This was groundbreaking news to the Jews—the truth that forgiveness is not conditional on performance or compliance to the law
but, rather, that forgiveness is through this man Jesus Christ. This
was a radical message with far-reaching implications—liberation
from the hopeless and heavy burden of perfect law keeping, a path
which never resulted in justification because no one could ever keep
the whole law.

This passage is reminiscent of many seen in Paul's epistles where
the righteousness of faith is contrasted with the righteousness of
the law. For example, in Romans Paul states:

> There is therefore now no condemnation for those who are in Christ
> Jesus. For the law of the Spirit of life has set you free in Christ Jesus
> from the law of sin and death. For God has done what the law,
> weakened by the flesh, could not do. By sending his own Son in the
> likeness of sinful flesh and for sin, he condemned sin in the flesh, in
> order that the righteous requirement of the law might be fulfilled in
> us, who walk not according to the flesh but according to the Spirit.
> (Rom. 8:1–4)

Acts 20:28b

The phrase "the church of God, which he obtained with his own
blood" (Acts 20:28b) was part of Paul's admonition to the elders of
Ephesus. It provides further insight into Paul's view of the centrality of the atonement. He declares the death of Jesus to be the great
ransom price by which Christ purchased the church and owns it
as his possession. The church is his, not simply because he rules
it, for in that sense the entire creation is already his. But as blood-
bought property, the church and its individual members are his by
right of purchase.

The people of Paul's day undoubtedly understood these words
to be analogous to the purchase of a slave. But no slave had ever
been purchased with blood, much less the blood of the Master—a

person of supreme value and dignity—the blood of God incarnate. The infinitely valuable Christ paid the infinite price, his own life, for this possession. And it then certainly follows that Christ forever holds the church near and dear to his heart. In view of the astonishing price paid by such a purchaser, Paul urged the elders to care for the church and its members with utmost diligence.

Only Christ, the God-man, can possess the church. No mere man can hold it, for no mere man can afford the redemption price. Redemption is as divine an act as creation, and he who claims us as his property must necessarily be divine. What an awesome mystery!

HEAVEY BURDEN
. GUILT OF SIN
. WEIGHT OF SIN
. TRYING TO BE PERFECT IN KEEPING THE LAW
. THE WEIGHT OF THE LAWS DEMANDS!

CHAPTER 6

The Epistles of Paul on "the Righteousness of God"

Taken together, the epistles of Paul provide the most comprehensive instruction and illumination on the doctrine of the atonement and its application. In general, he uses the same terms to describe Christ's sacrificial death as those employed by the other apostolic writers, terms such as redemption, reconciliation, forgiveness, propitiation, and peace with God. But there is one phrase that is distinctive about Paul's epistles: the righteousness of God.

The Bible uses the expression *the righteousness of God* in two distinct ways: the first as it applies to God, and the second as it applies to man. As an attribute of God, *the righteousness of God* refers to who God is in his holiness and perfect justice, and it ultimately means God's unswerving commitment to display his glory and uphold his name. As it applies to man, the expression refers to the righteousness that God requires from man, a righteousness no sinner can provide on his or her own. Thus, this phrase ultimately refers to the righteousness that is transferred from the sinless Christ to sinners as a result of his finished work on the cross.

This latter meaning of the expression relates to the outcome of the great atonement—Christ's righteousness imputed, credited, and imparted to sinners upon their becoming united to him by faith. Paul said it like this: "For our sake he made him to be sin who knew no sin, so that in him we might become the righteousness of God" (2 Cor. 5:21).

When this verse says, "we might become the righteousness of God," it certainly does not mean we become an attribute of God or that we are holy in and of ourselves. Instead, it displays the nature of the transfer of God's righteousness from him to us as the result of the work of him who knew no sin. Just as Christ was *made sin* objectively and by imputation, his people *become the righteousness of God* objectively and by imputation. This exchange, the Great Exchange, is inconceivably great, good news for sinners.

Martin Luther spent long meditations over entire days and nights wrestling with the phrase *the righteousness of God*. He wrote that when he finally comprehended and embraced the understanding of it, "thereupon I felt myself reborn and to have gone through open doors into paradise."[1]

If the expression *the righteousness of God* referred only to the divine attribute of justice, it would always carry with it the idea of God's wrath. However, Paul means more than that. Paul uses the phrase in relation to grace, revealing a reconciling and justifying God. This meaning of the righteousness of God, as the very essence of the message heralded in the gospel, is perhaps most distinctly shown in Paul's declaration, "For I am not ashamed of the gospel, for it is the power of God for salvation to everyone who believes, to the Jew first and also to the Greek. For in it the righteousness of God is revealed from faith for faith, as it is written, 'The righteous shall live by faith'" (Rom. 1:16–17).

Paul frequently uses this same meaning of the *righteousness of God* to depict the working of Christ's great atonement in contrast to the law. In addressing Jewish believers in particular, he uses this term to erode their attachment to the works of the law and their adherence to legal ceremonies as the basis for their approval by

God. For example, in Romans, Paul refers to righteousness obtained apart from the law and through faith (Rom. 3:21–22). Throughout Galatians, he enforces the grand theme that the righteousness of God through faith is the sinner's only valid plea before God, and he declares that the law could not impart life or righteousness (Gal. 3:21–22). In Corinthians, he holds that Christ is our righteousness (1 Cor. 1:30), and that the ministry of righteousness far exceeds the ministry of the law in glory (2 Cor. 3:9). He goes on to show how in Christ we become the righteousness of God (2 Cor. 5:21). In Philippians, we find Paul toward the end of his life exclaiming:

> Indeed, I count everything as loss because of the surpassing worth of knowing Christ Jesus my Lord. For his sake I have suffered the loss of all things and count them as rubbish, in order that I may gain Christ and be found in him, not having a righteousness of my own that comes from the law, but that which comes through faith in Christ, the righteousness from God that depends on faith. (Phil. 3:8–9)

Paul commonly placed this phrase, *the righteousness of God*, in direct antithesis to our own righteousness. This righteousness is a gift for those who have no righteousness of their own; this righteousness is the gracious provision of God. Paul writes in Romans, "If, because of one man's trespass, death reigned through that one man, much more will those who receive the abundance of grace and the free gift of righteousness reign in life through the one man Jesus Christ" (Rom. 5:17). This gift of righteousness is free. One cannot earn a gift; otherwise it can no longer be called a gift. Instead it becomes a wage deserved. And no sinner deserves to be credited with righteousness.

Christ's atoning work as a free gift supplies the righteousness that is due from man as a creature made in the image of his Creator. What the first man, Adam, should have produced as was proper for a creature made in the image of God, God produced and supplied to fallen man—the perfect sacrifice as our substitute met what was lacking in our righteousness. Since God possesses absolute righteousness as an innate attribute of who he is, and since man is required to produce this perfect righteousness but is in no way able

to do so, only a God-man, uniting the two natures ir
could provide this righteousness. Perfect righteousness
be accepted by God, becomes a human possibility only ͏
transferred to those who are united to the God-man by faith.

Upon receiving Christ and his righteousness by faith, a legal
union between God and the regenerated sinner is formed, resulting in immediate, perfect, and permanent justification. The sinner's
standing before the divine tribunal changes from *guilty* to *declared
righteous*. Then, forever joined in a living union with him, the sinner begins the process of sanctification with its outward evidence
of a changed heart as the sinner becomes who he is in Christ—a
new creation. As Paul states:

> Therefore, if anyone is *in Christ*, he is a new creation. The old has
> passed away; behold, the new has come. All this is from God, who
> through Christ reconciled us to himself . . . in Christ God was rec-
> onciling the world to himself, not counting their trespasses against
> them. (2 Cor. 5:17–19)

Therefore, in our union with Christ, the righteousness required
for our acceptance with God is transferred from Christ to us. Furthermore, our union with Christ is also the source of our entry into
the process of progressive transformation wherein we move toward
greater degrees of Christlikeness, that is, personal righteousness
empowered by the Holy Spirit and focused on bringing God glory.
Increasing levels of obedience display the outward evidence of
authentic union with Christ. However, even in the absence of a
perfect obedience, the righteousness of God is complete in itself,
resulting in perfect justification of the sinner. What a glorious joy
and hope it is to know that in the eyes of God, a sinner in Christ
is as righteous as Christ himself, "for Christ is the end of the law
for righteousness to everyone who believes" (Rom. 10:4).

Faith and the Righteousness of God

Faith and righteousness have distinct roles. It is important to develop a clear delineation between the meaning of the term *faith* and

the meaning of the term *righteousness*. Likewise, the relationship between these two terms is vital for believers to understand.

Paul wrote to the Philippians that he wanted to be "found in him, not having a righteousness of [his] own that comes from the law, but that which comes *through faith* in Christ, the righteousness from God that depends on faith" (Phil. 3:9). This verse makes the delineation and relationship between the terms evident: the righteousness of God is *through faith* in the atoning work of Christ. Faith is the instrument or vehicle by which the Holy Spirit unites the sinner to Christ; faith is not the actual righteousness. The object of our faith is Christ; he is the essence of the transferred righteousness. Thus, "the righteousness of God [comes] through faith in Jesus Christ for all who believe" (Rom. 3:22).

In other words, faith is the hand by which Christ and his righteousness is received, but the origin and source of the righteousness itself is in the person of Christ. There are two reasons for this arrangement: (1) Faith is the only mechanism by which a man or woman reaches out to rely on an object outside the self; and (2) faith is an act of the spirit, soul, and mind in which a man or woman relinquishes self-centeredness and self-dependency. The faith that unites a soul to Christ and appropriates his great atonement is a faith in something external to the self; by its very nature, this faith negates self-righteousness and attaches to an external, alien righteousness.

If faith were the actual righteousness, or if faith were required to purchase this righteousness, justification would be *of works* since it would require a human act. If that were the case, faith would in essence become a new law. But those who are justified are accepted without works of law, for as Paul says to the Romans, "We hold that one is justified by faith [in Christ's atoning work on our behalf] apart from works of the law" (Rom. 3:28; Rom. 3:21–27). Our righteousness was indeed purchased, not by our faith, but by our Christ. If faith itself were the righteousness, no one could be saved unless his or her faith were perfect, since God's law demands perfection (Rom. 14:23b).

Now if the basis for our acceptance was our faith, where would real righteousness be? What would satisfy the justice of God? And how would our consciences be cleansed? Even faith itself is a gift of God as Paul tells the Ephesians: "For by grace you have been saved through faith. And this is not your own doing; it is the gift of God" (Eph. 2:8). So, both our salvation and our faith are gifts of grace; neither our salvation nor our faith can be earned. God puts the faith in our hand, and then closes our hand to make sure we do not drop it. He even helps us with our unbelief by granting requests for help such as, "I believe; help my unbelief" (Mark 9:24b). It is all God.

Justification and the Righteousness of God

Just as we need to clarify the distinctions between *the righteousness of God* and *faith*, we must also be careful to clarify the distinctions between *the righteousness of God* and *justification*. God's righteousness is the material foundation and source of justification. Justification is a result of imputed righteousness, not vice versa. The basis for the justification of sinners united to Christ is twofold and simultaneous: (1) Believers are declared not guilty due to Christ's *sacrificial* death died on their behalf, and (2) believers are declared righteous due to Christ's *perfect* life lived on their behalf.

Jesus Christ, the perfect sacrifice, is absolutely everything a sinner needs for acceptance and standing before an absolutely holy God. And the justification he provides can be recoined, *just-as-if*-ication, that is, *just as if* I had never sinned. And yet it's more than that; it's also *just as if* I will never sin again for I am declared righteous before the Judge forever. God does not just put us back to square one where we start over with a clean slate. If that was all the justification we possessed, we would just start sinning again and be once more guilty before a righteous judge. No; our past, present, and future sins are justified in Christ.

The Righteousness of God: Six Summary Insights

The following are some key insights on the phrase *the righteousness of God* as used by Paul.

1) *This righteousness is actually an accomplished fact.* It is no less of an historical reality than our sin, but with equally real present and future results in an opposite direction. In Romans 5:12–18, Paul draws a parallel demonstrating that as death is the certain result of sin, life is the equally certain result of righteousness. He presents the two great counterparts of sin and righteousness as equivalent realities.

2) *The twofold nature of the Redeemer as God-man was necessary in order to accomplish the transfer of the righteousness of God to sinners.* Since it is impossible for God to die, we see the need for Christ to be human. But in order to be perfect, he must also be divine. As God, and as co-maker of the law, Christ was under no obligation on his own account to be under the law or to obey the law, and, as a result, he is capable of giving his voluntary obedience away.

By assuming humanity, Christ freely and willingly subjected himself not only to the limitations and temptations of being fully man but also to the law's requirement to live a sinless, obedient life in all respects. Having fulfilled the law of God as a man by his personal obedience, he became qualified to satisfy the justice of God by dying as the Lamb of God. The law was then doubly satisfied, first by his sinless life (his *active* obedience) and then by his death as our substitute (his *passive* obedience).

In other words, both his life as the God-man and his death as the God-man were necessary to produce the twofold righteousness of God transferable to redeemed sinners: his life for fulfilling the law, resulting in our imputed righteousness as he obeyed in our place, and his death for sin, resulting in our forgiveness as he died in our place. When the Judge beholds his Son clothed with our humanity and the sinner clothed in the righteousness of God, the result is permanent reunion of God and man.

3) *Though operating through aspects—his life and his death—the righteousness of God transferred by the God-man is one, indivisible, finished work of one Christ.* We must take his sinless life (active obedience) and atoning death (passive obedience), together as one

vicarious obedience. This atoning obedience extended over the entire life of the Lord and was not limited to the few hours on the cross. Both his active and passive obedience began with the incarnation; he obeyed God both personally and vicariously in taking on flesh and blood. And both his active and passive obedience were at work on the cross where he obeyed God both personally and vicariously in allowing himself to be nailed there to suffer, bleed, and die.

Both aspects of Christ's obedience pervade every event in his wondrous life. They were not exercised at different times for different actions; they meet in all actions at all times over the entire life of Jesus, from the first moment of his incarnation to his last breath on the cross. We can see the scope of this active and passive obedience in Paul's affirmation:

> [Christ Jesus] who, though he was in the form of God, did not count equality with God a thing to be grasped, but made himself nothing, taking the form of a servant, being born in the likeness of men. And being found in human form, he humbled himself by becoming obedient to the point of death, even death on a cross. (Phil. 2:6–8)

Christ's obedience had impact on every relationship he had as a man, including his relationship to God, his family, his neighbors, the disciples, and even the government. He learned obedience in them all. And as his trials amplified, thickened, and deepened, his obedience became magnified as well. Amazingly, "although he was a son, he learned obedience through what he suffered. And being made perfect, he became the source of eternal salvation to all who obey him" (Heb. 5:8–9). This obedience was capable of increasing, even though it was always perfect. What a wonderful and beautiful mystery!

What should be added by sinners? What can be added? Nothing. Nothing of man, whether good works or perceived merit—no improvement can be made. To do so would be to declare his obedience insufficient and his righteousness inadequate. It would belittle the great atonement and insult the love of God.

4) *The standard of this righteousness is the law of God and divine justice*. God made man in his image, and the law is the mold in which man's nature was formed, since God's holy nature is reflected in the law. The law does not lose its authority just because people cannot keep it. Wherever the phrase *righteousness of God* occurs, there is always either an explicit or implicit reference to subjection to conformity with the law as the standard or measure of righteousness.

Paul presents two aspects of the law as applying to both Jews and Gentiles alike. First, the law is absolutely inflexible in its demands for sinless obedience. Second, it comes armed with a curse for even a single violation. This is made utterly clear in the letter to the Galatians where Paul wrote, "For *all* who rely on works of the law are under a curse; for it is written, 'Cursed be everyone who does not abide by *all* things written in the Book of the Law, and do them'" (Gal. 3:10). Sinners who violate the law, even one part of it, are rightly under its curse.

In the perfect wisdom of God, in order for Christ to be able to bear this curse for us, Christ was made incarnate *under the law*, in order to redeem the law-breaking sinners he represented. For, "when the fullness of time had come, God sent forth his Son, born of woman, born under the law, to redeem those who were under the law, so that we might receive adoption as sons" (Gal. 4:4–5).

By fulfilling the requirements of the law both personally and for us (i.e., vicariously), Christ became the end of the law for obtaining righteousness to everyone who believes (Rom. 10:3–4). For believers, both the fulfillment of the law and the end of the law's power to condemn are found in Christ.

Thus, by providing "the redemption that is in Christ Jesus" God remains just, even while justifying sinners through imputed righteousness. Paul says this was to "show [God's] righteousness at the present time, so that he might be just and the justifier of the one who has faith in Jesus" (Rom. 3:26). The life of Christ fulfilled the law on our behalf, and the death of Christ paid the penalty of the law on our behalf. So the law is then doubly fulfilled in the life and death of Jesus.

5) *The righteousness of God is a substitutionary righteousness, lived out by Christ in our place and for our benefit; the death of Christ is a substitutionary death.*

In Christ's substitutionary role as sinless sin bearer, he always remained conscious of his personal sinlessness. None of his suffering was for his personal guilt. Rather, it was all for guilt transferred to him as the representative wrath bearer. In like manner, the redeemed, in spite of all the assurance and security of imputed righteousness, never cease to bear personal sinfulness and unworthiness. In this life, we remember the sin that his death causes God to forget. Consequently, we should always remain humble, awed by his grace, knowing we are undeserving, insisting he gets all the glory.

For those representatively *in him*, there is nothing greater in the entire world's history than the substitutionary obedience in the life and death of Christ on behalf of his people. To them, the life and death of Jesus Christ is the central event of all time to which previous ages looked forward and subsequent ages look back. It is the only hope for all humanity in all times and places.

6) *Sinners are born spiritually dead and remain dead and incapable of any aspect of sanctification until faith unites them to Christ.* Only when the Great Exchange takes place in the heart of a sinner does life replace death. Once his righteousness is credited to us, only then is true transformation possible. Biblically speaking, "even when we were dead in our trespasses, [God] made us alive together with Christ—by grace you have been saved" (Eph. 2:5).

The profound process of growth, or sanctification, only begins once a sinner has been regenerated (born again); only then can the day-to-day, moment-by-moment process of transformation be set in motion. Clearly, dead men cannot grow, but once we have been regenerated by Christ's atoning blood we can grow. "If Christ is in [us], although the body is dead because of sin, the Spirit is life because of righteousness" (Rom. 8:10). As the Spirit is transforming us, we become more like Christ.

The righteousness referred to here is transferred righteousness, or *imputed* righteousness. The result is life, meaning a new life resulting from a new birth. Authentic reception of the gift of the righteousness of God will always initiate the lifelong process of sanctification. Forgiveness and imputed righteousness necessarily precede the sanctification process and must remain the working platform on which sanctification takes place. And though evidencing the authenticity of their union with Christ redeemed sinners become more Christlike, they are never more justified than they were upon true belief, when the transferred righteousness of God was placed over their life.

CHAPTER 7

Romans

In his epistle to the Romans, Paul provides an extensive outline of biblical doctrine. His main purpose is to depict the redeemed sinner's relationship to God and, more specifically, to illuminate the fact that Christ's great atonement, as the heart of the gospel, is the sole basis for the justification of sinners united to Christ through faith. After declaring that "the gospel is the power of God for salvation for all who believe" (Rom. 1:16), Paul launches into his major themes by quoting from Habakkuk 2:4: "For in [the gospel] the righteousness of God is revealed from faith for faith, as it is written, 'The righteous shall live by faith'" (Rom. 1:17).

Throughout Romans, Paul establishes the great guiding doctrines of Christianity by elaborating on the key elements of the atonement, including righteousness, faith, and life. He begins to bring these into clear focus starting in chapter three.

Romans 3:23–26

> For all have sinned and fall short of the glory of God, and are justified by his grace as a gift, through the redemption that is in Christ Jesus, whom God put forward as a propitiation by his blood, to be received by faith. This was to show God's righteousness, because in

his divine forbearance he had passed over former sins. It was to show
his righteousness at the present time, so that he might be just and the
justifier of the one who has faith in Jesus. (Rom. 3:23–26)

Here Paul lays the foundation for the doctrine of justification.
The building blocks he uses display the following five principles:

1) The grace of God is the driving force behind his gift of justification for sinners.
2) The gift of justification comes through a redemption that is
   in Christ.
3) The purchase price of our redemption is the blood of Christ.
4) The righteousness of God is an essential element in the process
   of justification; Paul will go on to show how this righteousness
   is transferred (or credited) to redeemed sinners.
5) Faith is the only instrument through which the gift of justification can be received.

Paul clarifies the connection between justification and Christ's
great atonement by focusing on three terms used to connect the
death of Christ to the needs of sinners: redemption, propitiation, and
righteousness. Although each term casts the atonement in a slightly
different light and points to the cross from a distinct perspective, all
three terms depict the same completed work of Christ:

- Redemption relates the atonement to man's captivity to sin
  and to death.
- Propitiation relates the atonement to man's exposure to divine
  wrath.
- Righteousness relates the atonement to man's relationship to
  God's law.

Paul's selection of these words to describe the same great truth
demonstrates that the atoning work of Christ is one work with
multiple applications, thereby holistically meeting all the needs of
redeemed sinners.

By using the concept of redemption, Paul indicates that sinners are in a captivity and that a ransom must be paid by a benefactor on behalf of the captives in order to secure their release. For sinners, the ransom or price of deliverance is *the blood of Christ*, a term synonymous with his death (1 Pet. 1:18–19; Rev. 5:9). The very person of Christ became the ransom. In addition, the very person of Christ *is* the redemption of his people (1 Cor. 1:30). Our redemption is *in* Christ Jesus. So our redemption is secure as long as Christ lives, and therefore, like Christ, our redemption is both infinite and eternal.

But what does Christ redeem or deliver us from? He redeems us from (1) God's wrath against our sin (Rom. 5:9); (2) the curse of the law (Gal. 3:13); and (3) the one who has the power of death, that is, the devil (Heb. 2:14). In other words, he redeems us from all the penal consequences of our sin.

Just as the term *redemption* presupposes captivity, *propitiation* presupposes anger, wrath, and threat of punishment justly due to sinners from God. The propitiation itself is the appeasement of the justly kindled wrath of God. When God put Christ forward as a propitiation, his wrath was completely absorbed, depleted, exhausted, removed, and eliminated by virtue of its being spent in its entirety upon Christ.

The apostle John used the same term, *propitiation*, to depict a result of the love of God toward us. He writes, "In this is love, not that we have loved God but that he loved us and sent his Son to be the propitiation for our sins" (1 John 4:10). It is abundantly clear from this verse that God's love does not absolve us of our sins in the absence of a just basis. No, God's wrath against sin must find an outlet through the infliction of punitive justice in one of two ways: either upon self-justified sinners outside of Christ or upon the God-appointed wrath bearer, Jesus Christ.

The concept of propitiation harkens back to the *propitiatory*, also known as the mercy seat—names given to the cover of the ark of the covenant into which the Law of Moses had been deposited. The propitiatory was sprinkled with the blood of the sin sacrifice on the annual Day of Atonement. This was the heart of the old covenant provision for sin. The symbolism can be seen in this: the ark contained the law, and the propitiatory covered its curse whenever it was sprinkled by the atoning blood. So Paul's use of the word *propitiation* connotes the appeasing of God's wrath by sacrificial blood. The old covenant propitiatory, therefore, foreshadowed the true propitiation—Christ—who would personally and forever exhaust the divine wrath at the appointed time.

But there is yet more rich symbolism represented by the mercy seat. Not only did it serve as the Old Testament place of atonement, it was also considered to be God's throne in the midst of his people (Ps. 80:1). It was the place of his divine presence, where the glory of the Lord abided. This shows that once the blood of Christ propitiates our sin, redeemed sinners are able to enjoy restored personal relationship with their holy God.

Romans 3:25–26 connects the righteousness of God with the atonement, and, therefore, the meaning of the phrase "God's righteousness" here does not refer to an attribute of God but to the righteousness God imputes to sinners as a result of the Great Exchange.

In Romans 3:21–22, Paul states, "The righteousness of God has been manifested apart from the law, although the Law and the Prophets bear witness to it—the righteousness of God through faith in Jesus Christ for all who believe." In other words, every believer, whether Jew or Gentile, is declared righteous—justified—in Christ. Paul affirms that this also applies equally to those who lived and believed before and after Christ's death, the propitiating event (vv. 25b–26).

Christ's retroactive bearing of sin is of particular importance because, as we noted earlier, the old covenant system of sacrifices did not atone for moral offenses; therefore, these sins could not be forgiven prior to the historical event of the cross. God showed forbearance toward these believing sinners; he restrained himself from executing judgment and wrath. He deferred the punishment of their sins and advanced tentative forgiveness because he looked to the eventual fulfillment of the foreshadow, the accomplished fact of Christ's great atonement. Only at that time would the required righteousness actually be transferred and forgiveness granted. In a sense, theirs was a righteousness on credit, a debt to be paid by a future atonement. Once Jesus lived a perfect life on their behalf and died a perfect death on their behalf, his obedience became theirs, and Christ's righteousness was finally manifested (made evident, revealed) and credited to their account.

For thousands of years before Christ, millions of Jewish believers living under the old covenant trusted in the atoning work of the Messiah, their Christ and our Christ. They placed their faith in the Suffering Servant based on the promises and prophecies of their Scripture, the Old Testament. In their case, as in ours today, God's righteousness is transferred through the instrument of faith in Christ and his work of the great atonement. In other words, those believers living before Christ's atoning death looked forward to the cross while believers living after his death look back to it.

We must never forget that our God is a God of justice, and that he therefore must always assert just verdicts and inflict just punishments. God is a holy lover of men's souls, but his love does not disengage from his holiness, and his holiness does not disengage from his love. There are no exceptions. Jesus Christ embodies and unites these seemingly opposed perfections of God, and his great atonement fulfills and displays them both; perfect justice and perfect love meet simultaneously and in full harmony at the cross. At the cross, God's holy justice is not compromised and neither is his loving mercy, because there the infinite price was paid to keep these two indispensable attributes perfectly and forever intact. Through the death of his only begotten Son, the perfect sacrifice, God reconciled his own justice and mercy.

The divine justice that seemed to be slumbering during the period of forbearance, when God restrained his wrath, was satisfied at the cross. If the actual satisfaction of divine justice had not been delivered, and the righteousness had not been transferred, God would no longer remain just. Instead, he would be defiled by virtue of passing over the former sins and pre-justifying the old covenant believers without due cause. Thus, the cross results in both the justification of sinners and the justification of the God who justifies them.

Romans 3:23–26 helps to circumvent two commonly accepted yet non-biblical theologies designed to make people feel better about themselves and their sin. The first of these mistakes, something we touched on earlier, is the view that God is solely absolute, unconditional love. Those who adhere to this one-sided theology of the atonement, in which the element of God's love is recognized but the element of God's justice is excluded, believe that a loving God would never condemn anyone to eternal punishment. But if God could justify sinners with no more basis than his love, what need would there be for a cross? The explicit and unmistakable message of the Bible is that God's great love was the motivation for him to provide for the satisfaction of his justice in his Son, as Christ himself clearly stated in the most famous Bible verse of all: "For God so loved the world, that he gave his only Son, that whoever believes in him should not perish but have eternal life" (John 3:16). It was God's infinite love that sent Christ into the world and in due course to the cross. It was the only way, because the penalty for sin had to be paid.

A sinner's position of acceptance by God is not unconditional. In the absence of God's justice being satisfied, there is no forgiveness, no imputed righteousness, and no eternal life but, rather, only eternal perishing. Hundreds of Bible passages show this. To espouse a theology that holds to the unconditional, absolute love of God without simultaneously acknowledging the justice and holiness of God is to belittle Christ and his atonement.

Another common ideological mistake is the belief that we are all God's children. The universal fatherhood of God, as it is called, is uniformly refuted by Romans 3:23–26 and by the Bible as a whole. Only those redeemed by the ransom payment of the blood of the Son hold God as their adopted Father. Paul shows this clearly when he writes to the Galatians, "But when the fullness of time had come, God sent forth his Son, born of woman, born under the law, to redeem those who were under the law, so that we might receive adoption as sons" (Gal. 4:4).

Apart from our redemption by his blood, there is no father-child relationship between a sinful human being and an infinitely holy God. Instead, the only relationship to God is as judge, a relationship that draws down condemnation, punishment, and wrath.

Romans 4:22–25

> That is why [Abraham's] faith was "counted to him as righteousness." But the words "it was counted to him" were not written for his sake alone, but for ours also. It will be counted to us who believe in him who raised from the dead Jesus our Lord, who was delivered up for our trespasses and raised for our justification. (Rom. 4:22–25)

In Romans 4, Paul uses the case of Abraham to prove that justification is through faith alone. The expression "faith was counted to him as righteousness" is a concise description of the process by which Christ's righteousness is transferred to believers, even Old Testament believers such as Abraham.

Counted is an accounting term, denoting a crediting to our account. The term is synonymous with *imputed*. Faith, then, is the instrument by which believers are united to Christ, and the transfer of righteousness from the sinless Christ to sinners follows the establishment of this union. Without faith, the union could not be formed, and without the union the righteousness could not be transferred.

In verse 24, Paul asserts that the faith which justifies is a faith centered on God in his capacity as the Christ raiser. God the Father is the one who accepted the perfect sacrifice as payment and propitiation, and then, with a profound, physical declaration that the payment is sufficient, caused the resurrection of Christ.

But this justification is not bestowed on all sinners; there is an indispensable qualification—we must believe. We must rely entirely on Christ's righteousness, not our own, as our sole basis for acceptance by the Judge. This is the essence of saving faith. Christ has completed the work in which he is both the ransom and the redemption. Nothing is left to us except to believe and receive his death as our payment and his righteousness as our own.

By substituting *because of* in place of the word *for* in verse 25, the essence of the sacrifice becomes clearer: Jesus our Lord was delivered up *because of* our trespasses. In other words, our sins caused Christ's death.

Therefore, if we had never sinned, Christ never would have died. Sin and death have a cause-and-effect relationship, namely, that sin causes death, as Paul affirms in a later passage: "The wages of sin is death" (Rom. 6:23a). This reality is just as true for Christ as it is for unredeemed sinners. It is a clear biblical fact that from the time of the garden of Eden forward, God punishes sin with death, even in the case of his own sinless, sin-bearing Son, our substitute who became sin for us.

Since Christ had no sin of his own to cause him to be delivered over to death, verse 25 implies that it was our sin that caused Christ's death by virtue of substitution (or transfer) from us to him, that is to say, because he changed places with us. He succumbed to the death we deserved as our surrogate or stand-in. However, as can be seen from the context, in order for our sins to be charged to the sinless sin bearer, a covenant relationship must be established through faith in which Christ and believing sinners become federally one, that is, legally one, in the eyes of God. Without such a legal union, our sins could not possibly have been charged to Christ and certainly would not have brought him to the cross or caused his death.

God himself handed his Son over for crucifixion according to his own "definite plan and foreknowledge" to be "crucified and killed by the hands of lawless men" (Acts 2:23). And he did it for one great reason: so Christ would receive the punishment due for the sins of the redeemed, thereby paying the price of their redemption. The Judge of all saw fit to deliver him judicially into the hand of sinners for the physical aspect of the punishment. As noted earlier, the arrest, trial, and crucifixion were the visible counterparts of the invisible-to-us events transpiring at the divine tribunal. In both courts, human and divine, the judges Pontius Pilate and God the

Father found Christ personally innocent and yet pronounced his condemnation. The divine tribunal is where Christ was charged with our guilt and justly condemned to bear the penal consequence—death. Therefore, with our sin upon him, all the acts of man's injustice that befell Christ on earth were actually only part of the just punishment doled out by God.

Christ endured much more than the observable agony of torture by the hands of evil men. In the ultimate execution of God's infinite wrath upon our sin, Christ received inconceivable anguish by the hand of God, an unstoppable surge of torment invisible to our eyes and unfathomable to our imaginations. Yet he did not deserve it; we did.

Just as sin and death has a cause-and-effect relationship for both sinner and substitute, so there is a causal relationship between God's acceptance of Christ's atoning work and his resurrected life. The resurrection is tangible evidence that Christ's atoning work actually accomplished the satisfaction of God's justice and that Christ's righteousness was deemed transferable to the redeemed. In other words, Christ's great atonement perfectly provided for the imputation of righteousness from Christ to us, and because his work was both finished and accepted, there was no reason for the sin bearer to remain dead. Thus, he is gloriously and triumphantly raised.

If Christ's work of atonement had been imperfect or lacking in any way, the resurrection of Jesus would not have taken place. Had we not been justified (declared righteous), Christ the wrath bearer would not have been released from the clutches of death because the price for the sins he bore would remain, having not yet have been paid in full. But the historic, bodily resurrection of Christ after his atoning death on the cross stands as final, authoritative proof that Christ's work of redemption is forever acceptable and complete. God's justice is perfectly satisfied, his wrath is absolutely quenched, all our sins are entirely atoned for, Christ's righteousness is credited to us, and, as sinners united to Christ by faith, we are fully and forever accepted by God.

In the verses that follow Romans 4:25, Paul enumerates the massive fruits of our justification, which include peace with God, access to God, a firm foundation in grace, and the hope of glory. Adversity cannot extinguish this hope; it grows and flourishes in the crucible of hardship, difficulty, and suffering. It is a hope that does not disappoint because we have been given the Holy Spirit through whom God's love continually flows within our hearts (Rom. 5:1–5). To be sure, our justification in Christ is a major part of what makes the good news of the gospel good news because it leads to the best good news—God himself.

Romans 5:6–11

For while we were still weak, at the right time Christ died for the ungodly. For one will scarcely die for a righteous person—though perhaps for a good person one would dare even to die—but God shows his love for us in that while we were still sinners, Christ died for us. Since, therefore, we have now been justified by his blood, much more shall we be saved by him from the wrath of God. For if while we were enemies we were reconciled to God by the death of his Son, much more, now that we are reconciled, shall we be saved by his life. More than that, we also rejoice in God through our Lord Jesus Christ, through whom we have now received reconciliation. (Rom. 5:6–11)

Paul uses four descriptive terms to portray our position before God apart from Christ: *weak, ungodly, sinners,* and *enemies.* It is certainly remarkable that God provides Christ's great atonement while we are still in this totally depraved condition. It is imperative that we recognize the significance of the chronology of God's redemptive action toward us as his enemies, because only then do we have a platform for appreciating the freeness and magnitude of his love as we come to the humble realization that it was all of him and none of us.

Amazingly, we are not required to purify ourselves before coming to Christ. Indeed, how could we, being entrenched in habitual sin and too weak to improve ourselves with any consistency? How could we, being his enemies in active rebellion against divine authority, filled with contempt for his indisputable divine rights as our Creator, and indignant at his ultimate control of all things? We may offer lip service with apathetic hearts toward him, but apart from Christ, our hearts are passionate only for our own temporal pleasure, and our minds are intent only on avoiding or numbing our own pain. We despise his control, and thus we despise him. "For the mind that is set on the flesh is hostile to God, for it does not submit to God's law; indeed, it cannot" (Rom. 8:7).

But apart from Christ, do all sinners really *despise* God? Isn't this taking it too far? Are there not many good, relatively moral, and even philanthropic sinners who are not consciously on the warpath as enemies of God? Though this may seem to be the case at first glance, isn't an attitude of self-righteousness and self-sufficiency in itself an insult to God? Such attitudes represent a quiet insubordination cloaked in good works and self-justification, and those who live by them do not feel the reality of their sin and desperate need for the cross. They see themselves as deserving the applause of God and man. They claim the glory as their own, and God's glory is belittled. As a result, like the Pharisee in the following parable they are excluded from justification:

> "Two men went up into the temple to pray, one a Pharisee and the other a tax collector. The Pharisee, standing by himself, prayed thus: 'God, I thank you that I am not like other men, extortioners, unjust, adulterers, or even like this tax collector. I fast twice a week; I give tithes of all that I get.' But the tax collector, standing far off, would not even lift up his eyes to heaven, but beat his breast, saying, 'God, be merciful to me, a sinner!' I tell you, this man went down to his house *justified*, rather than the other. For everyone who exalts himself will be humbled, but the one who humbles himself will be exalted."
> (Luke 18:10–14)

The reality is that all sinners outside of Christ are enslaved, held captive by sin, and therefore, by definition, hostile to God. They are incapable of becoming morally strong or godly, since a self-centered motive underlies every word and action. They are incapable of freeing themselves from habitual sin and incapable of making God their friend. They are not God's children (John 8:34–44). Paul, in another epistle, even identifies their condition as *dead* in sin (Eph. 2:1, 5).

To make the timing of Christ's death—while we were still sinners—even more astounding, in verse 7 God's love is contrasted with the love of one man for another. Seldom does a man love enough to offer his life on behalf of another. Perhaps a man would die for a good friend. But in the entire history of the world, it had never been heard that a man laid down his life to die on behalf of a true enemy. And yet, Jesus did just that.

Paul uses the word *for* four times in verses 6–8, each time displaying the concept of one dying on behalf of another. The word *for* cannot be construed to mean that Christ died to provide his followers with a virtuous or moral example to follow. Christ died for us as our stand-in or surrogate. He changed places with us and died the death we deserved.

What made Christ die this horrible death on the cross for God's enemies? Verse 8 makes it clear that God's love was the motivating force behind the design and implementation of his Son's great atonement. God's love *caused* him to provide the great atonement, which in turn provided for our redemption, justification, and reconciliation. His love, however, did not provide for absolute forgiveness in the absence of the satisfaction of his justice.

And so, just as Christ's atoning work on the cross is the ultimate satisfaction of God's justice, the cross is the ultimate expression of God's love. The cross is the most significant place we will ever see God's love in action. In the absence of his love, there would be no cross. The cross substantiates his love.

In verses 9 and 10, Paul displays two direct results of Christ's bloody death. The first is justification, in which redeemed sinners are declared righteous and given a new standing as accepted by God. He makes it clear that Christ's great atonement is the sole basis of justification, as there is no mention of any other prerequisites. It is not dependent on the personal virtue or amended lifestyle of the believer. Sin is completely canceled by Christ's atoning blood; it is as if we had never sinned.

The second direct result of Christ's bloody death displayed is reconciliation, the mending of the redeemed sinner's estranged relationship with God. The term *reconciliation* refers to a state where two alienated parties are reunited by the satisfactory removal of the cause of estrangement or offense. In the case of God and sinners, the alienation is mutual. On man's side it is caused by our inherent and natural hostility toward God (Rom. 8:7). On God's side it is caused by the wide gulf of separation created by his holiness and his inherent hostility toward unforgiven sin. Isaiah puts it like this: "But your iniquities have made a separation between you and your God, and your sins have hidden his face from you so that he does not hear" (Isa. 59:2).

But how do we obtain the benefits of reconciliation with God through Christ's atoning work on the cross? We receive this reconciliation in the free exercise of God's grace. Like justification discussed above, this reconciliation is not based on man's performance. Paul does not say that we were reconciled to God by cultivating an improved attitude toward him, that if we would just obey him more, he would become our friend. We can never obey him perfectly, and only perfect obedience is good enough for a holy God. Instead, blood-bought reconciliation is our only hope for friendship with God. Reconciliation is not earned but received.

Until the very moment we received his grace, we remained his enemies: "While we were enemies we were reconciled to God by the death of his Son . . . through whom we have now received reconciliation" (Rom. 5:10–11).

We did not take the initiative to remove the enmity—God did. God himself is the author of the great plan of reconciliation and the source of its provision. God reconciled us to himself, for "in Christ God was reconciling the world to himself, not counting their trespasses against them" (2 Cor. 5:19). God did the reconciling through Christ.

This message of reconciliation is the gospel, the good news, the message of Christ's great atonement for the sins of the believer. All who receive the atonement enjoy reconciliation. All who refuse the atonement are left standing on their own inadequate righteousness. For them, favor with God is impossible since they are, both by nature and by practice, sinners, and their sin is an offense to him. Manmade attempts to bridge the relationship with God are unable to turn away God's wrath. But in the gospel, with God as its originator and God in Christ as its reconciler, the believer has full certainty of acceptability; the basis of our relationship is secure. On man's side, there is only one requirement: entering this reconciliation by accepting the atonement as his sole basis for righteousness. On God's side there is nothing lacking, since the work of Christ's great atonement is a finished work, perfect and complete, on behalf of sinners.

We have been justified and reconciled by the death of the Son, but it does not end there. God augments this "much more" by adding the benefits of the resurrected life of the Son, our future and eternally secure salvation. Paul said that we are "justified by his blood . . . reconciled . . . by the death of his Son, [and] much more [than that] . . . shall we be saved by his life" (Rom. 5:9–10).

Those united to Christ share in his resurrection with all its glorious benefits in this life and in the life to come. What is eternal life? It is knowing God and the Christ whom God sent (John 17:3)—for our ever-increasing and everlasting enjoyment. Paul shows this glorious reality like this:

> But God, being rich in mercy, because of the great love with which he loved us, even when we were dead in our trespasses, made us alive together with Christ—by grace you have been saved—and raised us up with him and seated us with him in the heavenly places in Christ Jesus, so that *in the coming ages he might show the immeasurable riches of his grace in kindness toward us in Christ Jesus*. (Eph. 2:4–7)

Accordingly, Paul writes, "More than that, we also rejoice in God through our Lord Jesus Christ, through whom we have now received reconciliation" (Rom. 5:11). As recipients of this eternally valid reconciliation, our reasonable and appropriate response can be summed up in a single word—joy. This restored fellowship with our holy Creator is a cause for unlimited and endless rejoicing. Joy is the inevitable, uncontainable evidence that we have indeed been reconciled.

We will never exhaust this joy. Throughout the endless ages of eternity, we will continually discover and experience more and more of God. And since our joy is directly proportional to our experience of God, our joy will never plateau; our delight and pleasure and satisfaction and happiness will increase forever and ever. If that does not take our breath away, what will?

Romans 5:12–19

> For as by the one man's disobedience the many were made sinners, so by the one man's obedience the many will be made righteous. (Rom. 5:19)

In Romans 5:12–19, Paul sets out to explain how the obedience of Christ gains righteousness for many, and to do so he builds a comparison between the disobedience of Adam and the obedience of Christ.

The statement "by the one man's disobedience the many were made sinners" can only mean one thing—that Adam is the representative of all descended from him, and by his sin, the entire human race collectively inherited a fallen sin nature resulting in personal condemnation and sealing the death of all individuals. In other words, sin entered the world through one representative man, Adam, and the judicial consequences of Adam's sin are experienced by all those born *in Adam*. This can be understood from where Paul declares "*one* trespass led to condemnation for *all* men" (Rom. 5:18a).

Paul makes clear here that our condemnation is "the result of that one man's sin" (v. 16), "because of one man's trespass" (v. 17), and "by the one man's disobedience" (v. 19). This explains why he writes to the Ephesians that we are born dead, referring to our condition apart from Christ. "[We] were dead in the trespasses and sins in which [we] once walked . . . and were by nature children of wrath, like the rest of mankind. . . . We were dead in our trespasses" (Eph. 2:1–5).

Because we are born into Adam, our representative, we are born into sin. And yet it is not as if apart from Adam we would never personally sin—it is always only a short time until we participate as sinners by our own volition. This is made perfectly clear elsewhere in Romans, such as where Paul writes, "for all have sinned and fall short of the glory of God" (Rom. 3:23).

What is the essence of Adam's sin? It is choosing some other pleasure (a forbidden fruit) over *the* pleasure, the infinitely valuable God. Think of that! Was this not a deliberate devaluing and degrading of the worth of God? Yes, it was a radical, outrageous, and offensive act—one deserving of the curse of God. And yet aren't all of our sins similar in their essence and therefore equally outrageous and offensive? Maybe we don't choose a forbidden fruit over God. But have we not at times treated him with contempt by preferring other things over him? Have we shown apathy toward God by choosing television, the newspaper, sleep, or some irrelevant trifle over spending time with him in his Word? Has a favorite sport or interest or hobby taken priority over worshiping him at church? Has entertainment, money, or social life taken precedence over prayer? Almost anything can become an idol, diverting our focus and desire away from God, revealing that in our heart of hearts we deliberately dishonor him. We all too frequently choose self over God—comfort, security, pride, self-righteousness, self-sufficiency, self-justification, self-glorification, and the approval of man.

Each of us is guilty of thousands of such sins. Are we better than Adam in his choosing a forbidden fruit over God? What then do we deserve when every single sin we commit is, at its very core, a form of spitting in the face of God?

Once the first sin entered through Adam, the presence of sin spread to his every descendant. And beyond sin's mere presence, sin's power to enslave was inbred in the fabric of every human soul. Sin subordinated all humanity as an irrepressible tyrant, "so that . . . sin reigned in death" (Rom. 5:21a).

Death is the culmination of sin's reign. From the beginning God pronounced death as the penalty for sin (Gen. 2:17), so it is not surprising to find death to be another common denominator for all descendants of Adam. In Romans 5:21 Paul undoubtedly implies physical death. However, he goes beyond just physical death. Since he draws a contrast with eternal life in the second half of the verse, it is safe to conclude that Paul means the broadest significance of the term *death*, which takes into account all the eternal misery that flows from permanent estrangement from God in the second death—that is to say, hell itself. John gives a horrific and sobering description of this in Revelation:

> Then Death and Hades were thrown into the lake of fire. This is the second death, the lake of fire. And if anyone's name was not found written in the book of life, he was thrown into the lake of fire. (Rev. 20:14–15)

To the extent that all of this is horrifying news for sinners, the second half of Romans 5:19 brings stunning relief to the many that will be made righteous by the one man's obedience. The reason Paul takes such pains to explain how one man's sin caused the condemnation of every person now becomes obvious. It is to illustrate and magnify his main point: just as sin is charged to all in Adam (all mankind), righteousness is credited to many (those in Christ). Just as the judicial consequences of Adam's sin apply to all in Adam, the judicial consequences of Christ's righteousness apply to the many who are in Christ. The identical principle of *the one on behalf of the many* applies to both representatives, God's first created man, Adam the sinner, and God's first begotten man, Christ the righteous. So just as all humans enter into condemnation and death solely by virtue of their connection to Adam in his representative sin, all the redeemed enter into justification and life solely by virtue of their connection with Christ in his representative righteousness.

In order to be accepted into favorable relationship with God, individual acts of righteousness are not required because Christ's representative righteousness is eternally sufficient. This is a proof that justification is by grace alone. To emphasize this point, the expression *much more* is used twice (Rom. 5:15, 17); it affirms the certainty with which Christ is able to represent the redeemed and make them righteous. If Adam, the sinner, could open the world's gate to sin and death, then Christ, the perfect one, could open the world's gate to imputed righteousness resulting in justification and eternal life.

This passage places the disobedience of Adam in direct antithesis to the obedience of Christ; the two men shed reciprocal light on each other. Christ incarnate and crucified is the great compensation set over and against the fall of Adam. The passage speaks as if there had been only two men in the world into whose obedience or disobedience their entire seed enters. These are the two, and the only two, representative men. Every other man and woman falls under the family headship of one or the other.

It was the Creator's prerogative to establish this principle of representation, and he did so from the beginning of man, applying it consistently to both the first man and the Second Man. It is not up to us to judge, rationalize, or modify God's chosen structure. In the exercise of his sovereign will, in which he is always holy, wise, just, and good, God determines the system, not we. As Paul said to his imaginary questioner, "But who are you, O man, to answer back to God? Will what is molded say to its molder, 'Why have you made me like this?'" (Rom. 9:20). This framework exists by the decree of God in the exercise of his ultimate, sovereign dominion over all things, including the human race and sin itself. This very plan was in place before time began (Rev. 13:8b).

Adam's trespass contains two parts: a personally violated command and a guilt incurred by his seed. Likewise, the Second Man must enter into both parts in order to satisfy divine justice. Christ must first personally obey all the Father's commands and then provide an obedience to be credited to his seed, redeemed sinners.

The personally sinless Christ perfectly obeyed all of God's moral will, and, as our representative, Christ fulfilled the law in our place. He loved *for us* when we hated God and man, he gave *for us* when we were selfish, and he was pure *for us* when we were polluted with sin. So, as we've noted, Jesus not only died for us, he also lived for us. All that Christ did in both his life and his death, he did in our place as our substitute.

Just as Adam's sin was in reality our sin, just as if we had committed it ourselves, Christ's perfect obedience to the law and his death to pay our penalty for breaking the law are just as much our obedience and death as if we had perfectly obeyed the law and had died on the cross.

At the conclusion of Romans 5, Paul extols the triumph of this grace over sin and explains that it is *through righteousness* that grace reigns:

> But where sin increased, grace abounded all the more, so that, as sin reigned in death, grace also might reign *through righteousness* leading to eternal life *through Jesus Christ* our Lord. (Rom. 5:20b–21)

As God's blessings in Christ are to those who deserve his curse, his grace is abundant and free and sovereign and life-giving and eternal, and it is offered to sinners exclusively through the righteousness of Christ. The reign of grace heralds the end of legalistic despair, the end of unrelenting guilt, the end of fear of punishment, the end of hopelessness in facing a holy God, and the end of death itself. Jesus can be wholly trusted for the righteousness we need. And in trusting him for our righteousness rather than ourselves, we honor, glorify, magnify, and exalt him. God gets all the glory.

Romans 6:1–12

> What shall we say then? Are we to continue in sin that grace may abound? By no means! How can we who died to sin still live in it? Do you not know that all of us who have been baptized into Christ Jesus were baptized into his death? We were buried therefore with him by baptism into death, in order that, just as Christ was raised from the dead by the glory of the Father, we too might walk in newness of life.
>
> For if we have been united with him in a death like his, we shall certainly be united with him in a resurrection like his. We know that our old self was crucified with him in order that the body of sin might be brought to nothing, so that we would no longer be enslaved to

sin. For one who has died has been set free from sin. Now if we have died with Christ, we believe that we will also live with him. We know that Christ being raised from the dead will never die again; death no longer has dominion over him. For the death he died he died to sin, once for all, but the life he lives he lives to God. So you also must consider yourselves dead to sin and alive to God in Christ Jesus.

Let not sin therefore reign in your mortal bodies, to make you obey their passions. (Rom. 6:1–12)

Paul anticipates a misunderstanding of the grace provided through the atonement and denounces the rationalization of sin in order to benefit from more and more grace. By no means should we do this (2a). Paul bases his point on death, this time not Christ's death alone but our dying with him, a death that changes everything.

To demonstrate the importance of this concept, Paul not only uses the expression "died with Christ" (v. 8), but he also uses three other related expressions: "buried . . . with [Christ]" (v. 4), "united with him in . . . death" (v. 5), and "crucified with him" (v. 6). All these terms refer to our participation in one act—Christ's great atonement. The words *with Christ* denote a union between Christ and the believer, as both are connected to the same atoning act.

For us, this death is not a bodily death but a spiritual one. In this death, we die to all self-justification and self-sufficiency as the basis for saving ourselves. We die to all claims of self-assured acceptability by God. All attempts to justify ourselves by independent performance-based schemes in order to satisfy God's justice apart from Christ are summarily killed.

By interpreting this passage in the context of Romans 5, where we saw Christ's great atonement as an act of one for many, it becomes clear that here in Romans 6 believers are described as doing what our representative did—dying. It is noteworthy that the fifth chapter of Romans describes all this in the third person, but the sixth chapter describes it in the first person, "we," making Christ's atoning death a personal death for both Paul and us. The corporate act of the atonement, described here from our point of view, demonstrates our personal participation in the transaction—we are in him, and he is in us in a mutual abiding.

This wonderful truth is illuminated again to the Corinthian believers as "one has died for all, therefore all have died" (2 Cor. 5:14b). When Paul uses this reciprocal phraseology, he is describing the same event from two different points of view. These deaths are not two distinct acts, one on Christ's side and the other on ours. Both deaths describe the single, public, corporate act performed by the Son of God that we share in by virtue of our union with him. Since we are in Christ, and since he represents us, when our representative died, all those in him died along with him. Christ's death for sin belongs to us as truly as if we had personally borne the penalty and accomplished the atonement ourselves.

Our dying with Christ results in a new relationship between us and sin, since the death Christ died he died to sin. And so Paul asks, "How can we who died to sin still live in it?" (Rom. 6:2b). He is not referring to an absolute and immediate deliverance from the presence of sin as an ongoing reality in our lives. Furthermore, he is not saying we are immune to the need for conducting warfare with sin as it seeks to tempt and re-enslave us. Rather, by uniting with Christ in his death we immediately become (1) dead to the guilt of sin. When we are made righteous (justified), we are legally dead to the condemnation and penalty of our sin. As well, we are (2) dead to the dominion of sin. We become dead to the reign of sin. This means we no longer have to sin. Its power to enslave is broken. "Our old self was crucified with him . . . so that we would no longer be enslaved to sin. For one who has died has been set free from sin" (Rom. 6:6–7).

Our joint crucifixion with Christ is the basis of our release from the bondage in which sin was our slave master, a tyrant that continually overpowered us. We are dead to its captivity, its dominion, and its reign. We are no longer controlled or compelled by sin. Thus, we no longer continue in sin as a habit or compulsion. By virtue of our oneness with Christ in his substitutionary death, we have done what he did, and so, as *dead to sin*, we are discharged from sin as our master. In dying with Christ, we are ushered into a new kingdom with a new king ruling over us—Christ, not sin. Paul puts it like this to the Colossians:

He has delivered us from the domain of darkness and transferred us
to the kingdom of his beloved Son, in whom we have redemption,
the forgiveness of sins. (Col. 1:13–14)

Therefore, we see again that our deliverance from sin's dominion
and Adam's headship and our transfer to Christ's dominion and
headship is based on our personal participation by faith in Christ's
great atonement.

Who or what is the *old self* that was co-crucified? It is our identity
under Adam's headship. In that identity, sin, guilt, bondage, and
death reigned. That identity, that *self,* is crucified when we participate in Christ's crucifixion. That is why we no longer have to be
controlled by the compulsion to sin. The foundation for our process
of transformation is set in place; we are on a path of progressive
change from sinfulness to Christlikeness. As we continue in union
with Christ, transforming power is provided as we depend on the
Holy Spirit's enablement in our ongoing battle against sin's presence
in our lives. Over time, these enlightening and powerful words of
Paul's become our own:

Now the Lord is the Spirit, and where the Spirit of the Lord is, there
is freedom. And we all, with unveiled face, beholding the glory of the
Lord, are being transformed into the same image from one degree
of glory to another. For this comes from the Lord who is the Spirit.
(2 Cor. 3:17–18)

Our union with Christ in his death is symbolized by baptism.
In this physical act, representative of the spiritual reality, we demonstrate our participation in Christ's representative death. Here
we do what he did. We symbolically and publicly undergo what
he underwent when he satisfied divine justice on our behalf. It is a
baptism into his death, an emblem of oneness with Christ in his great
atonement. It is fellowship with him in his death to sin. Baptism is
a symbolic performance; it is not an act that saves us.

In our union with Christ as our representative, we experience
new measures of life immediately and even more as we grow in
him. At his coming, we will experience fullness of new life in our

own resurrected bodies (1 Cor. 15:51–54; 1 Thess. 4:13–18). This fullness of new life is the same glory by which Christ was raised, as we read about here in Romans 6: "Just as Christ was raised from the dead by the glory of the Father, we too might walk in newness of life" (Rom. 6:4b). As those alive to God in union with Christ, we must count ourselves dead to sin's dominion, "for the death he died he died to sin, once for all, but the life he lives he lives to God. So you also must consider yourselves dead to sin and alive to God in Christ Jesus" (Rom. 6:10–11). Paul shows us how this works:

> But now that you have been set free from sin and have become slaves of God, the fruit you get leads to sanctification and its end, eternal life. For the wages of sin is death, but the free gift of God is eternal life in Christ Jesus our Lord. (Rom. 6:22–23)

Here in Romans 6:22–23 Paul declares our glorious end, eternal life, where we will savor unbroken harmony in fellowship with God forever. We must never forget this is the most precious gift of the gospel. It is granted exclusively by virtue of Christ's great atonement and given as a result of our union with his death and resurrection through faith. Our eternal life is *in Christ*. It is *from* Christ as the source, *through* him as the means, and *to* him as the ultimate destination.

Christ's death was the price of our life; his death secured our life as his unfailing reward credited to us. If we die with Christ, we will also live with him (Rom. 6:8) by a bond as sure as Christ's own death and resurrection. And because we are alive in Christ and dead to the guilt and dominion of sin, Paul declares, "Let not sin therefore reign in your mortal bodies" (v. 12). Dead men do not sin.

However, Paul does not say that Christians never sin; he does not indicate that holiness is automatic. So Paul tells us to "consider [ourselves] dead to sin and alive to God in Christ Jesus" (v. 11). He tells us, "Do not present [our] members to sin as instruments for unrighteousness, but present [ourselves] to God as those who have been brought from death to life, and [our] members to God as instruments for righteousness" (v. 13). But how does this happen?

Although we are already representatively dead to sin, and our old identity in Adam has been crucified, the reality of sin's continued presence in our lives, and the fact that we continue to need to fight against temptation, proves that sanctification is an ongoing, life-long process. It is a process in which we become in practice what we representatively are already—dead to every aspect of sin, including its presence and its ability to successfully assault us with temptation. So in essence, Paul is telling us to become what we are—perfectly righteous in Christ.

Since we participate in Christ's life and dominion, we cannot simultaneously participate in sin's death and dominion. In this truth we find the grand answer to the rhetorical question Paul posed at the beginning of Romans 6: authentic union with Christ in his death and life initiates and sustains a process of transformation that renders impossible a life dedicated to the continuance of sin.

Thus, the life-giving power of Christ provides an immediate and perfect vicarious holiness and then moves us toward a gradual, imperfect, experiential holiness in the body and, finally, to a perfect, actual, eternal holiness in heaven. His ongoing work in us, sanctification, is by a transforming power far above and beyond any exercise of mere human willpower. His sanctifying power is synergistic with our effort, but it always supersedes our effort since we are always dependent on him for the power to change. His power enables the change. His power is applied to us by the Holy Spirit.

So, dying with Christ is a death to our old self and to sin, immediately freeing us from sin's guilt and dominion and gradually freeing us from sin's presence and ongoing ability to tempt. We can see this death is also a death to the law. Paul writes:

> You also have died to the law through the body of Christ, so that you may belong to another, to him who has been raised from the dead, in order that we may bear fruit for God. (Rom. 7:4)

Where we used to have only rules to follow, which we could never fulfill, we now have a living relationship with the living Christ. We belong to him, and since we are indeed alive, we grow and bear fruit as we fulfill our purpose—belonging to him and bringing him glory.

Romans 8:3–4

> For God has done what the law, weakened by the flesh, could not do. By sending his own Son in the likeness of sinful flesh and for sin, he condemned sin in the flesh in order that the righteous requirement of the law might be fulfilled in us, who walk not according to the flesh but according to the Spirit. (Rom. 8:3–4)

Having explained the frustrating reality that, though secure in Christ we are not completely free from sin's presence in our lives, Paul goes on to declare adamantly, "There is therefore now no condemnation for those who are in Christ Jesus. For the law of the Spirit of life has set you free in Christ Jesus from the law of sin and death" (Rom. 8:1–2). What a glorious declaration! Sinners are no longer condemned to eternal punishment for their sins. Sinners are set free from bondage to the law that compels them to sin and then die as a result. In these verses, the term *in Christ Jesus* appears twice, making a plain qualification—these benefits apply only to a certain group of sinners, those united to Christ in his death and life. For the Christian, this is the pinnacle of hope in Christ.

Our deliverance from the law of sin and death is a unilateral act of God. This deliverance is not due to something we have done; it is due to something God has done. God is the originator and source of the atonement. He sent his Son. It was his act. It emanated from him like water from a fountain. The atonement could not be extorted from him; had he not devised and executed his own plan, we could never have forced him to provide for our sins. Furthermore, just as he is the source, he is also the authority by which the Perfect Sacrifice is accepted as a complete satisfaction of his justice. He has done it all.

The person by whom the redemption work is finished is God's own Son, from all eternity the second person of the Trinity. He is the Son of God in a unique sense, not by adoption, not by incarnation, not by resurrection, but by an act of eternal generation in which he was begotten, not made. Jesus Christ is not a created creature. Jesus existed in the beginning with God.

The atonement could only be the work of a divine person of infinite worth and dignity since the offence of our sin against a holy God is an infinitely appalling atrocity. No mere man, however good, could pay our due penalty—it took the God-man to accomplish it. As the atonement emanated from God the Father, it was consummated by the workmanship of God the Son.

There was a distinct purpose for Christ taking on the likeness of sinful flesh—it was to fulfill God's plan of redemption and to institute a new covenant. By God's sovereign will he established this plan, which was firmly in place before the world was made. Jesus "was foreknown before the foundation of the world but was made manifest in the last times for your sake" (1 Pet. 1:20). The Son of God was made incarnate at the perfect point in time.

Jesus took on a human body comprised of real, physical flesh and blood. Yet he is different from us in that he is personally sinless, for God could never unite himself to sin. And so we see the purpose of Paul's use of the word *likeness*—Christ was sent "*in the likeness of sinful flesh*," not *as* sinful flesh.

Since he took on human flesh through supernatural conception by a virgin, human mother and no physical human father, Jesus was never represented by Adam's headship. Christ was not subject to the imputation of Adam's sin. He was not born into sin or personally connected in any way to Adam's original sin by its nature, its guilt, or its consequences. As the Last Adam, the counterpart of the first Adam, Christ, is a representor, not a representee. And the Last Adam is the final representor; he will never be replaced by another.

Succumbing to temptation and personally sinning would have disqualified Christ for his work of atonement because sin would have invalidated his sacrifice and his ability to transfer vicarious obedience to us. If Christ had sinned even once, there would be no perfect sacrifice, no atonement, no redemption, no justification, no reconciliation, and no resurrection. One sinner cannot change places with another.

The phrase "in the likeness of sinful flesh" (Rom. 8:3) implies, then, that except for his sinlessness, there is no significant or perceptible difference between Christ incarnate and men. He was "made like his brothers in every respect" (Heb. 2:17). He was not exceptional in personal appearance (Isa. 53:2b). He was subject to every human physical limitation. He experienced real fatigue and the need for sleep. He experienced joy and sorrow, anger and calm. He experienced grief. He wept. He experienced family life. He experienced poverty, prejudice, and persecution. He was subject to an ordinary earthly calling in which he would labor, sweat, and thirst. He experienced hunger. He felt real physical, emotional, and spiritual pain, and he agonized through all three. He was not exempt from the fear of death or from death itself. He experienced weakness and was tempted in every way.

Jesus Christ embodied the entire nature of man and lived in the entire circle of humanity and all it entailed as fully as could be experienced by one who was a sinless man and the beloved Son of God. Like all other men, he was obligated to obey the Father as he demonstrated when he "made himself of no reputation, and took upon him the form of a servant, and was made in the likeness of men: And being found in fashion as a man, he humbled himself, and became obedient unto death, even the death of the cross" (Phil. 2:7–8 KJV).

From the moment he was conceived until his glorious resurrection, there was only one difference between his flesh and ours—his was sinless, ours is sinful. Other than that, Jesus' humanity was so completely like ours in form and substance that no difference was perceptible to the human eye.

There is, however, an important distinction that needs to be drawn between the personal and the official aspects of Christ's life. The personally sinless Christ was exempt from the penal consequences of sin. It was only in his official role as our representative, and as the mediator between God and man, that he took on our sin, voluntarily and by substitution. Christ died for officially assumed sins, not personally inherited or committed sins. Christ was the official bearer of God's curse because he was the official bearer of man's sin.

Beyond this explanation, *in the likeness of sinful flesh* also means the sinless Jesus was completely on common ground with sinful men; that is, Christ took on imputed sin, judgment, a curse, a penal consequence, and death. Men are not let off the hook, and once he took on our sins, neither was Jesus. God's justice must be satisfied. His due wrath was inescapable, even for the sinless Son of God. If Jesus was to bear sin, he also had to bear unspeakable wrath and every aspect of death.

As we have previously noted, the word translated *for* in the English Bible usually means *because of* or *on account of*. But in this case, its meaning is more along the line of an exchange, as in a trade of one thing for another. Here, the phrase *for sin* refers to Christ as a sin offering, i.e., a sin substitute. Christ came in the likeness of sinful flesh and for sin, that is, his body was the atoning sin offering exchanged for the remission of the sin of the redeemed.

The word *condemnation* is a judicial term, and its application is legal in nature. A condemned person is declared guilty and sentenced to penal consequences. *Sin* is personified here in Romans 8 (as it is in the three previous chapters of Romans). Paul speaks of sin entering the world, reigning, and enslaving mankind. God sent Christ incarnate to engage the enemy, sin. Through Christ crucified, God overcame sin, judged sin, and condemned sin to a sentence of eternal impotence by removing its ability to penalize sinners, dethroning it from its reign over the redeemed. Through Christ's great atonement, redeemed sinners are justified, and justified sinners are no longer obligated to obey the rule of their previous master, sin, that now stands condemned.

Ironically, the law could never do this, for the law was weak and impotent from the beginning. It served to reveal sin and to make sin known in the flesh, and, therefore, the law condemns sinners to death; yet, it cannot save. But the law does not condemn sin itself; Christ's atonement alone condemns sin and breaks its power.

Furthermore, the law makes no provision for mercy; mercy is something that exists outside of law. We do not receive mercy by appealing to the law or to our partial obedience to the law. Christ fulfilled the entire law on our behalf. Therefore, we receive mercy by appealing to God on the basis of Christ's righteousness, transferred to us by our union with him through faith. Christ was made the sin offering, and God condemned sin in his flesh so that the righteousness that the law required would be fulfilled in us by the imputation of Christ's righteousness.

The phrase "the righteous requirement of the law might be fulfilled in us" (Rom. 8:4) has everything in common with Paul's statement, "For our sake he made him to be sin who knew no sin, *so that in him we might become the righteousness of God*" (2 Cor. 5:21). These expressions do not refer to the believer's own righteousness, because such righteousness is always incomplete and could never pass for a fulfillment of the law, which requires perfection. The phrase "the righteous requirement of the law" is descriptive of Christ's obedience as the work of the one for many (Rom. 5:18). When the righteousness required by the law is said to be fulfilled in us, it means that it belongs to us and is applied to us by virtue of our union with Christ. It is fulfilled in us, as if we had done it all ourselves.

Romans 8:31–34

> What then shall we say to these things? If God is for us, who can be against us? He who did not spare his own Son but gave him up for us all, how will he not also with him graciously give us all things? Who shall bring any charge against God's elect? It is God who justifies. Who is to condemn? Christ Jesus is the one who died—more than that, who was raised—who is at the right hand of God, who indeed is interceding for us. (Rom. 8:31–34)

Paul fires off questions to get us to think about the certainty of our justification in Christ: who can oppose us, or accuse us, or condemn us? In between the questions, Paul provides several hints to the triumphant answers:

- He did not spare his own Son but gave him up for us all.
- It is God who justifies.
- Christ Jesus is the one who died—more than that, who was raised.
- Christ Jesus is interceding for us at the right hand of God.

In this passage, Paul proclaims the privileges granted to those who are united with Christ, and who are thereby completely freed from condemnation. The atonement, where God gave up the Son on our behalf, was a real transaction—it purchased something monumental—the fullest security for us all. Paul confidently defies the enemies and opposition surrounding Christians on the basis of the fact that God is for us. He thus establishes a direct connection between Christ's atonement and the blood-bought blessings bestowed on us. What have we to fear if we are covered by this great atonement?

God did not withhold his Son. Jesus was not spared from assuming a human body as a prerequisite for his work, an act that in itself was an immeasurable humiliation compared to Christ's sharing the fullness of God. Jesus, "who, though he was in the form of God, did not count equality with God a thing to be grasped . . . made himself nothing, taking the form of a servant, being born in the likeness of men" (Phil. 2:6–7). As well, he was not spared from subjection to the full force and fury of God's holy and just wrath against our sin. In spite of the infinite and eternal love with which God regarded his Son, a love that never could be lowered or withdrawn from Christ personally, God did not spare him. As the sinless Son of God and as man's sin substitute, Christ was simultaneously loved and yet not spared.

This prompts a few questions: (1) Why? Why would God subject Jesus to the full force of his wrath? The answer is amazing: God did not spare his own Son so that he might instead spare us. He did not remove the cup of wrath from him so that it would never be presented to us. From this wonderful truth, additional questions naturally follow: (2) How well protected from God's wrath are those under Christ's shield? Are we still to fear some of God's mighty fury? The answer is that there is not a drop of wrath that Christ did not drink on our behalf. If we are in him, our punishment has already been endured in full, our rescue is assured, and we are infinitely and eternally safe.

The words "his own Son" (Rom. 8:32) convey the idea of a true son, an actual son of divine relationship. There is no aspect of adoption here; Jesus Christ is the genuine, authentic Son of God from eternity past through eternity future. Two underlying inferences flow from this: (1) there is an infinitely zealous love-relationship between God the Father and God the Son, and (2) the Son has infinite dignity and value by virtue of his sonship. It staggers the imagination to embrace the thought that *this* is the Son that was given up for us. What price tag can be put on the Son? He is a sacrifice of infinite price. This is the extraordinary measure of the Father's love for us.

God gave up the Son. In other words, it was God himself who delivered Christ into the hands of men to be treated as if he really was the blasphemous offender they accused him of being. Although Judas, the high priest, the council, Pilate, and the Roman cohort were involved, there was a hand above theirs; God was the ultimate cause of Christ's suffering and death. God was the invisible but actual conspirator, righteous judge, and executioner (Acts 2:23).

At this point, Paul gives a logical argument from the greater to the lesser: "He who did not spare his own Son . . . how will he not also . . ." (Rom. 8:32). If God was willing and able to do the most difficult thing and to pay the most infinite price, certainly he is willing and able to "graciously give us all things" (v. 32), a far less costly task than giving his Son. He whose love overcomes the greatest difficulties, and he who by his own miraculous and magnificent plan replaces our condemnation with justification based on his own Son's blood, this great and gracious God will not be thwarted by what is comparatively much less demanding. God's love for us caused him to deliver the Son he loves to spitting, blindfolding, taunting, beating, and scourging, as well as to allow him to be nailed to a cross, speared in the side, and taken to the grave—all for our benefit. Can he not, will he not, then, provide for us in every other way with every other blessing we could possibly need? Having refused to withhold his Son, will he withhold the lesser blessings and mercies bought by the same blood? If he did not spare the Son while we were enemies, will he treat us less lovingly now that we are friends?

God did not deliver up Christ simply to provide us with a good example to live by or a demonstration of superlative, inspiring unselfishness. No, it was much more than that. He delivered his Son to provide a substitutionary death, a death we should have died. He did it to provide a punishment in the place of those who deserved his wrath. He did it to supply redeemed sinners with an inexhaustible basis of confidence and an unquenchable hope.

God would have spared his Son had he not purposed to bestow on us all good things conceivable as demonstrated by Paul when he declares, "And we know that for those who love God all things work together for good, for those who are called according to his purpose" (Rom. 8:28). What an amazingly good and gracious God!

An important question is raised when Paul declares that God did this "for us all." Who is included in the word *all*? Does it refer to all mankind? Does it refer to every sinner? The answer to both questions is an emphatic no. The *all* refers to the Roman believers to whom Paul was writing, believers who joined Paul in forming a mutual body of believers. We see this as well in the beginning of this epistle where Paul addresses his audience as "you who are called to belong to Jesus Christ, to all those in Rome who are loved by God and called to be saints" (Rom. 1:6–7a).

While this is true, the more explicit answer, however, is that *us all* refers to those depicted and qualified in the context of Romans 8:28–30 where Paul says:

> Those who love God . . . those who are called according to his purpose. . . . Those whom he foreknew [and] predestined to be conformed to the image of his Son . . . those whom he called . . . justified . . . glorified.

In this context, *us all* signifies the true church—the redeemed, reconciled sinners that constitute the body of Christ as a whole by virtue of their participation under his representative headship whereby they have died with him and have been raised with him. These, and only these, are the ones for whom God gave up Jesus. The promise of "all things" applies only to them.

Those who will not have Christ as their ransom, redeemer, righteousness, and propitiation, including all those who perceive themselves as relatively moral and expect to present their own righteousness as if it were good enough to stand before a holy God, should not expect to receive God's blessings. They have spurned the love of God, the plan of God, and the provision of God. They are not united to Christ and his great atonement, and thus they are not free from the condemnation, wrath, and death penalty due from the hand of the God of justice for each and every single sin.

May we never spurn the great and proven love of the awesome holy God and the Son he did not spare. Let us pray for enablement to turn to Christ and trust in his atonement and cling to him in a union that can never be undone. Then we will proclaim alongside Paul, "For I am sure that neither death nor life, nor angels nor rulers, nor things present nor things to come, nor powers, nor height nor depth, nor anything else in all creation, will be able to separate us from the love of God in Christ Jesus our Lord" (Rom. 8:38–39).

CHAPTER 8

1 Corinthians

S ometime during the three years the apostle Paul lived in Ephesus, he received news from Corinth that serious error in doctrine had crept into the recently founded church there, which resulted in severely misguided behavior and religious practices. He responded by writing his first epistle to the Corinthians, a letter filled with correction, warnings, and a call for the immediate exercise of discipline (1 Cor. 5:1–5). Although Paul prescribed a variety of specific remedies, each corrective measure had its root in the correct understanding and application of Christ's great atonement.

1 Corinthians 1:11–13

It doesn't take long to see this theme emerge in the epistle. Paul writes:

> For it has been reported to me by Chloe's people that there is quarreling among you, my brothers. What I mean is that each one of you says, "I follow Paul," or "I follow Apollos," or "I follow Cephas," or "I follow Christ." Is Christ divided? Was Paul crucified for you? Or were you baptized in the name of Paul? (1 Cor. 1:11–13)

The first correction given to the Corinthians addressed the division arising from the undue attachment of believers to individual human teachers. Paul exposes the absurdity of this practice by asking three rhetorical questions, the second of which zeroes in on the cross: "Was Paul crucified for you?"

No human beings, including preachers, teachers, and even apostles, are ever to be put on a pedestal, because no matter how sanctified or transformed to the image of Christ they become, as sinners, their blood is not qualified to save. Their righteousness is neither perfect nor transferable, and their resurrection cannot bring life to others. There is only one sinless sin bearer. His sacrificial blood is infinitely precious, and his redemptive work is unique and forever unfailing. The best man or woman, by comparison, is no comparison, for *all* have sinned and fall short of the glory of God (Rom. 3:23). There is an immeasurable gap in righteousness, authority, and power to save between Christ and every human ever born, beginning with Adam. Even the martyrdom of the saint with the most personal holiness and piety is of insignificant worth next to the value of the great atonement of Jesus Christ. Even the great apostle Paul was a sinner in need of Christ's atonement, just like everyone else.

The question "Was Paul crucified for you?" (1 Cor. 1:13) contrasts Paul's work with Christ's and shows that Christ's death was for a wholly different purpose than that which can simply be applied to one man's act on behalf of another. The benefit of the death of one man for another may well be to rescue one from physical death or to provide a lesser benefit. But the death of Christ is in reference to our sin, and its benefit extends into eternity. A man can dive in front of a bus or train or bullet to save someone, but only Christ can bear sin and its consequent curse and eternal death by substitution. In referring to the idea of one man dying for another in his letter to the Romans, Paul wrote:

> For one will scarcely die for a righteous person—though perhaps for a good person one would dare even to die—but God shows his love for us in that while we were still sinners, Christ died for us. (Rom. 5:7–8)

Christians may be called upon to risk life and limb for one another (Col. 1:24), not to suffer or die for their sins but to show confidence in the truth of the gospel and contribute to the building up of the faith of others by the demonstration of faith. There is a world of difference between this and Christ's vicarious sufferings and death as a propitiation for sins.

1 Corinthians 1:17–18

> For Christ did not send me to baptize but to preach the gospel, and not with words of eloquent wisdom, lest the cross of Christ be emptied of its power. For the word of the cross is folly to those who are perishing, but to us who are being saved it is the power of God. (1 Cor. 1:17–18)

Another aberration and sin in the Corinthian church was the undue admiration of human eloquence, the wisdom of words. Here again Paul exposes the error by placing it in the light of the atonement, referring to the simplicity and saving power of the cross. The gospel is the good news of the "word of the cross"—the simple yet life-transforming message that Jesus died for our sins and was buried and rose again on the third day.

Paul understood Christ's call to abstain from lofty words designed to gratify the Greek passion for eloquence and rhetoric. He also understood that the cross of Christ must not be drained of its power by hearers turning their attention away from its simplicity toward the persuasive arguments about or the style in which it might be presented. The truth, not the skillful presentation of the truth, is what matters.

It cannot be denied that Paul was capable of using powerful rhetoric. This very letter includes several such examples (see 1 Corinthians 15). But in the preaching of the gospel, Paul deliberately did not employ his command of human philosophy, his oratorical skills, or even his intellectual power of persuasion. This fact often seems to go unrecognized today in an era when attempts are made to make the gospel more palatable in the name of seeker sensitivity. But Paul never did that.

Paul was convinced that foreign matter or rhetorical refinement would only serve to distract from the message of the cross and thereby subvert the gospel. He was also convinced that the gospel had absolute sufficiency in itself to bring conviction to the sinner's conscience and salvation to the sinner's soul. The true gospel required no embellishment and no sugarcoating to make it easier for the masses to swallow. It required no rhetorical grease to slide it past the resistance of those opposed to its message. To Paul, such modifications only cause men to value style above substance and to glorify man, the messenger, above Christ, the message.

In remarkable contrast, Paul declares, "The word of the cross is . . . the power of God" (1 Cor. 1:18). What a remarkable statement! God's almighty, supernatural power is connected to a specific "word"—the message of the cross—the preaching of the great facts of Christ's atoning sacrifice as the provision of God's love for guilty sinners. When this gospel of Christ's great atonement is preached, God's miraculous power to regenerate, restore, and renew sinners is displayed in those who are saved by it.

This is the true gospel, the only gospel that unleashes the power of God by which those dead in sin are saved from the guilt, the consequences, and the enslaving power of their sin. Therefore, Paul was "not ashamed of the gospel" because this message of the cross "is the power of God for salvation to everyone who believes, to the Jew first and also to the Greek" (Rom. 1:16). Substitute anything for the cross or add anything to the cross, whether good works or human philosophy, and the preaching is stripped of God's power—for it is no longer God's message. It ceases to be the gospel.

Paul reveals that the "word of the cross" is joined with God's power, which demonstrates that the atonement is forever valid as the means of the believing sinner's acceptance before a holy God, since the eternally omnipotent power of God speaks it and supports it. And yet this "word" and "power" are not effective for all. This word and this power—this gospel—are and will be outright foolishness to anyone not united to Christ by faith. The wise among the Corinthians—philosophic minds attached to some of the famous schools of philosophy—thought it was folly to represent the Son of God dying on the cross. At the same time, the cross offended the Jews in Corinth, because they saw it as incompatible with the prophecies of the Messiah's everlasting reign, a Messiah that would be too noble and mighty to accept even the least form of suffering.

In the midst of all this resistance, Paul never altered his message. He did not attempt to accommodate the objections of the day. On the contrary, he stuck to the message in spite of the fact that the "Jews [demanded] signs and Greeks [sought] wisdom." He preached "Christ crucified, a stumbling block to Jews and folly to Gentiles" (1 Cor. 1:22–23), knowing this was how they felt and what they thought. He adds:

> I, when I came to you, brothers, did not come proclaiming to you the testimony of God with lofty speech or wisdom. *For I decided to know nothing among you except Jesus Christ and him crucified.* And I was with you in weakness and in fear and much trembling, and my speech and my message were *not in plausible words of wisdom,* but in demonstration of the Spirit and of power, that your faith might not rest in the wisdom of men but in the power of God. (1 Cor. 2:1–5)

Is it not abundantly clear that this approach was effective, that the power of God was demonstrated, in the wake of Paul's preaching the word of the cross? Does history not record the long-range, world-changing impact of Paul's message of Christ and him crucified? This stands as a lesson and a testimony to those who would influence the world today. We dare not compromise the message of the atoning power of the cross by molding it around the perceived viewpoints of our audience. Instead, like Paul, we should deliberately limit our presentation to the simple elements of the gospel and display Christ and him crucified in a clear, undiluted form: God's holiness, man's sin, Christ the sinless God-man, his finished work of sin bearing, his resurrection, and our response by repentance and faith and ongoing transformation. Anything more or anything less risks deadly error.

1 Corinthians 1:30

> And because of him you are in Christ Jesus, who became to us wisdom from God, righteousness and sanctification and redemption. (1 Cor. 1:30)

From the context of 1 Corinthians 1:30, we know that Paul's primary intention is to address the same error we considered above—the undue dependence on human eloquence. Paul reveals that men partake of Christ not by the wisdom of man but by the gift of God. Keeping in mind that the theme of this passage is Christ crucified, it is apparent that the four terms used here describe what the crucified Christ becomes to his people: wisdom, righteousness, sanctification, and redemption.

God's gift of the crucified Christ becomes all the wisdom we will ever need—wisdom to find acceptance before God and wisdom to live among those who think the gospel is foolish. Christ himself *is* the wisdom; all the treasures of wisdom and knowledge are hidden in him (Col. 2:3).

The person and finished work of Christ perfectly meets man's need and desire for wisdom. Because of who he is and what he's done, we have ready access to all the wisdom Christ has, which is infinite. Do you have a burning question? Jesus is the answer. Are you in a tight predicament? Jesus is the solution. Are you in the dark? Jesus is the light. Apart from Christ crucified, no sinner would have the wisdom it takes to become right with God or to live in a manner pleasing to God.

God's gift of the crucified Christ becomes all the righteousness we will ever need, for in the Great Exchange, we are seen by God to be as sinless as Christ himself. This would be impossible for us sinners were it not for two essentials. First, a qualified sacrifice must be made on behalf of our sin, and second, a perfect and alien righteousness must be credited to us. Both of these requirements were met in Christ on the cross. In a mind-boggling twist of grace, God credits Christ's death as payment in full for our sin, and he credits us with the real, lived-out righteousness of Christ as if we had personally, perfectly fulfilled the law. The value of this transferred righteousness is also incalculable.

As we have seen, God's gift of Christ crucified becomes both the basis and the means for our sanctification. Jesus expressed this purpose for going to the cross in his prayer in the garden prior to his arrest: "For their sake I consecrate myself, that they also may be sanctified in truth" (John 17:19). So the cross is the foundation not only for our justification but also for our sanctification. Apart from Christ crucified, there would be no sanctification of sinners.

1 Corinthians 5:7–8

> Cleanse out the old leaven that you may be a new lump, as you really are unleavened. For Christ, our Passover lamb, has been sacrificed. Let us therefore celebrate the festival, not with the old leaven, the leaven of malice and evil, but with the unleavened bread of sincerity and truth. (1 Cor. 5:7–8)

In 1 Corinthians 5:7–8 Paul addresses the problem of the Corinthian church tolerating sin and neglecting holiness. Once again, he centers his argument on the cross and the power of the crucified Christ to transform a leavened (sinful) soul into an unleavened (sin-free) soul. The sacrificial blood of Christ has changed us from the inside out, and Paul tells us to become what we are: righteous, holy, and sanctified in Christ.

There is rich symbolism to be seen in the Jewish Passover (Exodus 12). The event of the first Passover involved, at God's direction, the sprinkling of blood on the lintels and doorposts to preserve each Jewish household's firstborn from death on the night the destroying angel visited every home in Egypt. This deliverance led to the even larger deliverance of Israel out of slavery to the Egyptians.

But beyond simply the deliverance from death and slavery, the Passover launched the turning point for Israel. From that point on they would be set apart among all the nations. The Passover established a clear distinction: the people of the covenant were to be a holy people, a people consecrated to God, both in unique ceremony and in *unleavened* personal holiness. The Passover gave significance to all the other sin offerings. No Jew could neglect it, and no stranger could partake of it. There was now to be a new relationship between God and Israel, as well as a new law. God said, "I am the LORD who brought you up out of the land of Egypt to be your God. You shall therefore be holy, for I am holy" (Lev. 11:45).

God declared the Passover to be an annual celebration feast to memorialize the blood-bought deliverance that set Israel apart and preserved them as the covenant people of God (Ex. 12:24). God told the people:

> You shall say, "It is the sacrifice of the LORD's Passover, for he passed over the houses of the people of Israel in Egypt, when he struck the Egyptians but spared our houses." And the people bowed their heads and *worshiped*. (Ex. 12:27)

The Passover was celebrated annually as the pinnacle occasion for worship, confession, and the acknowledgement that no personal merit exempted the Israelites from the exacting of the divine wrath the neighboring families experienced. In designing the Passover, God took his own chosen people and set them apart for himself, specifically for his own glory.

Now that we understand the concept of the Passover better, we can see how Paul applies it in this section of 1 Corinthians. Paul compares the sacrifice of Christ to that of the Passover lamb of the old covenant. The similarities are quite apparent. The lamb was unblemished; Christ was sinless. Both were vicarious, sin-bearing substitutes slaughtered on behalf of and for the benefit of another. Both were blood sacrifices made by the institution of divine appointment. And both were sacrifice-based means of deliverance.

1 Corinthians 5:7 shows that the atoning work of Christ is the reason the church is directed to clean out the old leaven of sin. We are to become in experience what his sacrifice has already made us before God—pure, clean, and holy. This means, then, that because Christ has been sacrificed for the church, its members should strive to stop sinning and move toward becoming as pure as Christ himself, "who gave himself for us to redeem us from all lawlessness and to

purify for himself a people for his own possession who are zealous for good works" (Titus 2:14). Our participation in Christ's atonement means that, like Christ himself did, we are to "present [our] bodies as a living sacrifice, holy and acceptable to God, which is [our] spiritual worship" (Rom. 12:1).

It is certainly no coincidence that the Last Supper took place as Jesus and the disciples celebrated the Feast of the Passover. On the night before he became our Passover lamb, Jesus, the ultimate unleavened bread, offered himself saying, "This is my body, which is given for you. Do this in remembrance of me" (Luke 22:19; 1 Cor. 11:24).

For the believer, the celebration of the Lord's Supper is a God-ordained, periodic reminder that the entire Christian life is to be a continual keeping of the redemption feast of Christ's Passover—a celebration of our deliverance from our previous captors, sin and death. All our life—in fact, the entire period of the Christian church on earth—is to be a joy-filled festival, for the Son of God was sacrificed that we might receive a blessing of such a great, unimaginable magnitude as to take our breath away. It is infinitely better than deliverance from death, angels, or nations, since it delivers us from the curse and the wrath of God that we deserve and replaces it with eternal blessing, justification, and adoption.

The finished sacrificial work of Christ, the true Passover lamb, the fulfillment of the symbolic, is a cause for great celebration. And indeed sinners have never had a greater reason for festivity, merriment, and rejoicing, nor will there ever be.

Our celebration is to be free of the old leaven of malice and evil. Instead, we celebrate with the unleavened bread of sincerity and truth, that is, with inward and outward holiness. Partaking of Jesus, the bread of life, sets Christians apart from the world as holy and blameless, first as justified sinners and then as sanctified sinners. Peter puts it like this:

> As obedient children, do not be conformed to the passions of your former ignorance, but as he who called you is holy, you also be holy in all your conduct, since it is written, "You shall be holy, for I am holy." (1 Pet. 1:14–16)

Our call to holy conduct is a call from a holy God, and he provides the power to live this way—an infinitely powerful source—the word of the cross, the gospel.

1 Corinthians 6:19b–20

> You are not your own, for you were bought with a price. So glorify God in your body. (1 Cor. 6:19b–20)

Once again Paul addresses the sinful practices that had crept into the Corinthian church, shining the light of Christ's atonement on their sin. He exposes their immoral sexual behavior as inconsistent with the position of those who belong not to themselves but to the purchaser. Paul reminds them, "You are not your own, for you were bought with a price."

By laying down his life for us at the cross, Christ purchased us for God—all parts of us, body, soul, spirit, and mind. As a result, God owns us. But this goes beyond the rights God can inherently claim as our creator; we are doubly owned by him, first by virtue of his creator rights and then by virtue of his redeemer rights.

But what did the atonement purchase us from? To place this passage in its cultural context, we must understand that in the first century there was a prevalent custom whereby a slave could be redeemed upon the full payment of a costly price called a ransom. The slave would then pass from the ownership of one master into the service of another. Although the terms *ransom* and *redemption* are not employed in this passage, the concepts clearly apply, for Paul is referring to the purchase of men. The ransom is the purchase price, and redemption is the purchase process. Paul further develops this idea in a sermon in which he refers to the purchase of the "church of God, which [Jesus] obtained with his own blood" (Acts 20:28b). There are three distinct aspects of this purchase:

1) *The buyer is the God-man, Christ crucified.* Paul tells Titus, "our great God and Savior Jesus Christ . . . gave himself for us to redeem us from all lawlessness and to purify for himself a people for his own possession who are zealous for good works" (Titus

2:13b–14). And because what he gave was himself, Christ the redeemer is also our ransom and our redemption (1 Cor. 1:30). Titus 2:13 identifies Christ not only as our "Savior" but also as "our great God." As Isaiah proclaims, "Thus says the LORD, the King of Israel *and* his Redeemer, the LORD of hosts: 'I am the first and I am the last; besides me there is no god'" (Isa. 44:6).

2) *The price—the ransom for our deliverance from captivity to sin's curse and dominion—is too high. We cannot pay it ourselves.* No amount of good works or tithing or personal righteousness or self-sacrifice can free us. But the price our Redeemer paid in our place and on our behalf was sufficient (Matt. 20:28). The amount he paid is displayed in the nature, intention, and scope of Christ's obedience to the point of death, even death on a cross (Phil. 2:8). His is a glorious price, and for eternity the hosts of heaven will sing a new song, "Worthy are you to take the scroll and to open its seals, for you were slain, and by your blood you ransomed people for God from every tribe and language and people and nation" (Rev. 5:9). Just one of the countless reasons Christ is worthy of all praise is that he paid the ransom price that was too high for any other to pay.

God's perfect holiness and inflexible justice, as well as the inviolable authority of his law, render the liberation of guilty sinners simply impossible without an adequate ransom paid on their behalf. But the good news of the gospel is that just as Christ himself is our redemption, he is also our all-sufficient ransom. For "there is one God, and there is one mediator between God and men, the man Christ Jesus, who gave himself as a ransom for *all*, which is the testimony given at the proper time" (1 Tim. 2:5–6).

The "all" of this passage in Timothy certainly does not refer to every descendant of Adam, for that would contradict every passage pertaining to judgment and hell; to believe that would require ignoring countless pages of the Bible or discrediting the Word of God in its entirety. No, the "all" are those for whom Jesus is mediator, all he redeemed.

3) *The receiver of the ransom is God.* Was the ransom price we are discussing paid to Satan? By no means! Satan is but the ultimate executioner of God's justice, delivering the soul to hell and eternal torment and death. The ransom is paid to God, our original owner, the one to whom the debt is owed. The ransom is paid to satisfy God's justice, the very justice we have disregarded by our sin. It is paid to God to free us from his curse and from the dread of his holy wrath. It is paid to God to free us from subjection to his executioner, Satan.

Christians have been bought by their Redeemer by the price of his own blood, so Paul gives us the practical, logical conclusion that "you are not your own," i.e., you should serve the one who possesses you as master and owner, "so glorify God in your body" (1 Cor. 6:19b, 20b).

Glorifying, magnifying, and making much of God is to be our response to the great love God demonstrated in Christ's purchase of us while we were yet sinners (Rom. 5:8). The purpose for our very lives, that to which we must submit our very bodies, becomes living for the will, pleasure, and service of our ransom payer and new master, Christ.

Paul later put it another way when writing to these same believers at Corinth:

> For the love of Christ controls us, because we have concluded this: that one has died for all, therefore all have died; and he died for all, that those who live might no longer live for themselves but for him who for their sake died and was raised. (2 Cor. 5:14–15)

A powerful motive for glorifying God with our bodies comes from recognizing the fact that we have been bought at such a great price. Far from opening a door to continuing in sin, the grace provided by the great atonement compels us to recognize that as redeemed sinners, we have no right to use our bodies simply as we please or for our own pleasure, because they are the rightfully purchased property of another. Furthermore, because the parts that make up our body are "members of Christ" (1 Cor. 6:15), they belong not to us but to him. We are even told that our bodies constitute the temple of the Holy Spirit (1 Cor. 6:19), the member of the triune Godhead "by whom you were sealed for the day of redemption" (Eph. 4:30).

The price was so high that the transaction bought us completely; no part remains unpurchased or unowned. Our previous master, sin, has been completely disempowered; there is nothing left of its ownership, rule, or power to control us. Our buyer, Christ, owns all of us forever. We will never be sold again.

1 Corinthians 8:11

> And so by your knowledge this weak person is destroyed, the brother for whom Christ died. (1 Cor. 8:11)

Another error that crept into the Corinthian church was the improper exercise of Christian liberty, and Paul again exposes and corrects this by placing it in the light of the atonement. The specific issue addressed here involved the question of eating meat that had been offered in sacrifice to idols, a practice some Jewish Christians considered defiling. Many Gentile Christians felt free to partake without restraint, but their reckless use of this liberty caused damage to the faith of their weaker brothers by inducing them to participate in a practice that offended their less-mature, weaker conscience.

The principle behind Paul's instruction is that we should abstain from any free expression of Christian liberty if it will harm a brother. And the motivating force behind our restraint is the atonement. Any believer who needlessly puts another's spiritual welfare at risk for the sake of asserting his or her own liberty devalues the cost of the ransom. He loves neither his brother nor the Christ who bled.

Now, clearly, within the context of 1 Corinthians 8, we know the word *destroy* does not refer to eternal condemnation. One man could never destroy another in that sense—only God can employ the means to destroy the soul and body in hell (Matt. 10:28). No one for whom the Good Shepherd offered himself can be eternally destroyed by a mere man. By the merit provided by transferred righteousness, believers stand forever justified in spite of a weak conscience that may be further damaged by an unloving brother. Jesus said:

> My sheep hear my voice, and I know them, and they follow me. I give them eternal life, and they will never perish, and no one will snatch them out of my hand. My Father, who has given them to me, is greater than all, and no one is able to snatch them out of the Father's hand. I and the Father are one. (John 10:27–30)

Still, one brother may put a stumbling block in another's way and thus diminish his peace, defile his conscience, and cause weakness, trouble, sin, and sorrow. We must never do this to one for whom Christ voluntarily died. As Christ himself put it:

> I am the good shepherd. I know my own and my own know me, just as the Father knows me and I know the Father; and I lay down my life for the sheep. . . . No one takes it from me, but I lay it down of my own accord. I have authority to lay it down, and I have authority to take it up again. This charge I have received from my Father. (John 10:14–15, 18)

The most important part of the task committed to Christ by the Father consisted in his laying down his life for those he knew to be his sheep. A Christian is thus one whom Christ intimately knows and for whom Christ personally chose to die, including all those united to him by faith, even those whose faith is weak.

1 Corinthians 11:23–27

> For I received from the Lord what I also delivered to you, that the Lord Jesus on the night when he was betrayed took bread, and when he had given thanks, he broke it, and said, "This is my body which is for you. Do this in remembrance of me." In the same way also he took the cup, after supper, saying, "This cup is the new covenant in my blood. Do this, as often as you drink it, in remembrance of me." For as often as you eat this bread and drink the cup, you proclaim the Lord's death until he comes.

Whoever, therefore, eats the bread or drinks the cup of the Lord
in an unworthy manner will be guilty of profaning the body and
blood of the Lord. (1 Cor. 11:23–27)

Paul takes this occasion to expound on the celebration of the atonement in the institution of the Lord's Supper. He does so in the context
of addressing reports about abuses of its practice in the Corinthian
church. Paul's authority to speak on the subject is clear; he was transferring to them what he had received firsthand from the Lord.

The Lord did not leave it up to Paul or the other apostles to institute the Lord's Supper after his departure. Christ regarded it as
so important that by his own authority, and while still present in
the flesh, he instituted it at the most solemn time—on the night of
his betrayal, immediately before going to the garden and then to the
cross. The events of the Last Supper would surely be remembered,
so by instructing the disciples in the Lord's Supper, he extended the
meaning and application of his broken body and shed blood to all
redeemed believers of all times and all places.

For emphasis, the phrase "Do this in remembrance of me" appears twice in this passage, once related to the bread and again in
reference to the cup. What does Christ intend for us to remember?
His teaching? His example? No. It is his death as the atoning sacrifice for sin, as verse 26 makes clear: "For as often as you eat this
bread and drink the cup, you proclaim the Lord's death until he
comes."

The sacramental elements themselves clearly point to the cross. Of
the bread he said, "This is my body," alluding to his humanity in which
he rendered perfect obedience both for himself and for redeemed sinners—the body which was nailed to the cross on their behalf. Of the
cup he said, "This cup is the new covenant in my blood," alluding to
the atoning blood sacrifice, the blood by which the new covenant was
formed. Because of the blood of Jesus, our Passover lamb, this new
covenant would supplant and replace its foreshadow, the old Sinaitic
covenant, and this new feast, the Lord's Supper, would supplant and
replace the Jewish Passover. In their new covenant standing by the
blood of Christ, those who were far off become a holy people and

may sit as guests without danger or dread at the Lord's table. Joy and peace and hope replace fear and dread because "now in Christ Jesus you who once were far off have been brought near by the blood of Christ. For he himself is our peace" (Eph. 2:13–14a).

As believers we are not merely to commemorate the Lord's death as a historic event. We are to remember it in personal terms, its inestimable value as the atonement for *our* sin. His body was broken for us. His blood provides a covenant standing for us. His blood has brought us near. He is our peace with God.

The emblems—the bread and the cup of wine—are physical reminders of a greater reality: Christ's body was the true Passover sacrifice, and Christ's blood was the true Passover blood, the basis and means of the new covenant. The emblems were to furnish food for the understanding and the heart, vividly recalling the nature of the redeeming love of Christ crucified.

Thus, the action of eating and drinking denotes our participation in his body and blood. By faith we receive what the elements signify. Biblically speaking, "The cup of blessing that we bless, is it not a participation in the blood of Christ? The bread that we break, is it not a participation in the body of Christ?" (1 Cor. 10:16). Our partaking in the covenant is founded entirely on appropriating Christ's "blood . . . which is poured out for many for the forgiveness of sins" (Matt. 26:28). There is no other requirement, and there is no other mediator.

The expression "as often as" occurs twice in 1 Corinthians 11:23–27, making it abundantly clear that Christ's atoning death is to be frequently and repeatedly celebrated by believers through the sacrament of the Lord's Supper. This ordinance has remained foundational throughout all the twists and turns of church history. The celebration is to be perpetual until Christ comes again, at which time its own splendid replacement finally comes—the wedding feast of the Bride of Christ (Rev. 19:7–9). For now we remember; then we will celebrate and consummate the marriage.

The Lord's Supper heralds the essential proclamation of all time: that the death of Christ has made atonement for sinners. Is there a more joyful message to be found? Is there other news that should be sounded higher or remembered with more esteem? Is anything else nearly as significant or momentous? Let us remember his death, and let us proclaim it until he comes. This is the core of the gospel. No, it *is* the gospel. Take Christ crucified out of the gospel message, and it ceases to be the gospel.

1 Corinthians 15:3–4

> For I delivered to you as of first importance what I also received: that Christ died for our sins in accordance with the Scriptures, that he was buried, that he was raised on the third day in accordance with the Scriptures. (1 Cor. 15:3–4)

Attempting to correct another error, one related to a wrong perception of the timing of the resurrection of believers, Paul sets the stage by defining the gospel. As is clear from 15:1, it is *the gospel* that is the matter of preeminent importance. This is the message Paul received and delivered to the Corinthians, who, in turn, received it. It is the good news of Christ crucified for sin—buried and raised. It is the fulfillment of the Old Testament foreshadows—atoning animal sacrifices and prophesies. This is the gospel that has the power to save believing sinners who continue faithful to it.

Concerning the error occurring in Corinth, Paul wrote, "If Christ has not been raised, your faith is futile and you are still in your sins" (1 Cor. 15:17). It stands to reason that if Christ had remained dead, the payment he made is either insufficient or is still being made. No confirmation that we are now and forever forgiven would exist. If Christ had not risen, it would be because the price he paid was unacceptable, and, therefore, the justice of God would not have been satisfied. But Christ did rise, and with his glorious resurrection came undeniable evidence that our sins had been forgiven because of his death. Our faith and resurrection and eternal destiny are secure.

CHAPTER 9

2 Corinthians

The apostle Paul's second epistle to the Corinthians, written a short time after his first, is somewhat different in tone from the former letter. The church had responded well to most of Paul's corrective instructions, and yet there were still divisions within the church. Some were questioning Paul's apostolic authority since he had not been with Jesus in the days of his flesh. Consequently, in this letter Paul defends his apostleship by sharing the nature of his calling and his direct experience with Christ. In the process, he interweaves several facts about the atonement.

2 Corinthians 5:14–15

> For the love of Christ controls us, because we have concluded this: that one has died for all, therefore all have died; and he died for all, that those who live might no longer live for themselves but for him who for their sake died and was raised. (2 Cor. 5:14–15)

In the chapters leading up to 2 Corinthians 5, Paul refers to the extreme adversity and hardship he had experienced while engaged in his passionate labor for the gospel (2 Cor. 1:8–10; 4:8–12). He

143

also reveals the basis for his intense motivational drive for pressing ahead—the redeeming love of Christ. His awareness of Christ's love for him literally controlled him and moved him to action. (It was not Paul's love for Christ that controlled him; if that were the case, he would have said, *our* love *for* Christ controls us, but instead he says, "The love of Christ controls us.") As Paul considered the great love that is proven and demonstrated in the incarnation and in obedience to the point of death (Phil. 2:8), a death personally rendered in Paul's place as a sinner, this God-centered, unimaginable love permeated and impacted his life in such a way as to command every thought, word, action, and intention.

This discussion of Christ's love leads him directly into the substitutionary nature of the atonement. Paul informs the Corinthians that it is sinful man who is deserving of condemnation and the death penalty, and that Christ stepped forward in an exercise of boundless love and suffered and died in our place.

Christ's death is not a case of a hero exposing himself to danger or death for the benefit of his countrymen, or the case of a friend dying for the benefit of a friend (Rom. 5:7). The proper translation of these words is critical because the purpose and result of Christ's death is far beyond his simply dying *for the benefit of* a sinner. He died *instead of* the sinful one who should have borne the full penalty of his sin. To limit the meaning here to "for the benefit of" would disregard the fact that we deserved the death he died, as well as the fact that sinful man can in no way atone for his own sin, much less that of another, nor can he in any way by his own means propitiate God's just wrath. To do that, Christ had to become our substitute.

There are those who would construe the word *died* in the clause "therefore all have died" (2 Cor. 5:14) to mean that Christians merely die to a life of self. But this simply cannot be the case, because Paul, a great master of language and deduction, wouldn't have been likely to use the same word, *apothnesko*, in two different ways (literally and figuratively) in the same sentence. The Greek word translated *died* is best taken in precisely the same sense in both clauses of the sentence. If everyone for whom Christ died has also died, their death must also have occurred through the process of transfer, that is, through imputation or crediting. In other words, Christ died as our representative head, and whatever our representative did, we are regarded as having done in him. In union with Christ, his death *is* our death, just as his righteousness *is* our righteousness, and his resurrection *is* our resurrection. Every aspect of the substitution is reciprocal—sin, death, righteousness, life—all are both personal and substitutionary. We are not to regard Christ as performing one act and the Christian as performing a separate act parallel or similar to his. On the basis of our connectedness to him, we participated in the atoning death of Christ, and it is accepted by God as our own death.

John Owen masterfully demonstrated in *Death of Death in the Death of Christ* that the *all* for whom Christ died is the same *all* who have died in him, with no wider or more general translation acceptable. They are the ones who have become united with Christ as their representative in death, and thereby have received the forgiveness and the redemption purchased by the great atonement. Christ died only for *all* the ones who have also died in him.

To attempt to say that Christ died for those whom he failed to save is to distort and misrepresent the atonement and deny its nature as a single, whole, complete, vicarious transaction. The death of Christ must save all for whom he died, and all for whom he died must participate by faith in his act of representative, substitutionary death in which he completely changed places with the redeemed.

This is not to deny that unbelievers derive great benefits from the fact of Christ's atonement. They enjoy a period of God's patience and all the common graces of living among the people of God. But these blessings do not mean that the Lord died in a double way—for some vicariously, and for others to give them only a temporary advantage—for that would undermine the biblical truth that all for whom Christ died also died in him.

To further affirm this vital point, Paul points out that all those for whose sake Christ died and was raised will have a new, radically transformed life as a direct result of their participation in his representative death. They "no longer live for themselves but for him." This new life is a spiritual and eternal life resulting from their sharing in Christ's perfect obedience and perfect sacrificial death on their behalf.

This new life is a dedicated life, one in which we no longer live for ourselves—for our own profit, gratification, or honor. Instead, we are dedicated to live for him—his purpose, his pleasure, and his glory. This transformation of heart and mind stands as evidence of one's personal participation in the death of Christ. Once united with him, the risen Son shares his reward with his chosen ones, just as he said: "For as the Father raises the dead and gives them life, so also the Son gives life to whom he will" (John 5:21).

So for us, the love of Christ, seen and shared in his atoning death, results in a new, transformed, and eternal life—a life controlled by our awareness of and gratitude for Jesus and his finished work on the cross.

2 Corinthians 5:18–19

> All this is from God, who through Christ reconciled us to himself and gave us the ministry of reconciliation; that is, in Christ God was reconciling the world to himself, not counting their trespasses against them, and entrusting to us the message of reconciliation. (2 Cor. 5:18–19)

In 2 Corinthians 5:18–19 we find Paul shedding even more light on the nature of the atonement. As we've seen before, the term "reconciled" implies that God was at one point our enemy, and we were his enemies. The enmity was mutual—us against God and God against us. But God the Father, though offended and provoked by our sin, provided the means by which we are instead reconciled (restored) to a favorable relationship with him. Paul clearly shows here that God the Father is the initiator and the source of our reconciliation; God took the first step toward us, a single step that is all-sufficient for its recipients, a step infinitely able to bear away all his curse and wrath and to replace his fury with friendship.

Just as it is impossible for unregenerate sinners to adequately appease the just anger of God, it is equally impossible for them to bridge the resultant relationship gap by their own means. Man's natural inclination is not Godward; we are, rather, by very our nature, predisposed to more and more sin. Left to our own devices, the enmity between God and man would stand forever. Out of his great love and grace, God reconciled this relationship with us.

There has been much debate in theological circles about how we are to understand the phrase "the world" (v. 19). As we noted earlier, the expression cannot refer to the entire human family when both the Bible and our day-to-day experience tell us that the majority of people remain relationally alienated from God. No, in context we must understand this to mean *sinners united to Christ*. This is confirmed by the next clause, "not counting their trespasses against them," a reference that most certainly does not apply to everyone in the world, for the Bible makes it abundantly clear that God will judge and condemn many in the world:

> When the Lord Jesus is revealed from heaven with his mighty angels in flaming fire, inflicting vengeance on those who *do not know* God and on those who *do not obey the gospel* of our Lord Jesus. They will suffer the punishment of eternal destruction, *away from the presence* of the Lord and from the glory of his might, when he comes on that day to be glorified in his saints, and to be marveled at among all who have believed, because our testimony to you was believed. (2 Thess. 1:7b–10)

So, there are those in this world who are not reconciled, and they will remain unreconciled throughout eternity. But those who know God by submitting to the gospel—that is, those who come to God on his terms and by his appointed means—are reconciled. These will see the glory of the might of Jesus. These will glorify King Jesus forever by marveling at him in person.

This is a completely God-centered reconciliation. Not only did God initiate it, but God himself is the object of it. He reconciled us "to himself." Our reconciliation is a very personal reconciliation to a very personal God. As a result, he draws us close, welcoming us into his presence. He invites us:

> Come, everyone who thirsts,
>   come to the waters;
> and he who has no money,
>   come, buy and eat!
> Come, buy wine and milk
>   without money and without price. (Isa. 55:1)

We have done nothing to earn it, for we could never pay the price of our sin except by eternal condemnation and separation. Man does not by his own decision or will cause Christ to be made sin for him. It is blasphemy to think otherwise. Christ's sin bearing is not applied to a sinner by a mere human act such as participating in the physical act of baptism or the infusing of religious emblems, such as eating a communion wafer dipped in wine. Yes, there was a price, an infinitely high price. And it was paid to God on our behalf by Jesus Christ. And now we are his. Now we are God's friends. More than that, we are his cherished adopted sons and daughters.

The word "counting" can and probably should be regarded as an accounting term here. God does not count, or charge, our sin to our account; rather, he charges it to Christ instead by the process of substitution. The result is that we are debt free. We stand reconciled to God because we no longer owe him anything as payment for our sin. This being the case, it is no wonder in the next verse Paul implores the Corinthians, "on behalf of Christ, be reconciled to God" (2 Cor. 5:20b).

2 Corinthians 5:21

> For our sake he made him to be sin who knew no sin, so that in him we might become the righteousness of God. (2 Cor. 5:21)

Here Paul captures the vital concept of substitution in a single, monumental sentence. He precisely and concisely conveys the essential elements of the atonement—the inner workings and logic of the Great Exchange. Jesus became sin, and in him we become righteousness. It would not be an understatement to view this verse, properly understood, as the single key verse of the entire Bible.

God made Jesus Christ to be sin, that is, God took the initiative to make the great miracle of substitution happen, as Paul pointed out when he said, "All this is from God" (2 Cor. 5:18). We must not mistakenly take this to mean that Jesus did not go to the cross voluntarily. Long before sin entered the world, yes, even before the world was created, we know the Father and Son conspired together to display the glory of their grace in the gospel, as anyone that patiently unpacks these five breathtaking verses will eventually discover:

> Blessed be the God and Father of our Lord Jesus Christ, who has blessed us in Christ with every spiritual blessing in the heavenly places, even as he chose us in him *before the foundation of the world*, that we should be holy and blameless before him. In love he predestined us for adoption through Jesus Christ, according to the purpose of his will, *to the praise of his glorious grace*, with which he has blessed us in the Beloved. In him we have *redemption through his blood*, the forgiveness of our trespasses, according to the riches of his grace, which he lavished upon us. (Eph. 1:3–8)

Jesus, the founder and perfecter of our faith, endured the cross for the joy that was set before him (Heb. 12:2) and became the blood-bought guarantee of the new covenant in which the Father appointed and sent the Son to assume our human nature and bear our guilt.

Christ's personal obedience to God's law was flawless; he "knew no sin." Men could not convict him of sin (John 8:46), and even Pilate found no guilt in him (Luke 23:4). But these facts are of little significance compared to the overriding reality that Jesus proved to be absolutely sinless in the very eyes of God the Father, whose eyes have infinite ability to scrutinize. The One who "made Jesus to be sin for our sake" did so because he knew Jesus to be perfectly qualified to accept the transfer of our guilt by vicarious sin bearing.

Jesus committed no sin, either of commission or omission. No selfish motives. No prideful feelings. Not a single word of gossip. Not an impure thought. This from a man "who in every respect has been tempted as we are, yet without sin" (Heb. 4:15b).

The clause "he made him to be sin who knew no sin" results in one of the best descriptions of Christ as our atonement. Paul is careful to make a distinction between the personal sinlessness of Christ and his being *made sin* in his official, representative capacity in his position as sin bearer. Jesus was not *made a sinner*. No! He was *made sin*.

This is the first half of the Great Exchange—the sinless Jesus becomes our sin. Because of his union with us, our sin is transferred to Christ. Although Jesus is personally sinless in the all-knowing eyes of God, he was regarded by God as perfect sin personified. The punishment was no different than if Jesus had personally committed all the sins of those "in him." Herein lies proof that our guilt was transferred; if it were not, the punishment of the personally sinless Son would not have transpired. The perfectly obedient Son of God could not have become the object of the Father's loathing or aversion in his personal capacity as the only begotten and perfectly obedient Son. Christ could only have been subjected to God's wrath in his official, representative capacity as sin-bearing substitute.

But just because Jesus was a representative sin bearer did not mitigate or dilute the raging justice of the holy God. Just as we are made specifically aware of our guilt, Jesus was fully conscious of that unimaginable load of sin. Jesus' being made sin encompassed every consequence of sin, including the unthinkable: the separation that shocked Jesus into crying out from the cross with a loud voice, "My God, my God, why have you forsaken me?" (Mark 15:34).

> Though he was in the form of God, did not count equality with God a thing to be grasped, but made himself nothing, taking the form of a servant, being born in the likeness of men. And being found in human form, he humbled himself by becoming obedient to the point of death, even death on a cross. (Phil. 2:6–8)

It is essential that we do not overlook the meaning of the phrase "in him." This expression occurs twice in 2 Corinthians 5:21, both times possessing the same meaning—the reception of our sin by the sin bearer, and the reception of Christ's righteousness by the sinner. Both occur only to a qualified population of sinners, namely, those united to Christ by faith as their representative.

2 Corinthians 8:9

> For you know the grace of our Lord Jesus Christ, that though he was rich, yet for your sake he became poor, so that you by his poverty might become rich. (2 Cor. 8:9)

In this section of 2 Corinthians, Paul illustrates the Great Exchange by showing that we have traded places with our Lord Jesus Christ. He took our place so that we could join him in his. Once again Paul uses financial terms—rich and poor—to show how this exchange took place.

With these words, Paul positions us to discover the definition of grace. Some have used the acronym G.R.A.C.E., God's Riches At Christ's Expense, which would seem to flow from this verse. But this definition is inadequate in that it fails to include a key element of the verse—we are poor. As sinners we are destitute, bankrupt, poverty-stricken, and completely unable to begin to pay any of our debt. Before we can capture the full meaning of this verse—and of grace itself—it is critical that we acknowledge our inability to pay even a fraction of our debt. To help with this, we might substitute this definition for the acronym G.R.A.C.E.: "God's riches at Christ's expense to those who deserve his wrath and his curse."

In order to "know the grace of our Lord Jesus Christ," we must attempt to fathom the extent of the riches Christ abandoned in order to redeem us, because both our abject poverty and his abandoned riches have exactly the same magnitude, and both are important parts in understanding grace. Prior to his conception, throughout all of eternity past, Jesus Christ enjoyed every aspect and benefit of equality with God. We get a glimpse of this in Colossians where Paul states, "For by [Christ] all things were created, in heaven and on earth, visible and invisible, whether thrones or dominions or rulers or authorities—all things were created through him and for him. And he is before all things, and in him all things hold together" (Col. 1:16–17).

The apostle John demonstrated these truths as well. He opens his Gospel stating, "In the beginning was the Word, and the Word was with God, and the Word was God. He was in the beginning with

God. All things were made through him, and without him was not any thing made that was made. In him was life, and the life was the light of men" (John 1:1–4). We know from the context that this passage refers to Christ because John goes on to say, "The Word became flesh and dwelt among us, and we have seen his glory, glory as of the only Son from the Father, full of grace and truth" (John 1:14).

As the one through whom the entire universe was made, Christ's material wealth was all-inclusive. In addition, his spiritual wealth had no limits. In the garden of Gethsemane prior to his crucifixion, we receive remarkable insight into Christ's intimacy with the Father and the glory and position provided to Christ by the Father. There Jesus prayed, "And now, Father, glorify me in your own presence with the glory that I had with you before the world existed" (John 17:5), demonstrating his place in the Godhead, his original co-existence and co-preeminence with the Father.

Christ existed in perfect harmony, fellowship, and pleasure in the Trinity throughout all of eternity past. He spoke creation into being (Heb. 1:3) to display his glory and grace, not for the purpose of filling up a void or to complete his personal happiness. He had no unmet needs, as Luke shows us:

> The God who made the world and everything in it, being Lord of heaven and earth, does not live in temples made by man, nor is he served by human hands, *as though he needed anything*, since he himself gives to all mankind life and breath and everything. (Acts 17:24–25)

Blaise Pascal once said that man has a God-sized vacuum inside that only God can fill. But the reverse is *not* true: God does not have a man-sized vacuum that only man can fill. He was perfectly content and gloriously happy within the fellowship of the Godhead. To think otherwise is tantamount to blasphemy, because it lowers God at the expense of elevating man.

Because Christ's riches were infinite, it follows that he paid an incalculable price for us. In taking on our sin on the cross, the all-glorious, infinitely wealthy, completely perfect Christ died the most horrific, inglorious, degrading, and humbling death, the death of a wretched criminal. He gave up infinite perfection for infinite pain and ignominy. That is incredible love.

Jesus became poor from the moment Jesus, God's equal, became Jesus, the God-man. This point in time is marked by the immaculate conception by the Holy Spirit in the womb of a human mother, Mary, the moment Jesus took on humanity. There, "being found in human form, he humbled himself by becoming obedient to the point of death, even death on a cross" (Phil. 2:8).

The entire earthly life of Jesus—from the point at which he left the Father's side until he sat down at the Father's side once more after the resurrection—was a further "becoming poor" for our sake. And, therefore, all of it comprised his payment of our sin penalty and his trading places with us. The price was being paid constantly as Jesus lived on earth in perfect obedience to the Father without property or the comforts other men enjoyed. He was born in an animal trough. After his birth his parents fled to Egypt to protect him. He was raised in the shabby, second-rate town of Nazareth. As he labored and sweated as a carpenter's apprentice, the King of kings experienced hunger, thirst, and fatigue. At one point he said, "Foxes have holes, and birds of the air have nests, but the Son of Man has nowhere to lay his head" (Luke 9:58). Apparently he had no permanent residence after he started his ministry.

In view of the fact that he was personally sinless, he deserved none of this. He deserved absolute worship and adoration as a member of the Godhead. So, clearly, it can be concluded that his entire life was a progression of curse bearing, right up through his death on the cross and his resurrection.

The reason Jesus became poor was twofold, as we noted earlier. It certainly was for our sake, to redeem a people who could otherwise not be redeemed. But that was not his ultimate purpose.

In love [God] predestined us for adoption through Jesus Christ, according to the purpose of his will, *to the praise of his glorious grace*, with which he has blessed us in the Beloved. In him we have redemption through his blood, the forgiveness of our trespasses, according to the riches of his grace. (Eph. 1:4b–7)

Here Paul gives us further insight into what ultimately motivated Father and Son—the display of his grace forever on display at the cross, exalted for all time. God would get all the glory and give us all the grace. It was brought about by the exchange of infinite riches for infinite poverty, a substitution in which the owner of incalculable wealth became absolutely desolate in every way, so that we might receive immeasurable, never-ending wealth—God himself—and he would gain all the praise and glory.

In exactly what ways have we "become rich" (2 Cor. 8:9)? While the atoning obedience of Christ is one complete, finished work, we may see its various aspects applied to the specific needs of bankrupt sinners. Christ was humbled to atone for our pride. He became poor to atone for our covetousness. He experienced hunger and thirst to atone for our overindulgence and our eating of forbidden fruit. He became a captive that we might be set free. He became troubled that we might be comforted. He was tempted that we might have victory over temptation. He was dishonored that we may be glorified. He was scourged that by his stripes we might be healed. He died that we might have life.

The popular, modern-day prosperity gospel would have us believe that this verse refers to material possessions or affluence, that "if you become a Christian, God will bless you with health, wealth, and all forms of material prosperity." The Bible, taken in context, never comes close to asserting anything remotely resembling such a conclusion and often teaches the opposite, as the hundreds of passages on the subjects of Christian suffering and the true meaning of wealth testify. One example of this can be seen in Jesus' parable about the man who lives for wealth and ease and not for God (see Luke 12). Jesus doesn't commend him; he calls the man a fool.

Jesus offers no prosperity gospel. Christ is not a means to an end for the Christian—he *is* the end. He is the wealth we long for. The riches of Christ make the temporal, prideful, man-centered, conspicuous consumer riches pale and wither away by comparison. Evidence that we have these true riches will be manifest in a progressive deepening in our longing and desire for him rather than material possessions. A true understanding of our riches in Christ will make us follow him gladly, even into suffering or poverty, because for us to live is Christ and to die is gain (Phil. 1:21).

Through Christ's purchase of us with his blood we become children of God. And as Paul says in Romans, "If children, then heirs—heirs of God and fellow heirs with Christ, provided we suffer with him in order that we may also be glorified with him" (Rom. 8:17). If we are heirs of God, we have everything! So as to any apparent lack of material prosperity, Paul declares, "I consider that the sufferings of this present time are not worth comparing with the glory that is to be revealed to us" (Rom. 8:18). That is true wealth.

As a result of his perfect, personal, and substitutionary work in making us rich through his poverty, the risen Christ is now and forever restored to his exalted position.

> And being found in human form, he humbled himself by becoming obedient to the point of death, even death on a cross. Therefore God has highly exalted him and bestowed on him the name that is above every name, so that at the name of Jesus every knee should bow, in heaven and on earth and under the earth, and every tongue confess that Jesus Christ is Lord, to the glory of God the Father. (Phil. 2:8–11)

And those redeemed sinners who are *in him*, those Christ represents as a sin substitute, those who are cloaked in his righteousness, all share in his glory. As Paul wrote to the Colossians, "To [his saints] God chose to make known how great among the Gentiles are the riches of the glory of this mystery, which is Christ in you, the hope of glory" (Col. 1:27). How rich is that? How glorious? As rich and glorious as Christ himself.

CHAPTER 10

Galatians

The apostle Paul visited Galatia on two occasions. While there he preached the atonement, publicly portraying Jesus Christ as crucified (Gal. 3:1b). Within a short time after his second visit, a false and dangerous doctrine, legalism, began to gain a foothold, which asserted that our acceptance by God was dependent on observing certain Jewish rites and that participation in these ceremonies was necessary for the Christian to acquire righteousness.

Legalism occurs wherever a sinner attempts to earn God's favor by his or her personal righteousness instead of by Christ's transferred righteousness. Legalism demeans the value of Christ's work of atonement by requiring sinners to perform activities that are man-centered and, in essence, man-exalting. Even subtle, unspoken legalism sets forth a course that inevitably leads to spiritual pride and eventual defeat under the weight of unsuccessfully attempted law keeping. Paul reacted against all forms of legalism with force and focus, calling for those who teach such lies to "be accursed" (Gal. 1:8–9) and even wishing that those who were unsettling the Galatian Christians would "emasculate themselves" (Gal. 5:12). This is strong language. But such attacks by Paul do not seem shocking when we pause to consider what is at stake. By substituting man-centered performance as the basis for acquiring righteousness, the very essence and foundation of redemptive truth is compromised.

In this epistle, Paul shows that the atonement is the sole basis of man's forgiveness, righteousness, and acceptance by God—nothing can or should be added.

Galatians 1:4–5

> [Christ] gave himself for our sins to deliver us from the present evil age, according to the will of our God and Father, to whom be the glory forever and ever. Amen. (Gal. 1:4–5)

Nobody took Christ's life from him without his consent. Instead, he "gave himself for us." No one could have taken Christ's life if he had not presented himself as a voluntary sacrifice. Not the Jews or Pilate or the Romans or the crowds. Jesus made his willingness clear when he stated, "I lay down my life. . . . No one takes it from me" (John 10:17–18). He went to Jerusalem at the proper time for that very purpose. Before then no one could lay a hand on him, though many times they wanted to kill him for what he said or did (Luke 4:29–30). Even at his arrest in the garden of Gethsemane he could have saved himself by appealing to his Father with a single word (Matt. 26:53).

Clearly, Jesus' sacrifice was voluntary, in compliance with "the will of our God and Father." In the *giving*, Jesus provided the priestly action. In the giving of *himself*, Jesus provided the actual sacrifice. So Christ is the sacrificer and the victim in one. He is the priest of his self-sacrifice.

We must also take note that the sins mentioned here were not merely the sins of those who physically drove the nails into his innocent hands. These were our sins, as well. Therefore, you and I are personally culpable for his death. Death is always required as the payment for sin (Rom. 6:23a); the case of the sinless Christ was no exception. Our sin killed him, and no amount of fixing or patching ourselves up can change that fact. Our best personal righteousness is at best incomplete and therefore completely insufficient. Even if we never commit another sin as long as we live, the fact remains that our sin still killed him.

But there's good news. If Christ died for our sins as our representative, it follows that we are no longer required to die for our own sins. God does not punish the same sin twice. Because the justice of God was already satisfied on our behalf, there no longer remains any wrath, punishment, or death for us. Because of his death, we are no longer culpable for our sin. His death exculpated us; it freed us from the just accusation of our guilt because all-sufficient justice was served on the cross. Thus we are forever exonerated, acquitted, and declared not guilty.

And there's even more good news. The Lord Jesus Christ not only gave himself for our sins, but he also gave himself to deliver us from the present evil age—to set us free from our enslavement to the evil forces in today's world. In other words, Christ's death sets us apart for the process of transformation into Christlikeness. Not only did Christ's death accomplish our acceptance with God, it also launched the progressive renovation of our natures, the process of sanctification.

The order of the events here deserves notice. We sinners, previously dead in trespasses and sins are *made alive* together with Christ (Eph. 2:5) by the unilateral act of the Holy Spirit known as regeneration. Receiving and applying the gift of faith is the very first action in which we participate in our new life. In it we are united to Christ by participating in his redemptive work as our legal representative, resulting in our *justification*. Only after this legal union with Christ is established does the process of *sanctification* begin, as we are provided with ongoing access to the power of the Holy Spirit. In this living union we are progressively released from the forces that previously bound us to doing evil. So justification always precedes sanctification.

All of this is based on grace made ours through the atoning death of Christ. And because it is based not on man but on God, we do not get the glory; he does. As Galatians 1:5 declares, "To [God] be the glory forever and ever. Amen."

Galatians 2:20–21

I have been crucified with Christ. It is no longer I who live, but Christ
who lives in me. And the life I now live in the flesh I live by faith
in the Son of God, who loved me and gave himself for me. I do not
nullify the grace of God, for if justification were through the law,
then Christ died for no purpose. (Gal. 2:20–21)

Underlying Paul's words in this passage is his rebuke of the apostle
Peter, who feared that the legalists would condemn him for eating
with believers who hadn't been circumcised (vv. 11–14). Paul exposes
Peter's hypocrisy, pointing out that Peter's actions were motivated by
fear of the circumcision party. The circumcision party were legalists,
teaching that Christ's work on the cross was insufficient for salvation. What was needed, they said, was Christ and the ceremonial
rite of circumcision. In the wake of this, Paul states:

A person is not justified by works of the law but through faith in
Jesus Christ, so we also have believed in Christ Jesus, in order to be
justified by faith in Christ and not by works of the law, because by
works of the law no one will be justified. (Gal. 2:16)

Paul adds, "Through the law I died to the law, so that I might
live to God" (v. 19). Any and all hope of our being justified by our
personal performance of works of obedience must first be put to
death before we can *live to God*. We must embrace Christ as our
perfect Savior and our all-sufficient righteousness. This puts our
dependency on self-righteousness to death so that, like Paul, we
can say, "I have been crucified with Christ."

We are crucified with Christ when we deny our self-sufficiency
and declare it to be dead and thus unable to save us, embracing
Christ instead as our only hope and representative before the holy
Judge. In union with him through his death, we died to the guilt
of our sin and to enslaving power of sin over us, just as if we had
actually died. In addition, our futile attempts at self-justification
are killed as well.

In order to understand the nature of the way our union with Christ
works in this co-crucifixion, we must recall the way God designed

the entire human race. In Adam, one acted on behalf of all, and so all are born into sin and its consequences. In the same manner, one representative man—the God-man—obeyed on behalf of his redeemed and died in their place (Rom. 5:12–20). Therefore, God the Father views the entire redeemed church as if it were hanging on the cross with him.

In addition, we also share in his reward, so along with Paul we can say, "Christ lives in me." Paul, having just described our death in union with Christ, in the same breath describes our new life—a life attained by virtue of our union with Christ. Our death in him and our life in him are inseparable, just as Christ's death and life are inseparable, because we are one with him as our representative in both conditions. Christ is the source of our life—not just of our mortal, created, physical life, but also of our eternal, regenerated, spiritual life. Just as the union of soul and body sustains natural life, the union of the sinner's soul with the broken and resurrected Christ sustains spiritual, eternal life. The crucified and living Christ lives in me. This is the meaning of the living union between Christ and us.

This new life in Christ differs from our natural life in Adam in that it is never ending. It is secured forever, based on permanently satisfied justice that resulted from the finished, atoning work of Christ. The authority of God himself, by his own unchangeable plan and covenant, guarantees it.

This new life in Christ is similar to our natural life in Adam in that our experience of its reality occurs through the activity of the senses. That is to say, those who possess this new life "hear the voice of the Son of God" (John 5:25), they have eyes enlightened to the hope and calling of a rich and glorious inheritance (Eph. 1:18), and they taste that the Lord is good (1 Pet. 2:3). In spite of maintaining their distinct, individual identity and personality, believers live as active members of Christ's own body. Paul revealed this truth to the Corinthians when he said, "Now you are the body of Christ and individually members of it" (1 Cor. 12:27).

Just as the fact of natural life is evidenced by physical growth, the spiritual life is evidenced by growth as well in "holding fast to the Head, from whom the whole body, nourished and knit together through its joints and ligaments, grows with a growth that is from God" (Col. 2:19). All of those made spiritually alive by union with Christ will inevitably demonstrate it by growing in Christlikeness, and "the fruit of the Spirit" will be evidenced: "love, joy, peace, patience, kindness, goodness, faithfulness, gentleness, self-control" (Gal. 5:22–23).

However, the opposite is true as well. Where there is no growth, no fruit bearing, there is no evidence of the presence of the life that comes from union with Christ. In a profound statement to his disciples of the subject of union with himself, Jesus told the disciples:

> Abide in me, and I in you. As the branch cannot bear fruit by itself, unless it abides in the vine, neither can you, unless you abide in me. I am the vine; you are the branches. Whoever abides in me and I in him, he it is that bears much fruit, for apart from me you can do nothing. (John 15:4–5)

The union between Christ and his redeemed is reciprocal: he is "in you" (Col. 1:27; John 14:20; 2 Cor. 13:5), and, in passages too numerous to cite here, we are "in him." This union, this mutual abiding, is complete and inseparable, and at times our awareness of it is such that we cannot discern where one entity ends and the other begins, so that we exclaim, "It is no longer I who live, but Christ who lives in me." As our awareness of the fact of our union with Christ grows, we find the essence of abiding in Christ. We become increasingly satisfied with all that God is for us in Christ Jesus. Here he becomes our sole treasure and delight and desire as all others fade by comparison. Here we rejoice in exalting his glory. This is the essence of true worship. This is the essence of heaven on earth. At times like these, "we groan, longing to put on our heavenly dwelling" (2 Cor. 5:2) where we will be finally and completely at home with him forever.

All of this is dependent on the Great Exchange. If the Son had not intervened for us by offering his perfect obedience on our behalf and by becoming a perfect atoning sacrifice for our sin, this life could never have been bestowed on us sinners—even if we had committed only a single sin.

Paul repeatedly expressed the sentiments of a justified man glorying in an ongoing sense of acceptance and experience of grace. Our justification is not merely a single event in our past; we stand in the present reality of the righteousness of Christ every minute of every day. Paul continually sought to "be found in him, not having a righteousness of [his] own that comes from the law, but that which comes through faith in Christ, the righteousness from God that depends on faith" (Phil. 3:9).

Those in authentic legal union with Christ are irreversibly clothed in the righteousness of Christ in which they stand before a holy God. The faith that initially connected them to Christ for justification continues. They now live in his perfect, transferred righteousness, and at no time do they revert to depending on their own merit or goodness to gain God's blessing.

> Therefore, since we have been justified by faith, we have peace with God through our Lord Jesus Christ. Through him we have also obtained access by faith into *this grace in which we stand*, and we rejoice in hope of the glory of God. (Rom. 5:1–2)

Safely in Christ, we need not fear the wrath we deserve any longer; because of the atoning work of our all-sufficient wrath bearer, we are personally known, loved, and redeemed. The significance of this statement is impossible to overstate. It overshadows everything pertaining to us.

It is worth noting how significant it is that the verbs *love* and *give* are written in the past tense (Gal. 2:20). Christ's great atonement is a *fait accompli*, a finished work. It is fixed in history; it can never be undone. It culminated on the cross.

What is Paul's response to Christ loving him as a sinful wretch? Paul considered himself co-crucified with Christ and co-resurrected to "live by faith in the Son of God." If we are called to the same Shepherd, we are also called to the same response.

Paul turns to identify a sure way we can nullify this great grace of God. It is by failing to grasp the application of it to our lives. We fail to live in grace if we believe and trust that we are justified based on our personal obedience and live as if we can work our way to God by our performance. But the all-encompassing truth is that "none is righteous, no, not one" (Rom. 3:10). No one will stand on their own merit before the infinitely holy God of the universe. All who would be saved must trust the work of Christ alone.

As we saw in the case of Peter refusing to eat with the Gentile believers, it is absurd to claim that the observance of the law is required as a supplement to Christ's atonement, and that his death alone is not adequate by itself to save redeemed sinners. This lie was precisely the one to which the Galatians were falling prey. But how can an imperfect, personal obedience play any role in supplementing the reconciliation between a relatively good sinner and a perfectly holy God whose curse and wrath is upon the committer of a single sin? Any level of personal righteousness falls drastically short. Its perceived ability to reconcile is a fatal illusion, because often our sin is not even known to our deceptive and self-justifying hearts. We dare not trust in any righteousness apart from Christ's atonement. Paul didn't; he boasted only in the cross. We are deceiving ourselves if we think that our lives could in any way add any merit to the work of Christ. Furthermore, it is to demean the value of both his sacrifice and the new covenant. Is this not the preempting of God's Word, his plan, and his Christ? Is this not a form of blasphemy—an elevating of man to God's level? Is this not in itself the worst of sins? Our justification must stand completely on his work, not our own.

Paul's argument leads to a logical conclusion: if justification were through the law, then Christ died for no purpose. But the Son of God would not have died without a purpose—it would be inconceivable. Instead, the mission of Christ had the grandest purpose of all time: his incarnation and death ushered in an eternally perfect righteousness for sinners based on the transfer of his own obedience, a perfect obedience to the point of death, even death on a cross

(Phil. 2:8). This is the gospel of Jesus Christ; this is the message of God's Word and Spirit. Therefore, Paul challenges the Galatians with strong words to set aside the illogical notion that this perfect plan is lacking in any way, or that they can add to its effectiveness by human effort. Just a few verses later, he confronts them with a stinging question, a question we should ask ourselves often: "Let me ask you only this: Did you receive the Spirit by works of the law or by hearing with faith? Are you so foolish? Having begun by the Spirit, are you now being perfected by the flesh?" (Gal. 3:2–3).

Galatians 3:10, 13–14a

> For all who rely on works of the law are under a curse; for it is written, "Cursed be everyone who does not abide by all things written in the Book of the Law, and do them." . . . Christ redeemed us from the curse of the law by becoming a curse for us—for it is written, "Cursed is everyone who is hanged on a tree"—so that in Christ Jesus the blessing of Abraham might come to the Gentiles. (Gal. 3:10, 13–14a)

This passage in Galatians 3 bears a strong resemblance to 2 Corinthians 5:21, where Paul describes the transfer of our sin to Christ as our sin bearer: "For our sake he made him to be sin who knew no sin." Here in Galatians Paul describes Christ as curse bearer, the one that took away our curse, because he had taken on our sin that had placed us "under a curse."

God's curse extends far beyond the mere civil punishments inflicted by human judiciaries on law breakers. This curse refers to the consequences inflicted by God for disobeying his law:

> But if you will not obey the voice of the LORD your God or be careful to do all his commandments and his statutes that I command you today, then all these curses shall come upon you and overtake you. (Deut. 28:15)

Multiple layers of the consequences of being under God's curse are spelled out in detail in the verses that follow (Deut. 28:16–68). A fresh reading of this passage will shock and awe anyone who is aware of his or her own failure to perfectly obey. Careful meditation over this passage should immediately result in tremendous gratitude for Christ's work of curse bearing.

Adam and Eve were also subjected to a multifaceted curse for their single sin. It culminated in their banishment from God's presence in the garden of Eden (Gen. 3:23–24). Accordingly, for us, being cursed by God includes being subjected to God's pronouncement that "your iniquities have made a separation between you and your God, and your sins have hidden his face from you so that he does not hear" (Isa. 59:2).

God's curse applies to "everyone who does not abide by *all* things written in the Book of the Law" (Gal. 3:10b). Therefore, a single sin is an affront to a holy God and cannot and will not be overlooked by him. It is in no way acceptable, no matter how picayune. A person who has committed a single sin is a sinner. A sinner who is "relatively good" is still a sinner. There are no exceptions. As James said, "Whoever keeps the whole law but fails in one point has become accountable for all of it" (James 2:10).

Does this exclude the Galatians because they were Gentiles and not Jews? Certainly not, because:

> When Gentiles, who do not have the law, by nature do what the law requires, they are a law to themselves, even though they do not have the law. They show that the work of *the law is written on their hearts*, while their conscience also bears witness. (Rom. 2:14–15a)

And:

> For the wrath of God is revealed from heaven against all ungodliness and unrighteousness of men, who by their unrighteousness suppress the truth. For what can be known about God is plain to them, because God has shown it to them. For his invisible attributes, namely, his eternal power and divine nature, have been clearly perceived, ever since the creation of the world, in the things that have been made. *So they are without excuse.* (Rom. 1:18–20)

So, apart from Christ, Jew and Gentile alike are equally under God's curse and subject to his wrath. There are no exceptions.

The fact that Jesus actually bore the full weight and fury of our curse is quite apparent in the most agonizing aspect of his suffering when "at the ninth hour Jesus cried with a loud voice, 'Eloi, Eloi, lema sabachthani?' which means, 'My God, my God, why have you forsaken me?'" (Mark 15:34). Though many have gone to great length to display the intense physical agony, torture, and bloody scourging that Christ underwent for our sake, none of these constitute the most dreadful part of his suffering. The total separation from the Father was the vortex of his curse bearing.

Separation from the Father was something the Son had never experienced in all of eternity past. Even after his incarnation as a human, Jesus never experienced an inkling of separation from the Father. He enjoyed unbroken personal fellowship. As he told his disciples of the Father, "He who sent me is with me. He has not left me alone, for I always do the things that are pleasing to him" (John 8:29).

The curse necessitated separation; God could not simply overlook this part of the curse any more than he can overlook the separation of the eternal death that his just condemnation will bestow on all sinners who die outside of Christ's representation as curse bearer.

Galatians 4:4–5

> But when the fullness of time had come, God sent forth his Son, born of woman, born under the law, to redeem those who were under the law, so that we might receive adoption as sons. (Gal. 4:4–5)

Whereas redemption from the curse of the law was the subject of Galatians 3:13, this passage (Gal. 4:4–5) describes our redemption from the law itself. The process that secured our multi-faceted redemption began the day Christ started bearing our sin, that is, the day Jesus was conceived—an event planned before the creation of the world. God determined to send Christ to redeem us at the precise moment in human history when the fullness of time had come.

The timing of the central event in human history encompasses much mystery, much that is outside our realm and ability to grasp, because it goes beyond us to the infinite mind of God. However, as we noted earlier, the prophecies and foreshadows of the Old Testament offer indicators for recognizing God's perfect timing in providing the Redeemer and the ushering in of the new covenant.

Another aspect of "the fullness" was the fact that sufficient time had been provided to prove that all man-made schemes for reconciling sinners with God had failed—art and education, culture and civilization, even the law itself. All such attempts fell far short of removing man's guilt and restoring friendship and intimacy with God.

Jesus made it clear that "the Father consecrated and sent [Him] into the world" (John 10:36). The fact that God *sent* him indicates that the Son existed prior to his incarnation in Bethlehem's manger. Where was Jesus sent from, if not God's very presence? The clear implication here, then, is that Jesus is of divine origin (Heb. 1:1–3; John 1:1–3). Jesus was God's Son before he was Mary's son. There is no one like him; he is the God-sent God-man.

Paul states that the Son was "born of woman" (Gal. 4:4). No mention is made of a human father here, which is an allusion to the virgin birth of Christ. The immaculate conception of Jesus is yet another aspect of the uniqueness of the Redeemer's identity and qualification. The Son's humanity was not directly imparted to him by God. To share fully in our nature, it had to be derived as ours is—from a human mother. This is a vital element of the atonement. Without Christ's humanity, he would have no natural or legal relation to us or union with us, and he could not be our representative.

There is, however, a vital difference between Christ's humanity and ours—he is not personally represented in Adam. As a result, he was not born with a sin nature. Instead, Christ is the Last Adam, i.e., the last representative man (1 Cor. 15:45). Since Christ was personally exempt from receiving Adam's imputed sin, he became qualified and available to receive our sin.

In a stunning display of the redemptive power of the God-man's sanctifying blood shed on behalf of the redeemed sinners he represents, we are told, "He is not ashamed to call them brothers" (Heb. 2:11b). He thus became our kinsman-redeemer. Think of that! He shamelessly calls us, known sinners, his own brothers. No man ever imagined achieving a higher privilege, or one less deserved.

The fact that Christ had to be "born under the law" indicates that prior to his birth he was not under the law. Christ's existence prior to the incarnation was fully above the law's authority. He had no personal obligation to obey the law because, in triune union with the Maker of the law, he was above it. The law did not have authority over the Son; the Son had authority over the law. He placed himself under the law both voluntarily and at the direction of the Father (Phil. 2:6–8) in order to become the true substitute for the law-breaking sinners he came to redeem.

And ultimately he did it "so that we might receive adoption as sons" (Gal. 4:5). The final outcome of the eternal plan is this: we are adopted into the very family of God. We are no longer cursed outsiders. We are no longer enemies. We are made more than friends. We find ourselves ushered into a new standing as adopted sons and daughters. We find ourselves to have an adoptive Brother, the "first-born among many brothers" (Rom. 8:29), the very One who:

> is the image of the invisible God, the firstborn of all creation. For by him all things were created, in heaven and on earth, visible and invisible, whether thrones or dominions or rulers or authorities—all things were created through him and for him. And he is before all things, and in him all things hold together. And he is the head of the body, the church. He is the beginning, the firstborn from the dead, that in everything he might be preeminent. (Col. 1:15–18)

In this Great Exchange, we find ourselves arriving at God himself, adopted "through Jesus Christ, according to the purpose of his will, to the praise of his glorious grace, with which he has blessed us in the Beloved" (Eph. 1:5–6). And because we "are sons, God has sent the Spirit of his Son into our hearts, crying, 'Abba! Father!'" (Gal. 4:6) in an intimate expression of this new blood-bought relationship. Far from being slaves, we are now God-esteemed sons of God and Christ-esteemed brothers of Christ. And as if this were not more than enough, Paul points out the inconceivable fact that, if we are sons, then we are also heirs through God (v. 7). What can this inheritance possibly mean? What blessing can be excluded? What a reward, what grace, what a God, what a Christ, what a gospel!

Galatians 6:14

> But far be it from me to boast except in the cross of our Lord Jesus Christ, by which the world has been crucified to me, and I to the world. (Gal. 6:14)

Paul had many of the qualifications in which men of the day would have taken pride. He states:

> If anyone else thinks he has reason for confidence in the flesh, I have more: circumcised on the eighth day, of the people of Israel, of the tribe of Benjamin, a Hebrew of Hebrews; as to the law, a Pharisee; as to zeal, a persecutor of the church; as to righteousness, under the law blameless. (Phil. 3:4b–6)

But Paul forsakes all this and counts "everything as loss because of the surpassing worth of knowing Christ Jesus" (v. 8). Why does Paul take this radical step? Why does he hold this astonishing view? He tells the Philippians, "I count everything as loss . . . in order that I may gain Christ and be found in him, not having a righteousness of my own that comes from the law, but that which comes through faith in Christ, the righteousness from God that depends on faith" (Phil. 3:8–9).

In striking contrast to the error of the Galatians, who prided themselves in circumcision and other rites, ceremonies, and legal observances, Paul puts forth a single claim—Christ crucified. Recognizing the cross as the sole basis of his acceptance by the Father, he discards any allusions to supplemental offerings and "excludes" all personal boasting (Rom. 3:27).

However, Paul *does* glory in something; he glories in his participation in the cross. He implies that this type of boasting is one in which the Christian can never overindulge. We are to glory in the cross as the source of our blood-bought forgiveness, righteousness, redemption, reconciliation, propitiation, and adoption. This is the only form of boasting that rids man of pride and self-aggrandizement and glorifies Jesus Christ and God the Father. This should be the continual boast of our heart and mouth.

By declaring the cross to be the instrument "by which the world has been crucified to me, and I to the world" (Gal. 6:14), Paul removes all doubt that the cross will ever become a source of self-exaltation or self-promotion in the eyes of the world. Instead, those who participate in the blessings of the atonement also participate in a twofold crucifixion in which their connection with the world is terminated.

"The world has been crucified to me" denotes that we now see the world as if it were a crucified person—disgusting, unwelcome, and undesirable. Both the allure of the world and our tendency to claim relative legal righteousness in it are nailed to the cross. Neither has any greater influence over us than a cursed and crucified corpse can have.

On the other hand, Paul's expression ". . . and I to the world" denotes that we now see ourselves as if we were crucified people, dead to the world because another has won it over. Our tastes and desires for the world are to be as dead as those of a crucified man. No longer do we live for the world and its pleasures (James 4:4). No longer do we seek from it fame or fortune. Like dead men, we have lost our attachment to the world—it has become alien to us, no longer our home.

May we someday, by God's grace, sooner rather than later, be transformed into the image of Christ. May we say wholeheartedly with Paul, "For to me to live is Christ, and to die is gain" (Phil. 1:21), and, "If we live, we live to the Lord, and if we die, we die to the Lord. So then, whether we live or whether we die, we are the Lord's" (Rom. 14:8). This is the approach we will have to the world when Christ has captured our very hearts and minds.

However, being crucified to the world should not shut us off from its people. In practical terms, and in view of the fact that we remain "in the world" (John 17:11), we are called by Christ to take this gospel of hope to the world (Matt. 28:18–20). We also must not hate the people of the world (Rom. 12:20), although the world will certainly at times hate us (John 15:19). The animosity that we receive should not dim our enthusiasm to take the glorious message of the cross to the world. Knowing that Christ will be with us (John 17:24), and that his message will have glorious effect on all those he has called (John 10:26–29), we can rejoice in the kingdom work Christ has given us to do as we live and die to the glory of God.

CHAPTER 11

Ephesians

In his epistle to the Ephesians, the apostle Paul focuses on the person and work of Jesus Christ with a view to addressing the influence of Gnosticism, a cult distinguished by the belief that Christ was not human and that the physical realm is evil. Gnostics contended that freedom comes through diminishing the physical aspects of life while pursuing elusive and mysterious philosophical knowledge gained as Gnosticism is embraced.

Thus, in Ephesians *mystery* is a key word used by Paul six times. In the first chapter, Paul reveals that the mystery of God's will and purpose is "set forth in Christ as a plan for the fullness of time, to unite all things in him, things in heaven and things on earth" (Eph.1:9–10). Included in this mystery is the newly revealed truth that "the Gentiles are fellow heirs, members of the same body, and partakers of the promise in Christ Jesus through the gospel" (Eph. 3:6), which is to say, the Gentiles are saved the way the Jews are saved—through the atoning work of Christ.

Ephesians 1:7

In him we have redemption through his blood, the forgiveness of our trespasses, according to the riches of his grace. (Eph. 1:7)

172

Paul cannot get very far in this letter without centering his message squarely on the atonement. In the four verses leading up to Ephesians 1:7, Paul praises the God who has blessed us "in Christ with every spiritual blessing"—our election, sanctification, and adoption—all "to the praise of his glorious grace, with which he has blessed us in the Beloved." All of these blessings, the very foundation of our hope, are found in Christ or through Christ; they are based on our union with him as our representative. They cannot be obtained apart from him.

This redemption we have *in him* is our possession. As Paul states, "We *have* redemption through his blood." The full price was paid on our behalf, and we have it now, even as our final redemption draws nearer each day (Luke 21:28).

The price of this redemption is abundantly clear—it is "through his blood." Our redemption is as real as his blood. It is a real deliverance from a real captivity by a real ransom paid in blood. We really were captive to the dominion of sin and its resulting condemnation. Our sin nature dominated us, and the law condemned us to death. But Christ the beloved, as our representative, intervened on our behalf by dying a real and cursed death in our place. The ransom price was paid to God to satisfy his justice, and we were redeemed from our old owner to our new One with a perfect blood sacrifice acceptable to the Father.

It is also clear from this passage that just as our redemption is "through his blood," so is our forgiveness. There is a direct, causal relationship between Christ's atonement and our forgiveness. Without the substitutionary death of Christ, there would be no forgiveness—ever.

Nowhere in this passage, or in the Bible taken as a whole, do we find the requirement for us to add our own puny righteousness or good works to Christ's blood in order to receive forgiveness. There is no provision whatsoever anywhere for us to redeem ourselves by asserting that our good deeds outweigh our bad deeds. This strategy, though often attempted and practiced, will never be adequate in the presence of an absolutely perfect, holy, and unchangeable God.

Our personal righteousness is as filthy rags (Isa. 64:6) and is entirely worthless apart from the atoning work of Christ. If we stand on it as our hope for earning God's mercy and eternal salvation, it will merit us only hell, because it denies and diminishes and devalues God's own provision for the forgiveness of our sin—Christ crucified.

No, there is only one condition to warrant our salvation, and it is designated by the two little words "in him." These words have great weight and consequence because they assign us to a new representative, one that perfectly redeems sinners through his own all-sufficient blood.

All of this—our redemption, our forgiveness, and the blood of Christ through which it is provided—is bestowed on us "according to the riches of his grace which he lavished upon us, in all wisdom and insight" (Eph. 1:7b–8). From beginning to end, it is grace—God's blessings in Christ to those who deserve his curse—by which we are saved (Eph. 2:8–9). This grace is copious, bountiful, and abundant. It is never lacking. It never wanes. It is freely provided in the new covenant, sealed forever in blood by the God who cannot lie (Num. 23:19; Titus 1:2).

God's glory is displayed in this great grace. What other response can we have than to praise him, and praise him, and praise him some more?

Ephesians 2:13–16

> But now in Christ Jesus you who once were far off have been brought near by the blood of Christ. For he himself is our peace, who has made us both one and has broken down in his flesh the dividing wall of hostility by abolishing the law of commandments and ordinances, that he might create in himself one new man in place of the two, so making peace, and might reconcile us both to God in one body through the cross, thereby killing the hostility. (Eph. 2:13–16)

The context of Ephesians 2:13–16 is clear in the preceding verse (v. 12), where we find a description of our previous state: "separated . . . alienated . . . and strangers . . . having no hope and without God in the world." But something has happened to change all that, something objective, something historical, something of infinite value—the sacrificial blood of Christ has been shed to cover our sin.

But none of the wonderful blessings described in Ephesians 2:13–16 will be ours apart from our union with Christ in the Great Exchange. Paul's repeated references to our union with Christ, "now in Christ Jesus . . . in his flesh . . . in himself . . . in one body," emphasize the one essential qualification required to participate in the reconciliation that Christ's blood has granted us through his atoning work. If we stand before a holy God as sinners clothed only in our own righteousness, we stand in the direct path of God's curse, and our end is eternal separation from him. But the great good news is that *in Christ* and by his blood, we have been brought near to God.

Paul writes this phrase, "brought near," in the past tense, indicating once again that it is a finished work. We do not have to wait. We do not have to climb a stairway to heaven. We do not have to fix ourselves up, not even a little. Christ crucified is all-sufficient for us right now, and so we are near right now. If we are "now in Christ Jesus," we are "brought near" God now.

Stop and think about the all-surpassing value of this nearness. Instead of being distant, cast out from our glorious God, we are intimate with the God of the universe, the Creator, the infinitely holy God, the only God. Instead of being alienated by our great sin, we are cherished as adopted children though his great grace. We are cared for and constantly protected. We have immediate access to his throne of mercy and grace at all times (Heb. 4:16). We should not take this lightly. What amazing mercy! What a glorious thought!

Furthermore, as we in Christ trust in Christ's great atonement, Christ "is our peace" (Eph. 2:14a); that is, he is the peace offering that removes the mutual hostility between us and God and also between us and other believers. He is more than simply a peacemaker. Christ actually embodies our peace, because he has made peace between us and our God by virtue of his body broken for us. His body and blood are the basis of the new covenant (1 Cor.

11:24–25), a covenant which is literally a peace treaty between God and the redeemed sinner.

Likewise, Christ himself is personally the uniting force behind the peace between all believers. He "has made us . . . one and has broken down in his flesh the dividing wall of hostility" (Eph. 2:14b). In our mutual union with Christ, believers of all races, ages, genders, economic and social backgrounds, languages, and nationalities find a level playing field for relating to one another through a common death and a common life emanating from the application of a common participation in the atonement. In Christ there is no more hostility between God and believer, and there is no longer any ground for hostility between believers. All are one in Christ and should be working together to glorify, honor, and serve their Reconciler, Redeemer, Lord, and Master.

Certainly problems exist within the body of Christ, and much ink could and should be spilled in discussing this problem. But we will leave the problems within the church for another writer and another text and remain centered on the atoning work of Christ. It cannot be denied that in Christ crucified, we have the all-sufficient basis for peace with God and peace with all those fellow believers who treasure Christ and participate in his saving grace.

For over one thousand years before Christ, the Jews were under the Mosaic law—a law they could never keep. Christ's atonement fulfilled the Jewish law, an institution that formed a hostile division not only between God and sinner but also between Jew and Gentile. The dividing wall that surrounded the Jewish temple symbolized the law; it shut out the Gentiles from access. They could not participate in the atoning animal sacrifices, nor could they take part in Jewish ceremonial rites. Therefore, they were considered unclean, despised, and rejected. These Gentiles were sinners no better than dogs.

But Christ's atonement changed all that. "The law of commandments [expressed in] ordinances" (Eph. 2:15a) was fulfilled on our behalf by Christ's righteousness and sacrifice. The law was abolished, not by being revoked but by being fulfilled. The cross put a permanent end to the ceremonies, and with it the dividing wall.

All those united to Christ in the atonement are united to each other. In Christ, the dividing lines that create impasses between Jew and Gentile, black and white, male and female, rich and poor, and all other manner of alienation—all these dividing lines are erased. All are justified by the same Christ crucified, all enter into a similar path of sanctification, and all are commanded to love one another the way he has loved them (John 13:34). There is no longer any valid basis for any hostility between believers, just as there is no longer any basis for any hostility between believers and God. The cross removed both. Christ did this in order that "he might create in himself one new man in place of the two" (Eph. 2:15b), something absolutely profound and unheard of in the world, a true testimony of his power to transform lives.

Jesus said, "By this all people will know that you are my disciples, if you have love for one another" (John 13:35). Later in Ephesians 2, Paul describes this phenomenon of peace as a glorious unity in which all believers are fellow citizens and co-members of God's household (v. 19).

Ephesians 5:2

> And walk in love, as Christ loved us and gave himself up for us, a fragrant offering and sacrifice to God. (Eph. 5:2)

Ephesians 4:32 provides the context for Ephesians 5:2: we are to "be kind to one another, tenderhearted, forgiving one another." God's compassion and forgiveness toward us is to be our example, as is the fact that "Christ loved us and gave himself up for us."

Amazing as this may be, Christ's love is actually focused on us, that is, on those who corporately comprise his church, his bride. It is more than a sentimental love; it is an action-based love, prompting him to give himself for his beloved. And his action was all-encompassing; he "*gave* himself up." In the giving up of himself as a sacrificial offering on our behalf, he held nothing back. And he did this, not while we were radiant and beautiful, but, rather, while we were polluted and adulterous (Rom. 5:8). He loved us so much that he would, by his very blood, make his church presentable "in splendor, without spot or wrinkle or any such thing, that she might be holy and without blemish" (Eph. 5:27).

Jesus is the priest of his own sacrifice. And he did it all "for us" as a wrath-bearing or propitiatory sacrifice, made "to God" on our behalf. His was a "fragrant" offering, the fulfillment of the atoning offering prescribed in the law in which the priest:

> shall lay his hand on the head of the burnt offering, and it shall be accepted for him to make *atonement* for him. Then he shall kill the bull before the LORD, and Aaron's sons the priests shall bring the blood and throw the blood against the sides of the altar that is at the entrance of the tent of meeting. Then he shall flay the burnt of-fering and cut it into pieces, and the sons of Aaron the priest shall put fire on the altar and arrange wood on the fire. And Aaron's sons the priests shall arrange the pieces, the head, and the fat, on the wood that is on the fire on the altar; but its entrails and its legs he shall wash with water. And the priest shall burn all of it on the altar, as a burnt offering, a food offering with a *pleasing aroma* to the LORD. (Lev. 1:4–9)

The fact that Christ's offering was "fragrant" (Eph. 5:2) to God reveals an important point about the atonement: not only did his sacrifice turn away God's wrath, but it actually *pleased* God. It gave God pleasure, and as a result he looks on us with a favorable disposition. God doesn't merely accept us on account of our repre-sentation in Christ; he welcomes us with gladness.

Thus, the death of Jesus not only satisfied divine justice, but it altered God's attitude toward those who previously had been objects of his just displeasure. It had an effect, which was foreshadowed by Noah's sacrifice upon leaving the ark:

> The LORD smelled the soothing aroma; and the LORD said to Himself, "I will never again curse the ground on account of man, for the intent of man's heart is evil from his youth; and I will never again destroy every living thing, as I have done." (Gen. 8:21 NASB)

Ephesians 5:25–27

> Husbands, love your wives, as Christ loved the church and gave himself up for her, that he might sanctify her, having cleansed her by the washing of water with the word, so that he might present the church to himself in splendor, without spot or wrinkle or any such thing, that she might be holy and without blemish. (Eph. 5:25–27)

While in the process of instructing the Ephesians on the subject of family and labor relations (Eph. 5:22–6:9), Paul takes an opportunity to provide several key insights about Christ's atonement. While Paul points to Christ as the supreme example for the conduct of husbands, he makes it clear that his purpose goes beyond marital instruction. Pointing to the union between man and wife, in verses 29–30 Paul tells us that Christ "nourishes and cherishes . . . the church, because we are members of his body":

> "Therefore a man shall leave his father and mother and hold fast to his wife, and the two shall become one flesh." This mystery is profound, and I am saying that it refers to Christ and the church. (Eph. 5:31–32)

Personified as his bride, the church is the recipient and focal point of Christ's great love. Christ's death is the action—the proof—of his love. There is nothing vague or sentimental about this love. It is sacrificial in the most genuine, authentic sense of the word. What dowry did the God-man give? Not animals or money or property or anything external. As fully God, Christ gave up all his rights as God (Phil. 2:6–8). As fully man, he gave up everything—body, soul, and spirit. The God-man's giving consisted of all of himself. He excluded nothing. He paid the most costly price imaginable on behalf of "the church of God, which he obtained with his own blood" (Acts 20:28).

And yet, Paul clearly attempts to describe Jesus' giving of himself as the perfect sacrifice. He does so in the past tense, saying "Christ . . . gave" (Eph. 5:25). It is a finished work of love, historically valid and never to be repeated. It is real love to a real people, a prized people, chosen from eternity by his own wisdom and mercy (see Romans 9), redeemed in time, and called to union with him.

Jesus Christ loved the church and gave himself for her. The result is that we are his bride. No greater dowry price can be imagined. Christ delivered himself into the hand of God where he permitted himself to be seized and bound, tried and mocked, sentenced and beaten at the hands of men whom God appointed to execute his purpose (Acts 2:23; 4:28). Christ willingly surrendered himself to death. Of his life he said, "No one takes it from me, but I lay it down of my own accord" (John 10:18). He did it because of his great love "for her" (Eph. 5:25) to enact the marriage covenant in which nothing can separate us from Christ's love; not:

> tribulation, or distress, or persecution, or famine, or nakedness, or danger, or sword . . . neither death nor life, nor angels nor rulers, nor things present nor things to come, nor powers, nor height nor depth, nor anything else in all creation. (Rom. 8:35, 38–39)

Christ loved the church prior to her cleansing, while she was yet despoiled, contaminated with sin. He did not die for her because she was perfect. He gave himself up for her to make her perfect. In love, Christ sanctified her—that is, he set her apart as consecrated for his own exclusive possession, to have and to hold. He cleansed her by his atoning death for her, "so that he might present the church to himself in splendor, without spot or wrinkle or any such thing" (Eph. 5:27).

Because of Christ's atoning work, the church on earth stands pure, declared righteous based on the imputed righteousness of Christ, and becomes pure, based on the process of progressive sanctification. The presenting of the bride as finally pure will be culminated at the great wedding feast, when the vision given to the apostle John is fulfilled:

> "Praise our God,
>   all you his servants,
> you who fear him,
>   small and great."

I heard what seemed to be the voice of a great multitude, like the roar of many waters and like the sound of mighty peals of thunder, crying out,

> Then I heard . . .

> "Hallelujah!
> For the Lord our God
>   the Almighty reigns.
> Let us rejoice and exult
>   and give him the glory,
> for the marriage of the Lamb has come,
>   and his Bride has made herself ready." (Rev. 19:5–7)

CHAPTER 12

Philippians

T he apostle Paul was a prisoner in Rome when he wrote his epistle to the Philippians. He had received financial support from the Philippians while he was in Thessalonica, and he wrote this letter upon receiving a second contribution while in Rome (Phil. 4:10, 15). The Philippians had expressed concern about Paul's condition, but Paul was much more concerned to get to the passion of his heart—the cross of Christ. So after a brief update, Paul focused their attention on the joy of the atonement and on preparation for the Lord's coming.

He also used the occasion to provide a robust warning about those who were subverting the message of the atonement, asserting that acceptance with God required adherence to certain Jewish rites and customs. In Philippians 3, after identifying these heretics within the church as "dogs" and "evil doers" (v. 2), Paul laments, "For many, of whom I have often told you and now tell you even with tears, walk as enemies of the cross of Christ" (v. 18).

He presents his personal history as a stark contrast to this error. Referring to his stellar religious qualifications (vv. 4–6), he states, "I count everything as loss . . . and . . . rubbish, in order that I may gain Christ and be found in him, not having a righteousness of my own that comes from the law, but that which comes through faith in Christ, the righteousness from God that depends on faith" (vv. 8–9). Thus, the imputed, transferred righteousness from God—not merit from complying with the law—was the basis for Paul's hope of gaining and knowing Christ "and the power of his resurrection" (v. 10).

Philippians 2:6–8

[Christ Jesus], though he was in the form of God, did not count equality with God a thing to be grasped, but made himself nothing, taking the form of a servant, being born in the likeness of men. And being found in human form, he humbled himself by becoming obedient to the point of death, even death on a cross. (Phil. 2:6–8)

In exhorting the Philippians to live harmoniously with one another and to extinguish self-importance out of regard for one another (Phil. 2:1–4), Paul offers the supreme example—the life, obedience, and death of the God-man, Jesus Christ, who, before the incarnation not only existed in the form of God but also as God's equal. He is equal in essence, equal in attributes, and equal in glory.

After his incarnation, Jesus remained conscious of his equality with God. For example, he succinctly declared to both disciples and unbelievers alike, "I and the Father are one" (John 10:30). On the night before he went to the cross, in an intimate setting he told his disciples, "Whoever has seen me has seen the Father . . ." (John 14:9). As he stood before the council prior to his crucifixion, he was asked if he was the Christ. He replied to the high priest, "I am," in response to which the high priest tore his robes and cried "blasphemy!" (see Mark 14:62–64). Jesus had declared himself to be God.

And yet, though he was fully God, the Last Adam did exactly the opposite of the first Adam. Instead of aspiring to be equal to God (Gen. 3:5), Christ let go of his equality with God. The debasing of Christ began when he released his grasp on this equality, along with its rights and privileges.

Although Jesus never personally ceased to be God, by becoming the God-man there was an immeasurable—no, rather an incomprehensible—lowering of autonomy and power and glory in departing the infinite to enter the finite. By becoming a man, the Son of God underwent a condescension that is beyond measure. He went from infinite riches to base poverty, from omnipotent power to weakness, and from omnipresence to the limits of single time and place dimensions.

It was not enough that he went from being equal to the preeminent Person in the universe to being born in the likeness of men with all the limitations of a human body. In addition, he took on the form of an insignificant person among his human peers, a mere servant. Born in an insignificant place, an animal feeding trough, and trained as a carpenter's apprentice, an insignificant job in an insignificant town, Nazareth, the One through whom the universe was created went on to wash the feet of unworthy, insignificant men. Equally remarkable, he took on this new form willingly. He "made himself nothing" (Phil. 2:7) and "he humbled himself by becoming obedient" (Phil. 2:8).

In a mind-boggling twist of grace, the One who will judge the world, the One who should be obeyed and is obeyed among the heavenly host, the One who is sovereign over all the earth—this same One—became obedient. Whom did Jesus obey? Ultimately, it was not the Romans or the Jews; it was God the Father. The fact that the Son "took the form of a servant" upon himself, indicates that he remained above it; he could have rejected servanthood and its obligations at any time. Nevertheless, he chose to obey the Father's sending of "his own Son in the likeness of sinful flesh and for sin" to condemn "sin in the flesh in order that the righteous requirement of the law might be fulfilled in us" (Rom. 8:3b–4). In other words, Christ was not obligated to obey. He obeyed on behalf of others, so that his righteousness could be credited to them.

As we have previously explained, both Christ's active and passive obedience extended from the moment of his incarnation to his death on the cross. This is why Paul describes Christ's obedience as being "to the point of death" (Phil. 2:8), meaning up through and including that final act.

What limit did he place on his willingness to obey? None. His mission necessitated an all-encompassing compliance. It required the ultimate personal sacrifice. He experienced firsthand both physical and spiritual death in the most ignominious of places—on a cross, the emblem of shame and of the curse.

Philippians 2:9–11

Paul displays the results of Christ's perfect obedience as the God-man who fulfilled all that was required of him as the representative of redeemed sinners:

> Therefore God has highly exalted him and bestowed on him the name that is above every name, so that at the name of Jesus every knee should bow, in heaven and on earth and under the earth, and every tongue confess that Jesus Christ is Lord, to the glory of God the Father. (Phil. 2:9–11)

We see incomparable and reciprocal glory in these words. First, God has glorified Christ, and, as the last clause of verse eleven proclaims, Christ has glorified the Father. Furthermore, we see that God's exaltation of Christ and his name occurred immediately upon the completion of his work of atonement, as indicated by the verbs in past tense: "God *has* highly *exalted* him and *bestowed* on him the name that is above every name." And in the future, every knee—*every* knee—will bow to his name; and every tongue (no exceptions) will confess his supremacy.

Oh, that we would recognize Christ's glory, the blazing center of which is seen in the grace his obedience provided on our behalf at the cross. Oh, that we would savor him now as our great treasure and magnify his name among believers and unbelievers alike. In this way, we also glorify both Christ and the Father who glorifies Christ.

CHAPTER 13

Colossians

The apostle Paul wrote his letter to the Colossians from prison at approximately the same time he wrote his epistle to the Ephesians, and it likewise focuses on the person and work of Christ. Colossians specifically addresses the various errors of the Gnostic doctrines that threatened to undermine the church at Colossae, and Paul did this by placing the Gnostic doctrines in the light of the atonement. One category of error related to asceticism, a severe treatment of the body designed to deny physical needs and appetites in order to facilitate spiritual enlightenment. Another category of false doctrine involved the worship of angels and a fascination with a mystical spirit world consisting of a hierarchy of beings that mediated between God and man. Paul begins to clarify the creator-creature relationship between Christ and angels by declaring that Christ "is the image of the invisible God" (Col. 1:15), and the one by whom:

> all things were created, in heaven and on earth, visible and invisible, whether thrones or dominions or rulers or authorities—all things were created through him and for him. (Col. 1:16)

With this great display of the preeminence of Christ as a backdrop, Paul goes on to describe the true basis of our reconciliation with God, not in terms of the ministry of angels or of bodily denial, but on the basis of the atonement.

Colossians 1:19–22

> In him all the fullness of God was pleased to dwell, and through him to reconcile to himself all things, whether on earth or in heaven, making peace by the blood of his cross. And you, who once were alienated and hostile in mind, doing evil deeds, he has now reconciled in his body of flesh by his death, in order to present you holy and blameless and above reproach before him. (Col. 1:19–22)

Prior to the first man's fall into sin, all creatures, terrestrial and celestial, experienced harmony with their Creator and with each other, despite the fact that they had differing constitutions and capacities and provided different types of service. Adam's sin dissolved this harmony, resulting in separation from both God and angelic beings because, unlike Adam, the unfallen angels remained loyal to God and continued to respect all his rights as sovereign of the universe. God's will was no longer done in earth as it was in heaven, and the harmony between men and angels under one Monarch ceased.

As Paul's letter to the Ephesians revealed the cross as the basis for uniting all kinds of men, here in Colossians Paul shows that by the atonement, all kinds of beings, both angels and men, are restored into one family under one head. This extended benefit of Christ's death is important, because otherwise sinful men and sinless angels would have been forever at odds with one another. Since Christ's death removed God's wrath toward the redeemed, it likewise removed the wrath of angels. Because God sees those cloaked in the righteousness of Christ as sinless, the holy angels likewise see us that way, too. Thus, the entire universe of spiritual beings in earth and heaven are forever reconciled.

As the infinite lowering of the preeminent One, the Creator and sustainer of the universe on behalf of sinners unfolded according to God's own plan; it put his glorious grace on display before the host of heaven. It was a plan that included angels, and they frequently appear throughout the Gospel and apostolic accounts. Angels were present at the birth of Christ, glorifying God. They were present after Christ's temptation in the wilderness, in Gethsemane, and at the empty tomb. They stood by at the ascension. As a result of the atonement, the angels rejoice "over one sinner who repents" (Luke 15:10). They are "ministering spirits sent out to serve for the sake of those who are to inherit salvation" (Heb. 1:14). But apart from the cross, angels would be our powerful enemies and not our friends.

Paul makes it clear that "all the fullness of God was pleased to dwell" in Christ. It was the purpose of the Father that the Son be fully God even while he was fully man in order to execute a full reconciliation between God and man. In keeping with the fact that "whatever the LORD pleases, he does, in heaven and on earth, in the seas and all deeps" (Ps. 135:6), it pleased the Father to send the Son; there was no reluctance on his part.

When we express our gratitude to God for sending the Son to accomplish the atonement, God's response is, in effect, "I was pleased to do it."

Our reconciliation is not without a real mediator or a real price; both were required in order to remove the estrangement, hostility, and wrath and replace it with lasting peace. Both are found in Christ crucified. No other person is offered, nor any other way. Our Reconciler is himself our peacemaker.

The concept that reconciliation is provided only through the death of Christ is of such paramount importance that Paul was prompted to repeat it in the next sentence: "He has now reconciled [you] in his body of flesh by his death" (Col. 1:22). Furthermore, this statement is in opposition to the Gnostics who claimed that Christ is a mere spirit, that he never had a real, historical dimension, a flesh-and-blood body.

Next, Paul reveals the purpose for which he has reconciled us. It is "in order to present [us] holy and blameless and above reproach before him" (v. 22). In other words, we are reconciled in order that we may be sanctified, transformed into Christlikeness—a lifelong process in which perfection is finally reached only upon our departure from our body of flesh.

Once a sinner is securely reconciled through Christ's death, the process of sanctification always emerges and develops in the believer's life, because this, too, is a purpose behind the infinite price Christ paid by his atonement for us—to present us "holy, blameless, and above reproach before him." As these words indicate, he died so that we would be consecrated, set apart for God, and eventually become as holy in personal experience as we are by our representation in him. If this process of sanctification fails to take place, it is likely the reconciliation has not taken place. In such a case, the solution lies not in pursuing self-improvement as a prerequisite for reconciliation but in looking directly to Christ crucified for reconciliation and transformation.

Colossians 2:13–15

> And you, who were dead in your trespasses and the uncircumcision of your flesh, God made alive together with him, having forgiven us all our trespasses, by canceling the record of debt that stood against us with its legal demands. This he set aside, nailing it to the cross. He disarmed the rulers and authorities and put them to open shame, by triumphing over them in him. (Col. 2:13–15)

Paul declares that sinners are dead. The dead are incapable of action. They cannot do anything on their own behalf. This is the spiritual state of all outside of Christ—they are dead in trespasses and sins (Eph. 2:1). This is also the state of all Christians prior to their union with Christ. Therefore, apart from Christ it is impossible for justification, regeneration, reconciliation, sanctification, or any other spiritual activity to take place as a result of any man-designed, man-originated, or man-initiated action. The spiritually dead can do nothing to gain God's favor or earn merit before a holy God. There is nothing they can do to save themselves.

It is God, the exclusive creator of all life, who makes alive. God the Father, Son, and Holy Spirit act in unison to quicken the dead. Once we are made alive, we can do things such as worship, fellowship, grow, and serve, but even then we are dependent on his enabling power. In order for us to be made alive, *all* our sins must be forgiven, not merely some of them. Not just the big ones. If fact, there is no such thing as a little sin—all sin is an infinite offense because God is infinitely holy. Any type or amount of sin earns a death sentence. This even includes sins we are unaware of committing—there will be no pleading ignorance in the court of God's justice. Not only that, but in order to make us alive, he must forgive us of sins we have not yet committed!

So all the sins of those God made alive—past and future, big and little, known and unknown—all of them are permanently and irreversibly forgiven. How can God do this? "By canceling the record of debt that stood against us with its legal demands" (Col. 2:14) as the result of our sin. This required God to provide a qualified substitute on which to transfer our debt and its legal demands and then execute justice on him instead of us. This was the only way God could set it aside, forgive all our sin, and make spiritually dead sinners alive.

So according to his own plan and timetable, God accomplished all this by "nailing it to the cross" (v. 14). What exactly was the "it" God nailed to the cross? A piece of paper? No! It was the body of Christ which had become sin for us (2 Cor. 5:21) and a curse for us (Gal. 3:13).

Furthermore, in Christ's death on the cross, God "disarmed the rulers and authorities." This does not refer to the Jewish or Roman authorities but to satanic powers. They were armed with the law and its demand for justice. They were armed with authority to accuse sinners. They knew Jesus was the Son of God, and they assumed the ultimate victory was theirs when Christ died a shameful death. Instead, "by triumphing over them" in Christ's death, God disarmed them and "put them to open shame" (v. 15). But how does Christ's atonement conquer Satan and his cohorts? And where is the evidence of this disarming? First, Colossians 2:13–15 does not refer to Christ's resurrection but to his death. Yes, Christ also conquered death. "We know that Christ being raised from the dead will never die again; death no longer has dominion over him" (Rom. 6:9). But it is Christ's death that destroys Satan.

The key to understanding how this works lies in understanding that sin is the basis of Satan's authority, power, and strength on earth. If there were no sin, Satan would have no kingdom here. The moment "the record of debt that stood against us with its legal demands" was canceled and "set aside, [by] nailing it to the cross" (Col. 2:14), all the sins of the redeemed were forgiven because they were paid for on the cross. At that same moment, Satan's dominion over God's people was undermined; it no longer had any basis because its basis had been removed. Jesus explained, as he pointed to his imminent death, "Now is the judgment of this world; now will the ruler of this world be cast out" (John 12:31). At the cross, Satan bruised Christ's heel, but Christ crushed the serpent's head (Gen. 3:15).

When and where were the defeated enemies of God publicly humiliated? It was before the holy angels present at Christ's death. They witnessed the triumph of the cross as Satan's empire received a blow from which there was no recovery. There God displayed his justice and his love to the irreparable ruin, dismay, and confusion of satanic powers.

CHAPTER 14

1 and 2 Thessalonians

Irst and 2 Thessalonians were among the first epistles written
by the apostle Paul. The Thessalonian church was known for
brotherly love and a robust focus on the Lord's return. But
because they supposed Christ's second coming to be close at hand,
some of them neglected to provide for the material needs of their
families; they basically stopped living life to wait for Christ's return.
Paul set out to correct this. But at the time of Paul's writing, the
Thessalonians had not strayed into legalism, Gnosticism, or any
other form of man-centered effort to gain God's acceptance. The
Thessalonian church was a young but solid gospel-believing church.
Accordingly, there are only a few passages for us to review in these
epistles that shed light on the atonement.

1 Thessalonians 1:9–10 and 5:9–10a

For they themselves report concerning us the kind of reception we
had among you, and how you turned to God from idols to serve the
living and true God, and to wait for his Son from heaven, whom he
raised from the dead, *Jesus who delivers us from the wrath to come.*
(1 Thess. 1:9–10)

For God has not destined us for wrath, but to obtain salvation through our Lord Jesus Christ, who died for us. (1 Thess. 5:9–10a)

Though separated by several chapters, we will look at these passages together because they both address the issue of God's wrath. Taken together, they show that believers are continuously delivered from the wrath of God—past, present, and future. In the past, God did not destine us for wrath. Jesus, right now, in the present, "delivers us." And in the future he will deliver us from the wrath to come. The gospel is the sole basis of our deliverance—the death of the Lord Jesus Christ for our sins, "whom [God] raised from the dead" as a guarantee that his wrath toward us was fully extinguished.

Although this may be an unpopular topic, if one is to place his thinking under the authority of the Scriptures, it cannot be denied that the wrath of God exists. Both Old and New Testament alike provide abundant teaching and examples on the subject of God's just, holy, and imminent wrath with hundreds of references throughout his Word.

The wrath of God is synonymous with God's anger toward sin and sinner. Because this anger emanates from God's holiness, it is always righteous and just (Rom. 2:5). And it will always be expressed in action—condemnation and punishment. When God said, "I swore in my wrath" (Ps. 95:11; Heb. 3:11; 4:3), it indicates that wrath is a fundamental aspect of God's nature, an unchangeable attribute having its root in the moral perfections of God's own essence.

Nevertheless, there is a good reason God is not indifferent to our sin; it is an affront to his authority. God is intimately aware of our every word, action, and thought. He searches and knows us perfectly (1 Chron. 28:9; Ps. 139:1). Furthermore, he is always cognizant of his Creator rights over every creature, those created in his own image to reflect his glory. Our sin is a falling "short of the glory" (Rom. 3:23b); thus it is an elevating of ourselves over and above him, an exalting of the creature above the Creator (Rom. 1:23–25). In most cases, it is a deliberate, willful thumbing of our noses at God and Christ crucified. God is a living, personal being. That being the case, he takes our sin as a personal offense. The fact that it angers him shows that his response is emotional; he has a fervor and vehemence against our sin.

God's wrath is as real as his love. Thus we hear, "Jacob I loved, but Esau I hated" (Rom. 9:13; see also Mal. 1:2–3). God doesn't just hate the sin; he hates the sinner, too. His anger is not a mere figure of speech; it is real, literal anger.

God's wrath cannot be construed as merely divine sorrow or grief resulting from our failure to return his love. God's attributes of perfect holiness and perfect love do not dilute or nullify each other; rather, they simultaneously co-exist in full scope and force. God is not angry because he loves; he is angry because he is holy, and his holiness demands full-strength execution of his perfect justice.

When seeking to comprehend and apply this truth, however, we must be careful not to make wrong judgments about God. For example, God's wrath is not an inappropriate display of power against those who don't know any better. The Bible is clear—we all know, and there is no excuse (Rom. 1:18–21).

In addition, God's wrath does not exist because we have failed to meet a need of his. God has no needs. He existed for all of eternity past in perfect harmony, absolute contentment, and infinite happiness in the Trinity. He did not create man because he was lacking anything.

> The God who made the world and everything in it, being Lord of heaven and earth, does not live in temples made by man, nor is he served by human hands, *as though he needed anything*, since he himself gives to all mankind life and breath and everything. (Acts 17:24–25)

Because God is God and therefore has absolute Creator authority over his creation, it is just and right for him to prepare vessels to show both the splendor of his wrath and the splendor of his mercy. This is his divine prerogative (Rom. 9:22–24). We who have come to believe should marvel at the grace and mercy he has shown us in giving us the eyes to see "the light of the gospel of the glory of Christ, who is the image of God" (2 Cor. 4:4b) and to partake in the salvation from his mighty wrath. We should also pray earnestly that God will save the lost by pouring out this same mercy on them through Christ's great atonement.

Both Old and New Testaments refer to the wrath of God existing in a cup. Isaiah refers to those "who have drunk from the hand of the LORD the cup of his wrath, who have drunk to the dregs the bowl, the cup of staggering" (Isa. 51:17). Jeremiah quotes God referring to "this cup of the wine of wrath" (Jer. 25:15). The apostle John also used the cup analogy:

> He also will drink the wine of God's wrath, poured full strength into the cup of his anger, and he will be tormented with fire and sulfur in the presence of the holy angels and in the presence of the Lamb. (Rev. 14:10)

What grace that we will never taste that horrific wine, and what mercy that we are vessels of God's mercy! In the garden of Gethsemane, Jesus Christ knew the meaning of the cup of God's wrath:

> There he withdrew from the disciples about a stone's throw, and knelt down and prayed, saying, "Father, if you are willing, remove this cup from me. Nevertheless, not my will, but yours, be done." And there appeared to him an angel from heaven, strengthening him. And being in an agony he prayed more earnestly; and his sweat became like great drops of blood falling down to the ground. (Luke 22:41–44)

We know the content of Christ's more earnest prayer from Matthew's Gospel, where "again, for the second time, he went away and prayed, 'My Father, if this cannot pass unless I drink it, your will be done'" (Matt. 26:42). It was the anticipation of wrath bearing that caused the son of God to sweat as if it were blood. At the cross, the willing Christ swallowed the full cup of God's wrath on our behalf. There he felt every bit of every aspect of God's anger toward Christ's embodiment of our sin. He drank it all down so that not a drop would be left for us.

1 Thessalonians 4:14; 5:10

For since we believe that Jesus died and rose again, even so, through Jesus, God will bring with him those who have fallen asleep. (1 Thess. 4:14)

[Our Lord Jesus Christ] died for us so that whether we are awake or asleep we might live with him. (1 Thess. 5:10)

Here again we see the application of the atonement to believers who have already died. Paul aims to bring comfort to Christians mourning the loss of fellow Christians by pointing to the death and resurrection of Christ.

Christ's historical, bodily resurrection heralds the inevitable final outcome for all those united to him—"through Jesus, God will bring with him those who have fallen asleep." Represented by Christ, they follow Christ, as Paul makes clear in his first epistle to the Corinthians:

But in fact Christ has been raised from the dead, the firstfruits of those who have fallen asleep. For as by a man came death, by a man has come also the resurrection of the dead. For as in Adam all die, so also in Christ shall all be made alive. But each in his own order: Christ the firstfruits, then at his coming those who belong to Christ. (1 Cor. 15:20–23)

In physical death, believers retain the union with Christ that they enjoy in physical life. Through Jesus, that is, by the death of Christ, a redeemed believer's death is not a penalty but a falling asleep. This is true no matter what circumstances or sufferings are endured in the process of the death of the physical body. It is not a punishment, because as we have shown, all the wrath of God toward our sin was exhausted by the atoning death of Christ. Death is not accompanied with the curse. Because our sin is thoroughly atoned for by the finished work of Christ, death is deprived of its sting (1 Cor. 15:56).

The expression "fallen asleep" (v. 20) refers to a state of the body, not the soul. When Jesus tells the believing thief on the cross,

"Truly, I say to you, today you will be with me in Paradise" (Luke 23:43), it is apparent that he was not referring to a condition of the thief's physical body. Furthermore, Paul refers to disembodied souls having an immediate presence with God; they are not in an unconscious "sleep state" (2 Cor. 5:6–8). From this we can conclude that upon physical death, the body sleeps until it is raised as a glorified, resurrected body. In the meantime, the soul waits joyfully in the full awareness of God's presence. In a great mystery, both the church collective and the souls of individual redeemed believers are always with Christ. Paul declares:

> Your life is hidden with Christ in God. When Christ who is your life appears, then you also will appear with him in glory. (Col. 3:3b–4)

Jesus died for us so that our lives would be forever connected to his in a union that will never be severed, not even for an instant, whether our soul resides in a physical body, a resurrected body, or no body at all. Paul adds, "If we live, we live to the Lord, and if we die, we die to the Lord. So then, whether we live or whether we die, we are the Lord's. For to this end Christ died and lived again, that he might be Lord both of the dead and of the living" (Rom. 14:8–9).

After explaining the connection between the great atonement of Jesus Christ and our life after death, Paul makes the logical conclusion, "Therefore encourage one another and build one another up, just as you are doing" (1 Thess. 5:11). Indeed, there is monumental comfort in these truths because it is guaranteed by the infinitely valuable blood of Jesus Christ, our unfailing representative in death and in life. Our hope is secure. We can live without fear. So instead of fretting over death as the world does, those in Christ look toward his second coming, the great day when he will "be glorified in his saints, and . . . be marveled at among all who have believed" (2 Thess. 1:10).

CHAPTER **15**

1 and 2 Timothy

While both of Paul's epistles to Timothy contain specific references to the atonement (see 2 Tim. 1:10; 2:11), we will focus on one passage in the first letter:

1 Timothy 2:5–6

> For there is one God, and there is one mediator between God and men, the man Christ Jesus, who gave himself as a ransom for all, which is the testimony given at the proper time. (1 Tim. 2:5–6)

Paul declares that there is only one God and one mediator—no one else in the entire universe is qualified to mediate between God and man, because no one but the God-man, Jesus Christ, could begin or finish the necessary work of paying the ransom required to redeem sinners. The Mediator's mission is one that exemplifies the very definition of grace: he came to pacify God's wrath toward sinners and replace it with God's blessing and favor. He stepped into an infinitely wide gap and removed the cause of the separation by paying an infinite price, an act that made moving mountains look like mere child's play. This great mediator had to be more than a man—he had to be God.

Since Christ is a divine person, why does Paul refer to him as "the man Christ Jesus"? It is because he is about to speak of Christ's

198

sufferings and death—something God cannot do, but man can. In addition, Paul was taking an opportunity to oppose the false Gnostic teaching that Christ did not have a human body but only a phantom body that resembled a man. The Gnostics believed the physical body is evil, and therefore Christ could not have had a real body. The apostle John also denounces those who denied that "Jesus Christ has come in the flesh" (1 John 4:2–3). The apostles were adamant about the fact of Christ's true humanity, since without it, there was no death, and if there was no death, there was no atonement, and if no atonement, no satisfaction of God's justice, no forgiveness, and no reconciliation. Jesus Christ was fully human.

Jesus described himself to the disciples as "the Son of Man" who "came not to be served but to serve, and to give his life as a ransom for many" (Matt. 20:28). Demonstrating immeasurable love for us sinners and absolute obedience to the Father, Christ voluntarily surrendered all of himself—his entire life—to provide the ransom price by which he redeemed us from our captivity to sin and the otherwise inevitable eternal results: separation from God, condemnation, and punishment.

Here in 1 Timothy we once again find the word *ransom*, the price required in the first century to free someone from slavery. It was a transaction in which something was given in exchange for something else. This is exactly what Paul describes here. Put these elements together—the captives, the Redeemer, the ransom, and the receiver—and we have all the elements of a real transaction. Christ's atoning work of redemption is neither metaphorical nor metaphysical; it is real, historical, and finished. Once the ransom has been accepted, God forever embraces us as precious property purchased at an authentic, valid, and infinite price—his Son.

As we mentioned elsewhere, some would argue that the receiver of the ransom is Satan and not God. Certainly all the sinners standing outside the Mediator's representative atonement are forever subject to the captivity of Satan, death, and hell. So why then is the price not paid to him? It is because Satan is not the creator or owner of fallen man; God is. While it is true that Satan holds all unregenerate sinners captive, his dominion is subordinate. He only prevails because the Almighty Sovereign ordains it. Satan is nothing but the jailor; the only power he holds over captives is by *God's* authority. He has no authority of his own.

In human law, a jailor or executioner merely carries out a sentence determined by the representative of the governing authority, a judge. In a similar manner, the satisfaction of divine justice is paid to the ultimate Sovereign, God himself. And from the beginning of time, his plan was to discharge the captives only upon receiving the ransom of his Son's obedience and death.

Paul reveals that "God our Savior . . . desires *all* people to be saved and to come to the knowledge of the truth" (1 Tim. 2:3–4). Since "God . . . does whatever he pleases" (Ps. 115:3 NASB), and since he will accomplish all he has purposed (Isa. 46:10), and since "all the inhabitants of the earth are accounted as nothing, and he does according to his will among the host of heaven and among the inhabitants of the earth; and none can stay his hand or say to him, 'What have you done?'" (Dan. 4:35), and since the Potter's will cannot be thwarted by mere clay (see Romans 9), it is certain that the "all" in 1 Timothy 2:3–4 is undoubtedly "all" the elect. They are the "all" for whom the ransom was actually operative and effective, resulting in the completed transaction in which they were purchased out of slavery to sin. Of this "all," the Redeemer proclaimed, "This is the will of him who sent me, that I should lose nothing of *all* that he has given me, but raise it up on the last day" (John 6:39).

Paul refers to "the testimony given at the proper time" (1 Tim. 2:6). We have a "ransom," and we have a "testimony," and the two are connected. The ransom—that is, the atonement—*is* the testimony. That's why Christ's finished work of atonement must always be the beginning, middle, and end of our preaching. Like Paul, the proclaiming of the vicarious sacrifice of Christ is the purpose of our calling and the scope of our ministry as the next verse makes clear when Paul solemnly swears:

> For *this* I was appointed a preacher and an apostle (I am telling the truth, I am not lying), a teacher of the Gentiles in faith and truth. (1 Tim. 2:7)

CHAPTER **16**

Titus

aul's letter to Titus is another Pastoral Epistle, this one replete
with instructions for organizing and guiding the church at
Crete. Paul lists the qualifications for selecting elders and for
maintaining both sound doctrine and Christian behavior. However, it
is not surprising that in the process of laying the foundation for the
church, Paul takes time to reflect on the atonement. In this chapter,
we will examine a single verse related to our subject.

Titus 2:13b–14

> . . . the appearing of the glory of our great God and Savior Jesus
> Christ, who gave himself for us to redeem us from all lawlessness
> and to purify for himself a people for his own possession who are
> zealous for good works. (Titus 2:13b–14)

The bountiful and beautiful sentence that contains these words
begins in verse 11, where Paul proclaims the fact that "the grace
of God has appeared," showing that all that follows is rooted in
God's blessings in Christ toward sinners who deserve his curse.
Paul moves from past tense to present tense, where he reminds us
of two life-changing results of this grace: salvation and sanctifica-

tion. He then focuses our attention on the future, where we are "waiting for our blessed hope, the appearing of the glory of . . . Jesus Christ" (v. 13).

Before finishing the sentence by providing an indication of the key motivating forces behind Christ's sacrifice, Paul establishes the identity of our blessed hope and redeemer. It is a single person, Jesus Christ, with a double title, God and Savior. From the context, we can discern this meaning two ways. First, it is Jesus who will appear (v. 13), and, second, it is Jesus who gave himself (v. 14). Furthermore, a study of the original language shows that a single article is ascribed to the words *God* and *Savior*, indicating that both are predicated on one Person. Thus, verse 13 could be accurately translated: "waiting for our blessed hope, the appearing of the glory of Jesus Christ, who is both our great God and our Savior."

This brings us to the two grand purposes Paul gives here behind Christ's sacrifice. We get a glimpse into the Savior's heart, a two-part answer to the question, Why did Christ give himself for us?

First, it is "to redeem us from all lawlessness" (v. 14). We cannot help but marvel at the extent of our redemption. We are redeemed from *all* lawlessness—every transgression of God's law. No categories of sin are excluded. Both original sin (imputed to us by Adam), and our personal sin are paid for in full.

The second grand purpose behind Christ's giving himself is to purify for himself a people for his own possession. The word *purify* is one of several words used by the apostles to describe the effect of sacrificial blood on those defiled by sin. The list of words also includes wash, cleanse, sanctify, purge, and sprinkle. When we are purified, it means that our sin contamination is removed from us because it is transferred to a substitute who pays our penalty with his own death. By virtue of Christ's death, signified by his blood, we no longer must be excluded from fellowship with a holy God; instead we are made perfectly clean.

Why are we so highly treasured? Because the value Christ places on his possession—the collective body of redeemed, purified sinners—is equal to the value of the price he paid on its behalf. And the value of his sacrifice is infinite.

When we view ourselves as we are—his possession, redeemed and purified by his own precious blood—we are overwhelmed with gratitude. We cannot help but desire to perform good works that glorify him and magnify his name and his grace. But as we proceed along this path, we must never lose sight of the fact that only his blood redeems and purifies. We do not merit his blessing or acceptance by him for our performance of good works. Even our very desire—our zeal—for good works is a blood-bought blessing, for without Christ's atonement we would have nothing but self-serving, self-indulgent desires.

Furthermore, all truly God-honoring good works are God-enabled. They are not accomplished by our own strength or wisdom. They are the outcome of a synergistic process in which we remain dependent on the Holy Spirit's power and direction. Within this dependency, we work hard, even to the point of exhaustion. Paul described his ministry as a process in which he would "toil, struggling with all [Christ's] energy that he powerfully works within [us]" (Col. 1:29).

Paul told Titus to take these statements and demonstrate boldness and tenacity in applying them to the local church. He said, "Declare these things; exhort and rebuke with all authority. Let no one disregard you" (v. 15). A few verses later, Paul provides an outline of justification that builds on our discussion of Titus 2:14. In this picture we see our depravity, his love in providing a Savior, and the exclusion of our ability to earn merit by good works. We see mercy and grace in his provision of purification, regeneration, and justification. And the last clause of the passage takes our breath away:

> For we ourselves were once foolish, disobedient, led astray, slaves to various passions and pleasures, passing our days in malice and envy, hated by others and hating one another. But when the goodness and loving kindness of God our Savior appeared, he saved us, not because of works done by us in righteousness, but according to

his own mercy, by the washing of regeneration and renewal of the Holy Spirit, whom he poured out on us richly through Jesus Christ our Savior, so that being justified by his grace we might become heirs according to the hope of eternal life. (Titus 3:3–7)

This "eternal life" is nothing less than the undiluted, unimaginable glory of knowing God and Jesus Christ (John 17:3). In that timeless eternity, there will never be a single moment of boredom or pain. There will be a new heaven and a new earth in which there is absolute righteousness instead of sin (2 Pet. 3:13). There, as consecrated sinners saved by grace, we will continuously marvel at and worship Jesus our Lord and Savior and treasure.

CHAPTER 17

Hebrews

The epistle to the Hebrews is replete with deep and wonderful insights into the meaning and application of Christ's great atonement—a topic which this letter covers in more depth and detail than any of the other sixty-five books of the Bible. Therefore, along with Romans and Galatians, Hebrews ranks among the most important books in our study.

Hebrews was written by an unnamed apostle in about AD 70 prior to the destruction of Jerusalem. It addresses issues common to first-century Hebrew Christians living with strong opposition from the prevailing religious environment, Judaism, and its emphasis on legalism and ritualism designed to set Jews apart as superior to others.

The author sets out to compare and contrast the priesthood, covenant, and blessings of Christianity and Judaism in such a way as to strengthen these vulnerable, first-century Hebrew converts against attacks and persecution from religious Jews. For example, a common Jewish objection to Christianity was the humiliating way in which its founder was put to death as a weak and ordinary criminal. The apostle sets his sights to demonstrate that this was not only intentional, but that it was the only way, the glorious way of grace. The substitute had to "taste death" on behalf of those who deserved to die for their sin, in order that he would bring "many sons to glory" (Heb. 2:9–10).

At this point a note of clarification is necessary. It must be acknowledged that the author of this letter is not identified in the text. The last three verses of the letter show that the author sent his greetings from Italy and expected to be traveling with Timothy for a visit with those to whom the letter was originally written (Heb. 13:23–24). There has been much speculation as to whether it was Paul, Barnabas, Apollos, Luke, or perhaps even another author. While we deliberately will not enter into this debate here, we must acknowledge that the letter, nevertheless, is written with the authority of an apostle and breathes the spirit of Paul as seen through its statements on the person, position, and ministry of Christ, as well as on the doctrine of the atonement. These have much in common with the style and substance of Paul's letters. So, we believe we can with confidence say that if the epistle to the Hebrews did not originate directly from Paul, it is likely to have emanated from a close associate of his.

Hebrews harkens back to the Levitical priesthood and the symbolic animal sacrifices we discussed in chapter 3. At the time of this epistle, the temple services were operational; in fact, the Hebrew believers who originally read this letter most likely attended temple services regularly. The author sets out to demonstrate the superiority of Christ as the ultimate fulfillment of both the priesthood and the sacrifices. He shows that Christ, our Great High Priest and Passover Lamb, is the spiritual, heavenly, and eternal fulfillment of the material, earthly, and temporal found in Judaism. The symbolic aspects remain both significant and relevant for believers of all times and epochs because they provide a context in which a deep appreciation of the meaning of Christ's priesthood and sacrificial death may be gained.

Christ's Ministry as High Priest

The first, and perhaps the paramount point, the author makes is that Christ is superior to all created things. After clearly demonstrating

Christ's superiority to all heavenly beings in chapter 1, the author establishes the fact that Christ is superior to all earthly beings, including the Jewish high priest. A definite parallel is established between Christ and the Jewish high priest, where Christ is shown to be the substance and where the priest is shown to be the shadow. Much insight into Christ's atonement may be gained by studying this comparison.

Christ is not compared to an ordinary priest, one who performed the daily temple services. He is compared to the high priest in terms of his calling, qualifications, and ministry—as the one who approached God on behalf of sinners once each year as he entered the Most Holy Place with sacrificial blood on the annual Day of Atonement.

The Atoned Sins

The high priest offered the blood "for himself and for the unintentional sins of the people" (Heb. 9:7b). This sacrifice atoned only for ceremonial and unintentional sins, restoring the people to a condition in which they regained the privilege of participating in the temple services. But the Levitical priestly service and sacrifice were inadequate for removing the guilt of moral sin. Bulls and goats had no moral value, so their death could not adequately substitute for morally guilty man. The passage continues, "According to this arrangement, gifts and sacrifices are offered that cannot perfect the conscience of the worshiper, but deal only with food and drink and various washings, regulations for the body imposed until the time of reformation" (Heb. 9:9–10). By contrast, the Great High Priest ushered in the time of reformation:

> He entered once for all into the holy places, not by means of the blood of goats and calves but by means of his own blood, thus securing an eternal redemption. For if the blood of goats and bulls, and the sprinkling of defiled persons with the ashes of a heifer, sanctify for the purification of the flesh, how much more will the blood of Christ, who through the eternal Spirit offered himself without blemish

to God, purify our conscience from dead works to serve the living God. (Heb. 9:12–14)

We read in Romans that in God's "divine forbearance he had passed over former sins" (Rom. 3:25). This indicates that it was not until the time of Christ's death that the moral sins of pre-crucifixion believers were actually atoned for. The author of Hebrews resonates with this truth when, in the next verse, he describes Jesus as "the mediator of a new covenant, so that those who are called may receive the promised eternal inheritance, since a death has occurred that redeems them from the transgressions committed under the first covenant" (Heb. 9:15).

So while today's believers look back in time to the cross and become united to Christ by faith in the historical gospel, those living under the old covenant looked forward to the same event in which Christ "has appeared once for all at the end of the ages to put away sin by the sacrifice of himself" (Heb. 9:26b).

As he moves into the tenth chapter, the apostle emphatically argues once again that the old covenant sacrifices cannot actually remove sin:

> For since the law has but a shadow of the good things to come instead of the true form of these realities, [so they] can never, by the same sacrifices that are continually offered every year, make perfect those who draw near. Otherwise, would they not have ceased to be offered, since the worshipers, having once been cleansed, would no longer have any consciousness of sin? But in these sacrifices there is a reminder of sin every year. (Heb. 10:1–3)

The author makes a dogmatic conclusion in the next verse, where he declares, "For it is impossible for the blood of bulls and goats to take away sins" (Heb. 10:4). A few verses later he continues, "And every priest stands daily at his service, offering repeatedly the same sacrifices, which can never take away sins. But when Christ had offered for all time a single sacrifice for sins, he sat down at the right hand of God" (Heb. 10:11–12). Only the Great High Priest, Jesus

Christ, could take away all the sin of his redeemed, and that only by his victorious death.

The Sinner's Access to God

Under the Levitical priesthood, two divisions were marked out within the tabernacle or temple sanctuary. The first, called the Holy Place, was the site of the daily priestly service. The second, called the Most Holy Place, was separated by a thick curtain and was entered only by the high priest, only once a year, and only with the blood of the sin sacrifice (Heb. 9:7). The entrance to the Most Holy Place was always shut, except for the brief window of time each year when the high priest entered with sacrificial blood as the representative of the people. There he sprinkled the blood on the mercy seat, the covering of the ark in which the Law of Moses was kept.

While the return of the high priest to the assembly indicated the atonement was accepted by God, the intact curtain assured that direct access to God's presence remained closed to the people. Why? Because the high priest and the animal blood were ineffective at taking away sin and transferring righteousness, and therefore the people could never come directly into the presence of their holy God.

By contrast, at the moment of his death on the cross, the Great High Priest, as the priest of his own perfect sacrifice, sprinkled the mercy seat with his own infinitely valuable blood. This resulted in an amazing effect—at that very instant "the curtain of the temple was torn in two, from top to bottom. And the earth shook, and the rocks were split" (Matt. 27:51). When the significance and weight of this one-time event are understood and applied, the believing sinner is no longer separated from a holy and perfect God who had wrath against his sin but instead gains forgiveness, imputed righteousness, and "confidence to enter the holy places by the blood of Jesus, by the new and living way that he opened for us through the curtain, that is, through his flesh" (Heb. 10:19–20).

Believers under the old covenant would have died instantly had they entered the holy places (e.g., Num. 4:19). But because of the blood of Jesus, and because we are represented by his priesthood, we not only remain alive in the presence of our holy God, we are able to draw near with full assurance. And draw near with confidence we should.

Christ: The Great High Priest

Throughout the letter to the Hebrews, Christ is shown to be absolutely superior to any human high priest. "Now the point in what we are saying is this: we have such a high priest, one who is seated at the right hand of the throne of the Majesty in heaven, a minister in the holy places, in the true tent that the Lord set up, not man" (Heb. 8:1–2). So Christ is more than just another high priest—he is *the* Great High Priest. Let us consider several ways Christ uniquely exceeds the qualifications of high priest and surpasses all the others.

Christ, the Son, is a high priest by his Father's divine appointment. "So also Christ did not exalt himself to be made a high priest but was appointed by him who said to him:

> 'You are my Son,
>   today I have begotten you;'
>
> as he says also in another place,
>
> 'You are a priest forever,
>   after the order of Melchizedek.'" (Heb. 5:5–6)

Jesus is not a self-proclaimed high priest. He did not exalt himself to the position, nor was he elected by man. Instead, his priesthood was a direct assignment by his own Father, the fountain of all authority and law. The dignity and integrity of Christ's priesthood is unique because he is also the Son, a position held by no one else. As the only begotten Son, Christ's qualifications infinitely exceed the qualifications of all other high priests.

Only Christ is the fulfillment of both the Levitical and Melchizedek priesthoods. It noteworthy that this same passage also reveals Christ's unique twofold calling, first to fulfill the priesthood foreshadowed by the Levitical high priests and then to assume the eternal and royal high priesthood of Melchizedek. Such a calling was given to no other. When Christ ascended to his eternal and royal throne after his resurrection, it was in connection with the fulfillment of his Melchizedek priesthood. There Jesus is made "the guarantor of a better covenant" (Heb. 7:22). It is from this permanent position of his priestly and royal throne that he mediates for those he redeemed through his fulfillment of the Levitical high priesthood:

> Although he was a son, he learned obedience through what he suffered. And being made perfect, he became the source of eternal salvation to all who obey him, being designated by God a high priest after the order of Melchizedek. (Heb. 5:8–10)

There on that celestial throne "he is able to save to the uttermost those who draw near to God through him, since he always lives to make intercession for them" (Heb. 7:25). This dual priesthood, requiring absolute personal and representative perfection, can be held only by the Son of God himself. On earth, Jesus was a high priest who fulfilled the foreshadows of the Levitical priesthood by becoming the high priest of his own sacrifice. In heaven, upon his throne, Jesus fulfills his royal high priesthood not to purchase our redemption but to apply it as our advocate and mediator.

Christ is uniquely able to sympathize with sinners. "Therefore he had to be made like his brothers in every respect, so that he might become a merciful and faithful high priest in the service of God, to make propitiation for the sins of the people. For because he himself has suffered when tempted, he is able to help those who are being tempted" (Heb. 2:17–18). Every other high priest was sympathetic to sinners for the simple reason that they themselves were "beset with weakness" and "obligated to offer sacrifice for his own sins just as he does for those of the people" (Heb. 5:1–3). Not so with Christ. Like all high priests, Christ personally experienced temptation, but unlike the others he never sinned, not even once. As the author proclaims, "For we do not have a high priest who is unable to sympathize with our weaknesses, but one who in every respect has been tempted as we are, yet without sin" (Heb. 4:15).

So, unlike his human counterparts, when Christ is merciful in performing his high priestly role on our behalf, it is certainly not because he needs any mercy. It is because in his unique aspect within the triune Godhead, he has personally and fully experienced satanic temptation, physical need, pain, and death. He was "made like his brothers in every respect," and so he is capable of being touched by our suffering.

We see an excellent example of this in his earthly ministry at the time of his friend Lazarus's death. Jesus "was deeply moved in his spirit and greatly troubled" (John 11:33). Although Jesus was fully aware that this death was not permanent, that he would shortly raise Lazarus from the dead to prove his authority over all death to the glory of God, "Jesus wept" (John 11:33–35). He grieved with them. He felt their very pain and anguish, and then he came to the aid of Lazarus and his two sisters by calling Lazarus from the tomb. He was not aloof to their grief even though the whole situation was under his sovereign plan. What an amazing reality—Creator of the universe and compassionate friend!

Jesus Christ, Son of God and Son of Man, went so far in becoming just like his brothers and sisters as to learn "obedience through what he suffered" (Heb. 5:8). This is a great and wonderful mystery, and a powerful comfort to those who rely on him in their struggles against sin and temptation.

Christ was appointed high Priest for all eternity by a unique oath of God. One needs only to study the biblical account of God's oath to Abraham to gain the insight necessary to feel the weight of this remarkable passage:

> For those who formerly became priests were made such without an oath, but [Jesus] was made a priest with an oath by the one who said to him:
>
> > "The Lord has sworn
> >   and will not change his mind,
> > 'You are a priest forever.'"

For the law appoints men in their weakness as high priests, but the word of the oath, which came later than the law, appoints a Son who has been made perfect forever. (Heb. 7:20b–21, 28)

The author of Hebrews teaches that "when God made a promise to Abraham . . . he had no one greater by whom to swear, [so] he swore by himself" (Heb. 6:13). The oath of God is given by the supreme Oath Giver, and he swears by the supreme object—himself—and God's oath is inalterable and interminable; it can never change or fail. God cannot lie (Heb. 6:18).

The author concludes, "We have this [oath] as a sure and steadfast anchor of the soul, a hope that enters into the inner place behind the curtain, where Jesus has gone as a forerunner on our behalf, having become a high priest forever after the order of Melchizedek" (Heb. 6:19–20). The oath of God makes all the difference. When God swears by himself that the priesthood of the Son is eternal, then it is. The oath is what "makes Jesus the guarantor of a better covenant" (Heb. 7:22). Furthermore, all other priesthoods eventually fail due to the death of the priest. But Jesus "holds his priesthood permanently, because he continues forever. Consequently, he is able to save to the uttermost those who draw near to God through him, since he always lives to make intercession for them" (Heb. 7:24–25).

Permanent. Continuous. Eternal. Yes, he is able to utterly save his redeemed. He is our all-sufficient Great High Priest, our representative not just for a time but forever.

Jesus is the High Priest of a unique and superior sacrifice. "He has appeared once for all at the end of the ages to put away sin by the sacrifice of himself" (Heb. 9:26b). Jewish sacrifice consisted of the blood of calves and goats. The high priest had to repeat the same sacrifice year after year on the annual Day of Atonement. But the Great High Priest perfectly atoned for the sin of those he represents by appearing a single time with a single, infinitely valuable sacrifice that has never-ending efficacy.

When the author teaches that Jesus "entered once for all into the holy places, not by means of the blood of goats and calves but by means of his own blood, thus securing an eternal redemption" (Heb. 9:12), we can conclude that not only is the high priest superior but that the blood is also superior. It is therefore no wonder the outcome is superior. "For it is impossible for the blood of bulls and goats to take away sins" (Heb. 10:4). But the blood of the Great High Priest, the Son, the One appointed by the oath of God, that blood, and that death alone, makes all things possible.

Purified, Sanctified, and Made Perfect

Before we consider the key passages in Hebrews on the subject of the atonement, we will briefly unpack the meaning of three special terms. These terms would have been readily understood by the Hebrew Christians to which the letter was originally directed, but the distinctions and depth of their meaning have been largely lost to contemporary Christianity.

Purified (Heb. 1:3; 9:14, 22–23; 10:2). This term, also translated "cleansed" or "purged," implied the prior existence of stain or defilement, which resulted in exclusion from fellowship with God and his people. So being purified meant the stain was removed and fellowship was restored. When the author tells us that the Son made "purification for sins" (Heb. 1:3), he shows that sin is the cause of the stain, and by the unilateral action of the Son the stain and the consequence of the stain are completely eliminated. In other words, Christ's purifying action makes believers pure and holy in God's eyes. Again we see how Christ purifies us:

> Indeed, under the law almost everything is purified with blood, and without the shedding of blood there is no forgiveness of sins. (Heb. 9:22)

He purifies us by blood. Objectively, in the eyes of God the shedding of Christ's blood was the action that satisfied divine justice and canceled human sin. But there is also a subjective side to this truth: our awareness of the guilt and the weight and the hopelessness caused by our sin is also purified by the same blood:

How much more will the blood of Christ, who through the eternal
Spirit offered himself without blemish to God, purify our conscience
from dead works to serve the living God. (Heb. 9:14)

Once we embrace the objective fact that Christ's righteousness,
priesthood, and sacrifice on our behalf is all-sufficient for removing
our sin and restoring our fellowship with our holy God, we gain a
clear conscience, knowing that the price we owed was actually and
completely and forever paid by our Substitute. Our works are no
longer "dead," because they are no longer motivated by the false
pretense that by them we are somehow able to merit God's blessing.
Instead, our gratitude for the truly awesome, finished, redeeming
work of the atonement becomes our motivation to worship and
serve. No longer do we sense a need to make up for our offenses.
In fact, such thinking becomes repulsive to us, because it demeans
the value of his merit, priesthood, and sacrifice. His blood sets us
free from guilt, and we are now free for gratitude-centered service
that truly seeks to praise and magnify his glorious grace.

A purged conscience, however, does not mean we forget the fact
that we are sinners saved by grace—we will always remember that
we deserve condemnation and hell. But with our consciences purified by all-sufficient blood, instead of a gnawing awareness of guilt
and shame we rejoice in God's grace toward us as we experience his
blessings in Christ toward those who deserve his curse.

Sanctified (see Heb. 2:11; 9:13; 10:10, 14, 29; 13:12). This term,
sometimes translated "consecrated," is related but not identical to
the word *purified*. Both words assume the prior existence of sin,
which disqualifies the sinner from relationship with a holy God.
However, whereas *purified* refers to the objective and subjective
cleansing away of the effects of sin and its stain, *sanctified* literally
means believers are set apart for holy and sacred use.

It is useful to draw the distinction between the theological terms
definitive, progressive, and *final* sanctification. In definitive sanctification, the blood of Christ makes believers holy in God's eyes and
sets them apart as God's own. This is a single, moment-in-time event
that occurs when they first believe; they become united to Christ as

their representative and are thus considered holy by God because they are cloaked in Christ's righteousness.

Definitive sanctification is monergistic, i.e., God acts independently of man to cause the sinner to see the glory of Christ in the gospel. This is the sense in which the term *sanctified* is used in the above references in Hebrews, for example, "We have been sanctified through the offering of the body of Jesus Christ once for all" (Heb. 10:10).

When the Bible uses the word *sanctification*, it is frequently referring to progressive sanctification, which is the gradual transformation of the believer in his or her day-to-day experience. Progressive sanctification is synergistic; the believer works in cooperation with God in dependence on his providing the enabling power to change. The process of progressive sanctification continues from the moment of definitive sanctification until the believer vacates his body of flesh.

Final sanctification (sometimes referred to as completed or perfect sanctification) refers to the ultimate destination of all true believers upon their removal from the body—a sinless state of eternal existence in which "we shall be like him, because we shall see him as he is" (1 John 3:2). It is a condition described by the author as "the spirits of the righteous made perfect" (Heb. 12:23).

In sum, progressive sanctification is the evidence in the life of believers that they were united to Christ in definitive sanctification and are on their way to final sanctification. Definitive, progressive, and final sanctification—all three emanate from the atonement; none of them is possible without the atonement. In other words, we are not free to become experientially holy or to exist as finally holy until we are first set apart and considered holy by being forgiven and cloaked by Christ's transferred righteousness by virtue of our union with him as our representative in the atonement.

Make perfect (see Heb. 7:11, 19; 9:9; 10:1, 14; 11:40; 12:23). The use of this term is distinctive of the epistle to the Hebrews in the same way the term *righteousness of God* is distinctive to the epistle to the Romans. While the term *righteousness of God* relates to the legal aspects of the atonement, *make perfect* relates to the priestly aspects of the atonement. The author of Hebrews frequently uses the phrase *make perfect* to expose the inadequacy of Levitical priesthood and sacrifices:

> For since the law has but a shadow of the good things to come instead of the true form of these realities, it can never, by the same sacrifices that are continually offered every year, make perfect those who draw near. (Heb. 10:1)

By contrast, Christ, "by a single offering . . . has perfected for all time those who are being sanctified" (Heb. 10:14). By the single offering of himself, Christ "has perfected" the ones he has set apart for himself. Notice the use of past tense here—*has perfected*—indicating that those united to Christ in the atonement are already considered perfectly holy in Christ. In other words, as believers draw near to their holy God, they are accepted by him based on the superior priesthood and sacrifice of Christ. While they remain experientially imperfect, they are positionally perfect because of their union with their representative, their Great High Priest, who himself was "made perfect through suffering" (Heb. 2:10).

To *make perfect* literally means "to complete a work," which is displayed by the immortal three words of our dying Savior, "It is finished" (John 19:30). Those who embrace a right understanding of the atonement will tend to declare these three words to be the most excellent three words in all of language.

Hebrews 2:9–10

> But we see him who for a little while was made lower than the angels, namely Jesus, crowned with glory and honor because of the suffering of death, so that by the grace of God he might taste death for everyone. For it was fitting that he, for whom and by whom all things exist, in bringing many sons to glory, should make the founder of their salvation perfect through suffering. (Heb. 2:9–10)

The author of Hebrews begins his letter proclaiming that Jesus, the Son, is "the heir of all things" and the one "through whom also

[God] created the world." He describes Jesus as "the radiance of the glory of God and the exact imprint of [God's] nature." Then he makes a mind-boggling statement about the Son: "He upholds the universe by the word of his power" (Heb. 1:2–3). He goes on to prove from prophecy and by understatement that Jesus is absolutely superior to angels. It is against this backdrop that the author teaches the meaning of grace and its inseparable connection with the atonement: "That by the grace of God he might taste death" (Heb. 2:9).

As he traces the beginning of the manifestation of this grace, the author shows that the Son had to undergo infinite debasement in order to be in a position to meet the need of undeserving sinners. Thus, "for a little while [Jesus] was made lower than the angels." Then God, the one "for whom and by whom all things exist" found it "fitting that he . . . should make the founder of [our] salvation perfect through suffering" (v. 10). It was then, after fulfilling all righteousness by living a sinless life in a fully human body subject to temptation, that in the greatest display of grace imaginable, he tasted death for us.

But why was it *fitting?* It was fitting because the grace that saves hell-deserving sinners does not come without a price. Justice must be served to a holy God; the payment cannot be simply overlooked. The offence of treasonous sinners requires justice—the death penalty. The penalty is appropriate, and it is appropriate for God to demand it because there is no other way to keep all his attributes intact. And even if the personally sinless Christ is to pay our penalty, it must be paid *in full* by him. If the penalty were cheapened, our salvation would be cheapened as well. And so, by the grace of God, it was necessary that Jesus fully taste death for us.

The word "taste" indicates he experienced death (v. 9). Furthermore, he experienced death in its undiluted bitterness. He encountered everything we would have experienced had we paid our own penalty. This included spiritual death—that is, his agonizing separation from the Father. The bearing of our sin must include this aspect, as Isaiah stated:

> But your iniquities have made a separation
>   between you and your God,
> and your sins have hidden his face from you
>   so that he does not hear. (Isa. 59:2)

God's grace—that is, God's blessings in Christ toward helpless sinners who deserve only his curse—is the only reason Christ tasted death for us. Nothing we could do could cause or compel God to love us enough to send his Son to die for us. We only contribute one element to the formula of grace—our sin. We do not and cannot make grace happen—not by what we do and not by what we don't do. All we can "do" is fall on our faces, bankrupt before him, and receive grace from his almighty, holy, and loving hand while we acknowledge that none of this would be happening were it not for the historical fact that Jesus, "because of the suffering of death" (Heb. 2:9), tasted the full bitterness of the death we deserved.

The word *for* as it is used here (v. 10) means "on behalf of," "instead of," or "in place of." In other words, it means Christ's death was vicarious—he died as the substitute for the sinners he redeemed by his atonement. We find the same in Paul's words in Romans: "While we were still weak, at the right time Christ died *for* the ungodly" (Rom. 5:6). Likewise the apostle Peter affirms it when he declares, "Christ also suffered once *for* sins, the righteous *for* the unrighteous" (1 Pet. 3:18a).

Placed into the context of the whole Bible, the word *for* becomes a most important operational word, the very fulcrum of the Great Exchange—his substitutionary death *for* us means that our sin is traded or exchanged for his righteousness.

The gospel is written in the language of transaction. My sin is charged to Christ, and his righteousness is credited to me. And it all happened because Christ was qualified to provide a God-appointed, twofold substitution: his death *for* my sin becomes my death for my sin, and his sinless life lived *for* me becomes my sinless life, my righteousness.

But as we've noted before, Christ didn't undergo this vicarious death *for everyone*—that is, for all human beings and creatures in all times and places. We read that God brought "many sons to glory" (Heb. 2:10), which points to "those who are sanctified"—the ones who share his origin, the ones he "is not ashamed to call . . . brothers" (Heb. 2:11). Some cite verse 9 as a proof for universal atonement, but the passage is actually a proof for a specific atonement. The death of Christ was valid *for everyone* represented by him rather than by Adam. And those are the ones who are united to him by faith.

Hebrews 2:14–15

> Since therefore the children share in flesh and blood, he himself likewise partook of the same things, that through death he might destroy the one who has the power of death, that is, the devil, and deliver all those who through fear of death were subject to lifelong slavery. (Heb. 2:14–15)

Jesus Christ partook of all the things that constitute our human nature—flesh, blood, heartbeat, feelings, hunger and thirst, the ability to experience pain and fatigue, and the temptation to sin. Christ's human nature, like ours, included both body and soul. So he experienced feelings including anger, fear, sadness, and grief. He partook of all this in order to become our true representative; he experienced everything possible in common with those he represented. Furthermore, as fully human he had the ability to die like a human. This was a key prerequisite in order to die for us, because as God, he could not die. But there was one essential difference between Christ's human nature and ours—Christ was not represented under Adam, so he was not born with a sin nature that compelled him to sin. Christ could have sinned, but unlike Adam, he did not.

It may appear ironic that the weapon Jesus chose to secure victory over the devil's power of death was his own death. But from this passage we derive the reason behind this irony: Christ's death would be substitutionary for his redeemed. For how could his death "destroy the one who has the power of death, that is, the devil" if his death were simply his own?

It is worthy of note that the victory we've discussed here is ascribed to Christ's death, not Christ's resurrection. Now we know that "the sting of death is sin" (1 Cor. 15:56a), specifically referring to unforgiven sin, which is where the enemy's power of death lies. So since Christ's death constituted the atonement, which resulted in the forgiveness of the sin of his redeemed, it is his death, not his resurrection, that caused Satan's defeat. It bears repeating: Christ's resurrection was his victory over his own death, but his actual death was his victory over ours.

How did Satan gain the power of death in the first place (Heb. 2:14)? This domain of Satan does not exist because he has self-existent powers to judge, condemn, or punish people, but rather because God himself chose to assign unforgiven sinners to a captivity over which Satan is merely the jailor or executioner. Satan always was, and still is, a subordinate creature, and he has his power of death because it was granted to him by God for the purpose of executing divine justice.

In other words, Satan's power of death is applied when, by the will of God, he is granted possession of unforgiven, condemned sinners to execute their eternal ruin. So Satan's power of death extends to all who live apart from representative union with Christ's death, and, thus, who die in their own sin. At the time of unforgiven sinners' physical death, Satan acquires them as his possession while they await final judgment.

What does Christ's destruction of Satan look like? Ultimately, the Bible tells us he will be "thrown into the lake of fire and sulfur . . . tormented day and night forever and ever" (Rev. 20:10). By this we can see that Satan will never cease to exist. So his annihilation cannot be the meaning of "he might destroy the one who has the power of death" (Heb. 2:14). Instead, it means that Satan's power of death has been annulled for those that are united to Christ in his representative death. In other words, Satan's authority to condemn and punish forgiven sinners has been made void, because for them, God has already judged, condemned, and punished all their sin in Christ. Jesus referred to this truth when he said:

Now is the judgment of this world; now will the ruler of this world
be cast out. And I, when I am lifted up from the earth, will draw all
people to myself. (John 12:31–32)

Note the connection between Christ's being "lifted up from the
earth," a clear reference to the atonement, and the casting out of "the
ruler of this world," Satan. Paul makes the same connection in his
letter to the Colossians when he indicates that God had "forgiven us
all our trespasses, by canceling the record of debt that stood against
us with its legal demands. This he set aside, nailing it to the cross."
Thus he "*disarmed* the rulers and authorities and put them to open
shame, by triumphing over them in [Christ]" (Col. 2:13b–15).

All three of these passages show that it is by the death of Christ
that Satan was disarmed. Satan's weapon, the executing of eternal
death upon sinners, was removed for all those who gained forgiveness in Christ.

In addition to being delivered from the fact of eternal death, the
believer is also delivered from the fear of death. The fear of death
is connected to the sinner's guilty conscience—the sense that God's
wrath and punishment are deserved. But the infinitely valuable and
all-sufficient blood of Christ removes believers' sin and causes them
to be clothed in his perfect righteousness, thus cleansing their consciences (Heb. 9:14; 10:22). Because believers' confidence lies not
in their own righteousness, but in Christ's perfect righteousness, the
penalty of eternal death need no longer be feared. Instead, liberation
replaces fear to such an extent that physical death can actually be
welcomed, because it is connected with eternal life with Christ. As
Paul concludes, "For to me to live is Christ, and to die is gain. . . .
I am hard pressed between the two. My desire is to depart and be
with Christ, for that is far better" (Phil. 1:21, 23).

In addition, awareness of the union believers have with Christ
in his great atonement results in their deliverance from the fear of
the often painful process of death. Strengthened by the hope of
eternal life, believers are enabled to endure end-of-life suffering.
Likewise, their believing loved ones are enabled to treat the funeral
as a celebration of the victory earned by Christ's death. Faith like

this brings much glory to God, as the entire eleventh chapter of Hebrews testifies through example after example of those who died in faith (Heb. 11:13–16).

Those outside of Christ may observe our fearless behavior in our suffering and death and call us brave. But all our courage can be traced directly back to Christ, who took on flesh and blood and died as our atoning sacrifice. Through his substitutionary death for us, he delivered "all those who through fear of death were subject to lifelong slavery."

Hebrews 2:17

> Therefore he had to be made like his brothers in every respect, so that he might become a merciful and faithful high priest in the service of God, to make propitiation for the sins of the people. (Heb. 2:17)

Whereas the previous passage connected the human nature of Christ with his defeat of Satan by his death, Hebrews 2:17 connects Christ's human nature with his priesthood. This is the first mention of Christ as priest in the book of Hebrews, so it is no wonder that the author starts by pointing out that Christ was "made like his brothers in every respect," excepting, of course, in our sin nature. As the author clarifies later, "For we do not have a high priest who is unable to sympathize with our weaknesses, but one who in every respect has been tempted as we are, *yet without sin*" (Heb. 4:15). So it is by taking on all the other elements of our human nature that our sinless high priest becomes sympathetic and merciful. He personally experienced our weaknesses. He is connected, not detached, because he, like us, was made fully human. That, plus the fact that he did not sin, uniquely qualifies him to be our Great High Priest. And we can trust him to be faithful to us because he knows how it feels to be human. He understands.

Someone may wonder, does he *really* understand? Consider that he was born into poverty and lived among poverty. For at least a part of his life on earth, he was literally homeless (Matt. 8:20). Jesus was subjected to intense temptation to sin, and it is unlikely any human was ever tempted more than he (Matt. 4:1–11). His family turned on him; his friends deserted him. Jesus was subjected to injustice—to unfair ridicule, mocking, and scorn. He was falsely accused. Jesus was brutally and unmercifully tortured. Jesus experienced real physical death. And all of this fostered in him a sense of sympathy for our plight, and undoubtedly spurred him on to complete his mission as priest of his own sacrifice.

Furthermore, the sympathy, mercy, and faithfulness he acquired by this process are etched into history, never to change throughout all of eternity—how could he ever forget his experience as a human?

Our confidence in his ability to compassionately help us soars as we read the next verse: "For because he himself has suffered when tempted, he is able to help those who are being tempted" (Heb. 2:18). Christ is able both to understand and to help.

Jesus partook of our human nature in order to become our "merciful and faithful high priest" (v. 17), and next we are told why he became "a merciful and faithful high priest"—so that "in the service of God" on our behalf as high priest, he could "make propitiation for the sins of the people." The validity of his propitiation for us, like his priesthood, is everlasting. We will never face *any* of the wrath of God that we as sinners so fully and rightfully deserve, because Christ faced it for us and exhausted all of it on our behalf. Here is a staggering and true statement: God will always be friendly toward sinners who are truly united to Christ as their representative wrath bearer, no matter what they do or don't do.

Hebrews 5:7–9

> In the days of his flesh, Jesus offered up prayers and supplications, with loud cries and tears, to him who was able to save him from death, and he was heard because of his reverence. Although he was a son, he learned obedience through what he suffered. And being made perfect, he became the source of eternal salvation to all who obey him. (Heb. 5:7–9)

Hebrews 5:7 is a clear reference to the appeal Christ made in the garden of Gethsemane on the night before he went to the cross "to

[God the Father] who was able to save him from death." It was there, "being in an agony he prayed more earnestly; and his sweat became like great drops of blood falling down to the ground" (Luke 22:44). What was so agonizing? Why the "loud cries and tears?" Was it merely because Jesus was afraid of physical suffering? Absolutely not. We see the answer in the following gospel account:

> And he took with him Peter and James and John, and began to be greatly distressed and troubled. And he said to them, "My soul is very sorrowful, even to death. Remain here and watch." And going a little farther, he fell on the ground and prayed that, if it were possible, the hour might pass from him. And he said, "Abba, Father, all things are possible for you. Remove *this cup* from me. Yet not what I will, but what you will." (Mark 14:33–36)

It was the cup. Jesus was "greatly distressed and troubled" for a very good reason—he knew what was in the cup. The drink in it represented the undiluted force of the wrath of God against sin—not the sin of just one man, but every sin of every sinner ever to be redeemed.

The author reveals that Christ "was heard because of his reverence" (Heb. 5:7). This may seem to be a contradiction. How were Christ's appeals in the garden "to him who was able to save him from death" heard? After all, he wasn't saved from God's wrath; he was immediately and summarily subjected to the process of excruciating physical and spiritual death.

The answer lies in looking at Christ's exact words in the garden where "[he] prayed that, if it were possible, the hour might pass from him" (Mark 14:35b). Whatever Jesus absolutely and unconditionally asked was absolutely and unconditionally granted. But whatever he conditionally asked was answered in the way most expedient to the Father's plan and purpose. We hear Jesus saying, "Yet not what I will, but what you will" (Mark 14:36b).

In this attitude of perfect reverence for and submission to the will of the Father—a will Jesus voluntarily entered into with full agreement "before the foundation of the world" (Eph. 1:3–10)—Jesus was heard. God answered him immediately, as Luke's Gospel records:

"And there appeared to him an angel from heaven, strengthening him" (Luke 22:43).

The statement "he learned obedience through what he suffered" (Heb. 5:8) may seem alarming and perhaps confusing. How can the sinless Son of God, the one through whom the entire universe was made, "learn obedience"? As co-lawmaker with God, Christ is infinitely and eternally above the law. How, then, can he learn to obey? He learned this obedience through what he suffered. This means that his obedience gradually *grew* in its scope, intensity, and vigor, as more and more pressure was put upon it. The more intense the crucible of conflict became, the more obedience unfolded in Christ's experience. Hence the progression: Gethsemane, the cross, and "My God, my God, why have you forsaken me?" (Mark 15:34). As Paul affirmed of Christ, "Being found in human form, he humbled himself by becoming obedient to the point of death, even death on a cross" (Phil. 2:7–8).

Surely Christ could have appealed unconditionally to his Father, and he would have "at once [sent Christ] more than twelve legions of angels" (Matt. 26:53). But since this was not the Father's will, Christ obediently drank the cup instead, and he drank it perfectly and completely to its final, bitter dregs.

The process of Christ perfectly fulfilling all the requirements of the law on behalf of every redeemed sinner ended in the final establishment of confirmed perfection. All of this was for us, since Christ was already perfect before he partook of flesh and blood. He did not do this for himself. He did it for us as our substitute, our representative. He was "made perfect" so that in him we would be made perfect, too. "For by a single offering he has perfected for all time those who are being sanctified" (Heb. 10:14).

Note that "made perfect" is past tense. For those he represents, Christ's final, perfect performance becomes their final, perfect performance. The unholy are made holy—in him. The impure are made pure—in him. Redeemed sinners enlightened to this truth are glad beyond description that because Christ was made perfect, so are they.

In this passage, the author partially repeats what he has previously stated, saying, "For it was fitting that [God], . . . in bringing many sons to glory, should make the founder of their salvation perfect through suffering" (Heb. 2:10). There is, however, an important, though subtle difference. This passage refers to Christ becoming "the founder," or leader, of our salvation, whereas Hebrews 5:9 states that Christ became "the source" or the cause of it. Because he was made perfect through suffering, Christ is both the captain and the author of our salvation. To him be all the glory forever!

When the author qualifies the saved as "all who obey him" (Heb. 5:9), he is referring to the obedience of faith, that is, the very act of believing. The New Testament writers used this language frequently, as we can see where Luke records, "The word of God continued to increase, and the number of the disciples multiplied greatly in Jerusalem, and a great many of the priests became *obedient to the faith*" (Acts 6:7). John's gospel also equates believing and obeying: "Whoever believes in the Son has eternal life; whoever does not obey the Son shall not see life, but the wrath of God remains on him" (John 3:36).

However, as we have already shown, genuine obedience of faith is always evidenced by progress in the obedience of life. So it seems appropriate to end this section with the benediction Paul used as he closed his letter to the Romans:

> Now to him who is able to strengthen you according to my gospel and the preaching of Jesus Christ, according to the revelation of the mystery that was kept secret for long ages but has now been disclosed and through the prophetic writings has been made known to all nations, according to the command of the eternal God, to bring about the *obedience of faith*—to the only wise God be glory forevermore through Jesus Christ! Amen. (Rom. 16:25–27)

Those who respond to the gospel with God-enabled "obedience of faith" are also strengthened to live by that same gospel and that same God. To him be all "glory forevermore through Jesus Christ! Amen."

Hebrews 9:12–15

> [Christ] entered once for all into the holy places, not by means of
> the blood of goats and calves but by means of his own blood, thus
> securing an eternal redemption. For if the blood of goats and bulls,
> and the sprinkling of defiled persons with the ashes of a heifer, sanc-
> tify for the purification of the flesh, how much more will the blood
> of Christ, who through the eternal Spirit offered himself without
> blemish to God, purify our conscience from dead works to serve the
> living God. Therefore he is the mediator of a new covenant, so that
> those who are called may receive the promised eternal inheritance,
> since a death has occurred that redeems them from the transgressions
> committed under the first covenant. (Heb. 9:12–15)

Christ's priestly service consists of two parts: the earthly and the
heavenly. Upon his ascension, Christ assumed his heavenly, eternal,
royal priesthood, the fulfillment of all that was foreshadowed by
Melchizedek. It is from that throne that he intercedes for those he
redeemed, where "he is able to save to the uttermost those who draw
near to God through him, since he always lives to make intercession
for them" (Heb. 7:25). At the time this letter was written unbeliev-
ing Jews complained that Christianity did not have a standing high
priest to represent them. So, in refuting this the author of Hebrews
shows that we who believe have an infinitely better one—a seated
one—one who "after making purification for sins . . . sat down at
the right hand of the Majesty on high" (Heb. 1:3b). This is a grand
and encouraging truth, but this is not the priesthood the author
refers to in this passage.

Instead, this passage displays glorious truths related to Christ's
fulfillment of his earthly priesthood, the one foreshadowed by the
Levitical priesthood, where as the priest of his own sacrifice, he
"entered once for all into the holy places, not by means of the blood
of goats and calves but by means of his own blood" (Heb. 9:12).

Where did his priestly offering actually take place? In the immediate context, the previous verse tells us that the holy places Christ
entered were in "the greater and more perfect tent (not made with
hands, that is, not of this creation)." The tent "made with hands"
is an historical reference to the physical tabernacle, the center of

Jewish worship and the place where atoning sacrifices were made. Jews were quite familiar with the intricacies of this structure because the Scriptures are filled with details about it (e.g., Ex. 25:8–27:21). Accordingly, the first ten verses of Hebrews 9 describe this earthly tent and the priestly work that went on inside it. So the place where Christ acted on our behalf was the heavenly correlate of the earthly holy places.

> Thus it was necessary for the copies of the heavenly things to be purified with these rites, but the heavenly things themselves with better sacrifices than these. For Christ has entered, not into holy places made with hands, which are copies of the true things, but into heaven itself, now to appear in the presence of God on our behalf. (Heb. 9:23–24)

The "holy places" where Christ presented his offering were in heaven itself, in the very presence of God. When did this happen? Was it after he ascended? No. It was upon the moment of his death. The entrance of Christ "once for all into the holy places" is analogous to the earthly high priest carrying animal blood into the Most Holy Place on the annual Jewish Day of Atonement. As we've noted, in that process a substitutionary death took place at the altar and immediately following the death, the blood of the sacrifice was carried into the Most Holy Place and presented by sprinkling it on the mercy seat. In this symbolic foreshadow, these events happened sequentially. This would indicate that upon Christ's death, at the moment his body and soul were separated, he entered the heavenly sanctuary with his own blood (coinciding in real time with the rending of the earthly curtain in the temple [see Matt. 27:51]) to appear before his Father and our Judge to make atonement. Disembodied, yet still our Great High Priest, Christ sprinkled the heavenly mercy seat with his blood, the blood of the new covenant (Luke 22:20). Christ's resurrection on the third day, then, is the parallel of the return of the Jewish high priest from the earthly Most Holy Place; it was proof that the blood sacrifice had been accepted.

The expressions "he entered" (v. 12) and "Christ has entered" (v. 24) indicate a past event, not an ongoing process, as in Christ's royal Melchizedek priesthood where his priestly service consists of perpetual intercession for the redeemed. Furthermore, the expression "once for all" denotes that this entrance was a single historic event; it happened only once, and it is final and complete. It is finished.

Yes, there was a second entrance into heaven—a glorious and triumphal entrance indeed—when upon the ascension Christ sat down on his royal throne. There God said of the Son, in glorious and perfect fulfillment of the messianic prophecies recorded in Psalm 45:6–7 and Psalm 102:25–27:

> Your throne, O God, is forever and ever.
>   The scepter of your kingdom is a scepter of uprightness;
> you have loved righteousness and hated wickedness.
> Therefore God, your God, has anointed you
>   with the oil of gladness beyond your companions.

And,

> You, Lord, laid the foundation of the earth in the beginning,
>   and the heavens are the work of your hands;
> they will perish, but you remain;
>   they will all wear out like a garment,
> like a robe you will roll them up,
>   like a garment they will be changed.
> But you are the same,
>   and your years will have no end. (Heb. 1:10–12)

As if this weren't enough, God adds one more glorious statement, (this time showing fulfillment of Ps. 110:1): "Sit at my right hand until I make your enemies a footstool for your feet" (Heb. 1:13b). Should this not make us tremble with anticipation?

Why all this attention to detail and exactness about where and when the atonement took place? First, because thinking that the atonement took place after the ascension takes our eyes off the cross where they belong. We are not pardoned in some mystical way by Christ's resurrection or intercession; we are pardoned by his substitutionary death on the cross. And, second, because holding an accurate biblical view of the atonement is needed in order for us to experience maximum joy and to give God maximum glory by correctly seeing and savoring and proclaiming Christ in his great atonement as the greatest treasure of all time. To fall short of this is to limit our joy and diminish his glory.

The author sets up a contrast between "the blood of goats and bulls . . . with the ashes of a heifer" and "the blood of Christ" (Heb. 9:13–14). The former resulted in the outward and temporary purification "of the flesh." The later resulted in a spiritual and eternal purification of the guilt of "our conscience" (v. 14). Here the author refers to the old covenant provision for the sacrifice of a red heifer to remove the defilement caused by touching a corpse, a human bone, or a grave (Num. 19:1–18). Offenders participated in this sin offering through the service of a priest. The result was they were sanctified, that is, set apart as cleansed for the purpose of ceremonial worship. In other words, they gained renewed access to the sanctuary and to fellowship with God's people. In addition, they regained entitlement to privileges as citizens of Israel. And since they were no longer defiled, they escaped the death they deserved from a holy God for violating his ceremonial laws—laws designed to "sanctify," that is, to set Israel apart from other nations. God is so holy that offenders were subject to these penalties, even if the touching occurred unintentionally (Lev. 5:17–19). This is just one example of how the Jewish sacrificial system worked. Many other types of sacrifices were prescribed for other specific types of defilements (see Lev. 12–15). But the same principles applied to all—substitutionary death evidenced by sacrificial blood.

Since these sacrifices were completely unable to gain God's forgiveness or cleanse the conscience of guilt for moral sins, they fell far short of restoring personal relationship with God, for those with guilty consciences can never look into the eyes of a holy God. According to the old covenant arrangement between God and sinners, "gifts and sacrifices are offered that cannot perfect the conscience of the worshiper, but deal only with food and drink and various washings, regulations for the body imposed until the time of reformation" (Heb. 9:9–10). So the Jewish system of atonement operated in the earthly, physical sphere, and thus its range of effectiveness was restricted, and the longevity of its impact was limited.

But there are three important lessons to learn from these foreshadows of Christ's atonement. First, in providing the animal sacrifices, God was expressing grace, since the people did not deserve to be sanctified. Next, the sacrifices worked on the basis of vicarious substitution—the price was paid by the death of one for another. And third, the payment was made to satisfy God's due justice, which was pending because of sin.

While "it is impossible for the blood of bulls and goats to take away sins" (Heb. 10:4), the blood of Christ is an entirely different matter. "If the sprinkling of defiled persons with the blood of goats and bulls and with the ashes of a heifer sanctifies for the purification of the flesh . . . how much more will the blood of Christ . . . purify our conscience?" (9:13–14). The sacrificial "blood of Christ" shed on our behalf offers "much more" because it alone is able to purify our conscience; that is, it removes our subjective sense of guilt, that miserable internal sense of foreboding that tells us we rightly deserve God's condemnation and punishment as moral sinners.

Christ's perfect sacrifice is so all-sufficient for us that his blood can actually remove all "consciousness of sin" (Heb. 10:2). How can this be? Because as we see and savor our morally sinless Christ's finished work on the cross as our substitute, we are gripped by an overwhelming sense that he actually paid all that we deserved to pay. And his historical, bodily resurrection proves that God agrees.

So now, in spite of the fact that "no creature is hidden from his sight, but all are naked and exposed to the eyes of him to whom we must give account" (Heb. 4:13), we trust that the infinite value of Christ's blood makes us acceptable to God. Furthermore, "we have a great high priest who has passed through the heavens" (4:14) to intercede for us forever from the throne of his royal priesthood. Therefore:

> [We] hold fast our confession. For we do not have a high priest who
> is unable to sympathize with our weaknesses, but one who in every

respect has been tempted as we are, yet without sin. Let us then with confidence draw near to the throne of grace, that we may receive mercy and find grace to help in time of need. (Heb. 4:14b–16)

The weight of our guilty conscience is replaced with bold confidence, not in ourselves but in his blood; not in our own flawed righteousness, but in his all-sufficient transferred perfect righteousness; not in our frail and feeble works, but in his all-sufficient finished work resulting in readily available mercy and grace for us forever.

The author reveals that it was through the eternal Spirit that Christ's offering was made. The Holy Spirit filled Christ's humanity with compassion, zeal, and strength to accomplish his mission, impelling him forward until his atoning work was completed. Thus, Christ was uniquely enabled and empowered to make his infinitely valuable offering. The Holy Spirit provided such to no other.

Christ's offering was made to "purify our conscience from dead works" (9:14)—all that emanates from our alienation from the life of God. There are two categories of dead works. The first consists of the sins that defile our consciences. The second consists of works of the law performed with the aim of securing a righteousness of our own with which to justify ourselves before God.

The purifying of our consciences by the blood of Christ consists of the removal of our sense of the pollution and just condemnation caused by conscious guilt. Thus, both categories of dead works are eliminated, the first directly and the second because there remains no perceived need for developing and offering our own righteousness. When our consciences are purified, our agonizing sense of guilt ceases to plague our minds. It no longer accuses us with images of our standing guilty before God's court receiving the pronouncement of an eternal death sentence in accordance with God's law. Only the blood of Christ can purify our conscience like this, because nothing else is adequate to satisfy the justice of a holy God and pacify his due wrath. Objectively, Christ's blood actually does this for us, while, subjectively, "with our hearts sprinkled clean from an evil conscience" (Heb. 10:22), we no longer feel dirty, guilty, or condemned, and we no longer have reason to shrink back from his presence.

Christ's blood works to remove guilt where manmade psychology fails, because the cross offers a tangible, historical basis for guilt removal—conscience-satisfying evidence that an all-sufficient sacrifice was rendered on our behalf. In other words, believers in his properly understood and applied priestly representation do not deny that there is a price due for their sin. But they acknowledge that the price was paid by a perfectly qualified priest and sacrifice, one who was appointed by God, lived in a body like ours without sin, and fulfilled the law for us before dying in our place as our substitute. This is the only unassailable basis for obtaining freedom from a guilty conscience.

Therefore, it can be stated unequivocally that those who harbor feelings of guilt either misconstrue the gospel or its application. This is the arena we need to enter in order to help believers and unbelievers alike in their struggle with guilt. They need to know that Christ's atonement was not lacking in any respect. Nothing needs to be added; no sacrifice or righteousness on our part will embellish it. Indeed, it cannot be embellished by anything we do or anything we don't do. God delivered the exact amount of punishment to the Son needed to secure our eternal redemption—no more, no less. To harbor guilt then is to diminish the magnitude of his preeminent, finished work.

One may argue, "But I cannot forget my sin!" This is where Christ's Great Exchange relieves the believer. Remember, we have traded places with him; we have fully entered into the other's position by God's own unilateral action and judicial decree. Christ is our representative; therefore, what he did, we did. So the rebuttal to this common argument follows inexorably along these lines:

- My sin does not attach to me but to my substitute.
- Therefore, the punishment I deserve is no longer mine but his.

- He has already tasted death for me; as he said, "It is finished."
- He obeyed in my place; his perfect righteousness is credited to me.
- Therefore, in God's holy eyes I am already as perfect as Christ himself.
- In my union to Christ, both God and my conscience are pacified.
- All the merit is his, not mine, so I remain forever humble and grateful.
- The work or service I now perform in and for his kingdom is a joyful overflow of and response to his grace.

We become confident that the purifying of our conscience is appropriate when we see that the law suffers no wrong, and the divine attributes of holiness and justice suffer no indignity. We are freed by a substitutionary death that is "much more" than adequate for all our sin.

Furthermore, this death frees us "to serve the living God" (9:14). Having gained a clean conscience and the ability to look God in the eye through Christ's substitutionary atonement, we are now ready "to serve the living God." Clear-conscience serving is necessarily different from guilty-conscience serving in five key aspects:

1) It does not aim to appease God's wrath with personal sacrifice.
2) It does not aim to satisfy God's justice with personal righteousness.
3) It is motivated by gratitude for Christ's death.
4) It looks to God for enablement to serve and receives it.
5) It gives glory to God for any and all results.

Because believers with a conscience purified by the blood of Christ are intimate with God, they see where God is leading them to serve. And because they are serving "the living God," their works are no longer dead but alive, as evidenced by the fruit they bear. As Christ told the disciples:

> I am the vine; you are the branches. Whoever abides in me and I in him, he it is that bears much fruit, for apart from me you can do nothing. . . . By this my Father is glorified, that you bear much fruit and so prove to be my disciples. (John 15:5, 8)

Once our consciences are purified by him, our focus is to remain on him—on abiding *in* Christ. Our focus does not shift to the works or the fruit and definitely not to our own glory. Rather, the fruit is the natural result of abiding in the vine.

Upon his victorious death, Christ established "a new covenant" (Heb. 9:15) between God and redeemed sinners. Within this covenant, God and man are now mutually aligned in amiable fellowship. This covenant is based on the substitutionary death and transferred righteousness of Christ, who is personally its mediator forever.

In fulfilling his role as mediator, Christ continues to claim and apply his blood on behalf of those he represents. As we have already shown, he does this from the throne of his eternal, royal priesthood. And because Christ represents them there forever, "those who are called . . . receive the promised eternal inheritance."

Throughout his letter, the writer of Hebrews makes much of the differences between the old and new covenants, demonstrating that the new covenant is far better due to the fact that it is:

- enacted based on God's oath (Heb. 7:21–22);
- based on better promises (Heb. 8:6);
- brought to bear on the inward man (Heb. 8:10; 10:16).

And as the context of 9:11–14 shows, all these advantages can be traced back to the superior blood of Christ. It is blood that is indicative of a "death that . . . redeems . . . the transgressions . . . under the first covenant" (v. 15). For believers, the substitutionary death of Christ provides redemption for sins committed under the first covenant as well as under the new covenant, that is, sins committed both prior to the cross as well as sins committed after Christ died on the cross. This is yet another way Christ's sacrifice is better than the symbolic foreshadow that required annual repetition.

How does this work for those who never knew the name Jesus of Nazareth? As we have seen, the animal sacrifices did not and could not atone for the moral sins committed by Jewish believers under the first covenant (the old covenant). Those are the sins referred to in this passage, and they are forgiven on the same basis as ours—the blood of Christ. Paul also attested to this fact when he said:

> [All] are justified by his grace as a gift, through the redemption that is in Christ Jesus, whom God put forward as a propitiation by his blood, to be received by faith. This was to show God's righteousness, because in his divine forbearance he had passed over former sins. (Rom. 3:24–25)

The sins God "passed over" consisted of the moral sins committed under the old covenant. Paul shows that believing Jews who lived before Christ are justified exactly the way we are—by union with Christ through "faith"—hence the expression, "in Christ Jesus."

Whereas we look back in time to our historical substitute, they looked forward in time to their promised substitute. To pre-Christ Jewish believers, such as the prophet Isaiah, the impact of the finished work to come on their behalf was as good as if it was already past tense, as demonstrated by this remarkable Old Testament passage:

> But he *was* wounded for our transgressions;
>> he *was* crushed for our iniquities;
> upon him *was* the chastisement that brought us peace,
>> and with his stripes we are healed.
> All we like sheep have gone astray;
>> we have turned every one to his own way;
> and the LORD *has laid* on him
>> the iniquity of us all. . . .
> Yet it *was* the will of the LORD to crush him;
>> he *has put* him to grief;
> when his soul makes an offering for guilt. . . .

> Out of the anguish of his soul he shall see and be satisfied;
> by his knowledge shall the righteous one, my servant,
>> make many to be accounted righteous,
>> and he shall bear their iniquities. . . .
> He *poured out* his soul to death . . . ;
> he *bore the sin* of many. . . . (Isa. 53:5–6, 10–12)

In fulfillment of Isaiah's prophecy, Christ's great atonement displaced and supplanted the old covenant system of atonements and accomplished what they could not—permanent payment for moral sins—past, present, and future—for believers of all times and all epochs.

Hebrews 9:26b–28

> But as it is, he has appeared once for all at the end of the ages to put away sin by the sacrifice of himself. And just as it is appointed for man to die once, and after that comes judgment, so Christ, having been offered once to bear the sins of many, will appear a second time, not to deal with sin but to save those who are eagerly waiting for him. (Heb. 9:26b–28)

The author of Hebrews uses this powerful expression, "to put away sin," after reaffirming that Christ's historical appearance to offer "the sacrifice of himself" is never to be repeated; it is "once for all" time.

By the term "put away sin" the apostle does not mean we are no longer tempted to sin or that we no longer commit sin. Nothing in the immediate and extended context would indicate that. As well, such a rendering would contradict other Scripture (e.g., 1 John 1:8). Instead, the expression is equivalent to "canceling sin," that is, removing its guilt, condemnation, and penalty by applying it to a qualified substitute. Likewise, Paul indicated that our trespasses are forgiven by God's "canceling the record of debt that stood against us with its legal demands. This he set aside, nailing it to the cross" (Col. 2:14). Only when our sin is put away by the sacrifice of Christ do we become free to undergo the process of progressive sanctification.

With regard to mankind, we all have a divine appointment with physical death, an event that happens once. But this passage is focused on spiritual death as the penalty for unforgiven sin. That death, too, happens only once, when after physical death "comes judgment." Christ's sacrificial death was "offered [only] once to bear the sins of many" (Heb. 9:28). And then, immediately after his death, Christ entered into our place in judgment before the throne of God (9:24). And he did not come empty-handed. He came with blood, his own. Nothing remains for us to pay, so nothing remains for Christ to do with respect to our sin, death, and judgment. This is why Jesus, from the cross, uttered with his dying breath, "It is finished" (John 19:30).

All this is in the here and now. But Christ "will appear a second time, not to deal with sin but to save those who are eagerly waiting for him" (Heb. 9:28b). The second advent of Christ will be entirely different from the first, because sin has already been dealt the decisive blow. Christ will not come again as sin bearer because that work is "finished . . . once for all." His final appearance has a distinct purpose: to offer a glorious final salvation where we see him face-to-face. He does this only for a distinct group, "the many," whose sins were borne by his one offering. They are "those who are eagerly waiting for him." They are the blood-bought, conscience-purified sinners Christ redeemed.

Are you eager? If not, look to the cross and believe. Can you hardly wait? If so, look up, "for your redemption draweth nigh" (Luke 21:28b KJV). "For salvation is nearer to us now than when we first believed" (Rom. 13:11b).

Hebrews 10:1–4

> For since the law has but a shadow of the good things to come instead of the true form of these realities, it can never, by the same sacrifices that are continually offered every year, make perfect those who draw near. Otherwise, would they not have ceased to be offered, since the worshipers, having once been cleansed, would no longer have any consciousness of sin? But in these sacrifices there is a reminder of

sin every year. For it is impossible for the blood of bulls and goats to take away sins. (Heb. 10:1–4)

In the same way that a shadow of a man is not the man, the sacrificial system provided under the law lacked substance at its very core. It supplies a mere outline, a shadow of the "good things to come." When we see a shadow, we can trace the light back to the true, real object that casts the shadow. When we do that with the shadow called the Levitical sacrifices of the law, it leads us to Christ's great atonement, the reality, fulfillment, and substance. It leads us to Christ, the only one who really takes away all our sin and perfects us by cloaking us in his own perfect righteousness.

Can animal sacrifices "make perfect those who draw near"? The answer is a resounding, "Never!" For animals do not have a moral righteousness of their own to transfer to us sinners, and thus they cannot cleanse our guilty consciences. But they provide a shadow that serves a divine purpose, leading us to the sinless sin bearer. Only the perfect life and death of Christ provide us with justification, forgiveness, and the resulting permanent position of favor with the holy God. Christ's finished work of atonement provides us with something animal blood never could—God!

If animal sacrifices consisted of substance and not merely shadow, they would have resulted in the true perfection of believers. If such were the case, "would they not have ceased to be offered, since the worshipers, having once been cleansed, would no longer have any consciousness of sins?" (v. 2). In other words, it is impossible to "make perfect" an already perfected believer—if there is no consciousness of sin, why pursue another atoning sacrifice?

But this was clearly *not* the case. Thus, year after year the annual sacrifice was repeated. And year after year the believers held their breath until the high priest emerged from the Most Holy Place alive—indicating that the animal blood provided an acceptable substitute—at least for the past year's ceremonial and unintentional sins. From that point forward, as their awareness of fresh sins began to mount, their thoughts and dependency turned toward the next animal sacrifice. Far from providing a cleansed conscience, instead, "in these sacrifices there [was] a reminder of sin every year" (v. 3).

The consciences of old-covenant believers could only be truly cleansed the same way ours are—by the one true great atonement of their Christ and our Christ. They waited in anticipation; we look back to his single, all-encompassing sacrifice—his personally sinless yet vicariously sinful body nailed to the cross where his blood was shed until he died. They had promises of atonement embedded in foreshadow and prophecy. We have promises of atonement showcased in history. The promises are the same, and they work the same both for those who believed before the cross and for us who look back to the cross—by faith in a substitutionary death by a qualified substitute.

Here, with "It is impossible for the blood of bulls and goats to take away sins," the author reveals that sacrificial animal blood exists merely in the physical and symbolic realms. In the spiritual realm, it has no real value; it is mere shadow. Not so with Christ's sacrificial blood. There are three reasons Christ's blood can take away sins where animal blood cannot:

1) Because Christ truly took on our human nature, something no animal could or will ever do. Thus, he can become the true representative *of man* by stepping into their place with a substitutionary death.

2) Because he lived a perfectly sinless, moral life, also something no animal could or will ever do. Thus, he can become the true representative *of sinners* by providing a substitutionary righteousness on their behalf by which they are "made perfect" in him.

3) Because Christ's blood truly satisfied God's justice—something no mere animal could ever do for any sinner. Thus, Christ paid our penalty in full, resulting in true forgiveness for those he represents.

Furthermore, unlike sacrificial animals, Christ voluntarily came to "do [God's] will" (v. 9). Christ did this in accordance with the agreement he had with the Father from the beginning of time wherein he would die for "everyone whose name [was] written before the foundation of the world in the book of life of the Lamb that was slain" (Rev. 13:8b). In so doing, Christ provided what God desires from us; he provided that which truly pleased God. By virtue of his monumental substitutionary obedience and sacrifice, with respect to the old and new covenants, Christ "abolishes the first in order to establish the second" (Heb. 10:9). Animals can do none of this; they do not enter into plans that call for them to lie down willingly and have their throats slit on behalf of sinners. So once the second (i.e., new) covenant was established by Christ's superior atonement, there was no more use for the first (i.e., old) covenant. With Christ's dying words, "It is finished" (John 19:30), the old covenant was abandoned, abolished. It, too, was finished.

Hebrews 10:10, 14

> And by that will we *have been sanctified* through the offering of the body of Jesus Christ once for all. . . . For by a single offering he has perfected for all time those who *are being sanctified*. (Heb. 10:10, 14)

The all-sufficient offering of Christ has both past and present application to redeemed believers. First, as we noted previously, it sets us apart in definitive sanctification. Second, it has ongoing application as the believer is transformed into the likeness of Christ in the process of progressive sanctification throughout the believer's life.

In verse 14, the apostle also uses the past-tense expression "has perfected" in connection with Christ's same offering on behalf of "those who *are being* sanctified" (in the present progressive tense), thereby incorporating the idea of a finished work by which we are already positionally perfect in God's eyes, even while we are undergoing the process of progressive sanctification in our day-to-day experience. It means that we are becoming what we already are—perfect in Christ. Here, too, we find the answer to an important question. What is the evidence that we are already perfected? Is it that we live a sinless life? No. Instead, the evidence is that we are making progress toward living a sinless life; that we are "bear[ing] fruit in keeping with repentance" (Matt. 3:8). So, in a wonderful paradox, being on the path is proof that we are already there.

The fact that animal blood as sin offering required repetition proved that these offerings were inadequate and merely foreshadows. They were not perfect sacrifices, so they did not perfectly remove sin. In utter contrast, Jesus Christ, by his single, for-all-time offering, perfected his redeemed.

It is safe to conclude, therefore, on biblical grounds, that the doctrine and practice of *perpetual oblation* is in error. In other words, Jesus Christ is not sacrificed again and again as we partake in the sacrament of the Lord's Supper. The offering of the body of Jesus Christ is once for all. To argue against this is to declare his sacrifice deficient for future sins. But Hebrews 10:14 proclaims, "By a *single offering* he has perfected *for all time* those who are being sanctified." If Jesus were to be re-crucified for this week's sins, it would mean that "he would have had to suffer repeatedly since the foundation of the world" (Heb. 9:26a). But the Bible clearly shows that, instead, he "is seated at the right hand of the throne of God" (Heb. 12:2b). And at that throne, he is perpetually interceding, not suffering, for us. The author of Hebrews quotes from Jeremiah 31:

> "This is the covenant that I will make with them after those days, declares the Lord: I will put my laws on their hearts, and write them on their minds. . . . I will remember their sins and their lawless deeds no more." Where there is forgiveness of these, there is no longer any offering for sin. (Heb. 10:16–18)

Since Christ's work of atonement is finished, all the sins of those he represents are forgotten because they are forgiven. And because of this fact, "there is no longer any offering for sin." This proves that the process of "offering" has ended. He has forever discontinued the act of making the sacrifice because its purpose is permanently fulfilled.

This is also a good time to consider the words sandwiched between verses 10 and 14:

> And every priest stands daily at his service, offering repeatedly the same sacrifices, which can never take away sins. But when Christ had offered for all time a single sacrifice for sins, he sat down at the right hand of God, waiting from that time until his enemies should be made a footstool for his feet. (Heb. 10:11–13)

Under the old covenant, the priest's work was never done, and the sacrifices could never take away sins. Under the new covenant, when Christ had offered for all time a single sacrifice for sins, his work was complete, because all the sins his offering atoned for were permanently removed. "But as it is, he has appeared once for all at the end of the ages *to put away sin* by the sacrifice of himself" (Heb. 9:26b). Yes! Christ's great atonement is finished forever. So no wonder we find him seated at the right hand of God, waiting from that time until his enemies should be made a footstool for his feet. Where else would one expect to find him?

Those who are being sanctified are perfected for all time by his single offering. Can it be? Am I perfected forever and ever and ever? Perfected perfectly enough to fellowship with the all-powerful, impeccably holy, creator God, the absolute sovereign one who reigns? Is that not too good to be true? But it is true because of the sheer preeminence of the one who made this infinitely costly, infinitely sufficient single offering, and because we are united to him as our sole representative and hope. He and only he can do this. And he has. Because his offering on our behalf is forever acceptable to God, he has perfected still-sinful believers and made us acceptable to God for all time.

Hebrews 10:19–20

> Therefore, brothers, since we have confidence to enter the holy places by the blood of Jesus, by the new and living way that he opened for us through the curtain, that is, through his flesh. (Heb. 10:19–20)

Everything about this way is new, because it is the fulfillment of what was merely symbolic. An entirely new covenant was ushered in. And everything about this way is living, because Jesus did not remain dead, but he arose as the proof that his sacrifice on our behalf was acceptable. He lives and reigns forever. Jesus "holds his priesthood permanently, because he continues forever. Consequently, he is able to save to the uttermost those who draw near to God through him, since he always lives to make intercession for them" (Heb. 7:24–25).

And because we are represented by such a "great priest [who is] over the house of God," we "draw near with a true heart in full assurance of faith, with our hearts sprinkled clean from an evil conscience and our bodies washed with pure water" (Heb. 10:21–22). Because he and his atonement are overwhelmingly great, not even our consciences can now hold us back from enjoying an intimate relationship with God.

Jesus told the disciples about this way by connecting it with his personal identity. He said, "I am the way, and the truth, and the life. No one comes to the Father except through me" (John 14:6). Yes, he himself is the way, because he himself is the offering. And it is only through his offering that we can ever come to the Father. That's where the way leads. And what could ever be better than that? The end is God himself!

He offered his body (Heb. 10:10), his flesh. It was everything that was required for his entrance into our humanity by which he became our representative, the last Adam. So "his flesh" constituted his sin-bearing humanity and his atoning offering was executed the way atoning offerings are always executed—by dying in the flesh as a substitute for sinners.

The author here equates his flesh to the curtain of the Jewish temple sanctuary—that thick veil that shut sinners out and excluded them from access to God's presence in the Most Holy Place. As long as Christ was still alive in his flesh, his sacrifice had not yet been consummated. But at the very moment his flesh was torn from his soul, that is, upon his death on the cross, Christ actually "opened for us . . . the new and living way . . . through the curtain, that is, through his flesh."

This brings us to something that is so remarkable we are compelled to meditate upon this mystery over and over again. At the precise moment of Christ's death, "the curtain of the temple was torn in two, from top to bottom" (Matt. 27:51). This miraculous event heralded, commemorated, and forever illustrated the entrance of Christ's soul into heaven's Most Holy Place. And because he came carrying the evidence of the infinitely valuable substitutionary death—his own impeccable blood—he pierced right through the heavenly curtain, and the symbolic, earthly, physical curtain tore from top to bottom.

Thus, the way was opened for us; we were forgiven, made holy, and provided with limitless access to God himself by the blood of Jesus and through his flesh. When he entered as our representative, we entered with him into a perfect standing of intimate fellowship with God.

Hebrews 13:10–12

> We have an altar from which those who serve the tent have no right to eat. For the bodies of those animals whose blood is brought into the holy places by the high priest as a sacrifice for sin are burned outside the camp. So Jesus also suffered outside the gate in order to sanctify the people through his own blood. (Heb. 13:10–12)

The Jewish sacrificial system that foreshadowed Christ's great atonement contained two altars, the bronze altar of burnt offering in the court and the altar of incense in the holy place. Hebrews 13:10–12 clearly refers to the bronze altar, one that is also described as a table furnished with both bread and the flesh of slain sacrificial victims. The priests whose job it was to "serve the tent" there had the right to eat portions of certain sin offerings and thank offerings brought to this altar by individual sinners (Lev. 6:16–17; 7:5–6). However, no priest could eat meat from the altar in the case of the burnt offerings; those were to be entirely consumed. Similarly, they could not eat meat from the public sin offering made on the annual Day of Atonement.

As Christians we, too, have an altar. It corresponds to the fore-shadowed one upon which animals were sacrificed as sin offerings. It is the site of Christ's sacrificial death, the cross. Believers may freely eat the flesh of this altar; indeed, they must. For partaking by faith of his representative death constitutes our union with him. As Jesus said:

> "Truly, truly, I say to you, unless you eat the flesh of the Son of Man and drink his blood, you have no life in you. Whoever feeds on my flesh and drinks my blood has eternal life, and I will raise him up on the last day. For my flesh is true food, and my blood is true drink. Whoever feeds on my flesh and drinks my blood abides in me, and I in him." (John 6:53–56)

So the flesh of our altar, Christ crucified, cannot be eaten by those who continue to depend on the law and its foreshadowed system of atonement. In other words, "those who serve the tent have no right to eat" (Heb. 13:10) from Christ; he is not their sin substitute; shadows are. Through his own blood Jesus separated a group of people as his own. This being the case, the author invites all these special, blessed, undeserving people to join him in taking the only logical course of action they can pursue, saying:

> Therefore let us go to him outside the camp and bear the reproach he endured. For here we have no lasting city, but we seek the city that is to come. Through him then let us continually offer up a sacrifice of praise to God, that is, the fruit of lips that acknowledge his name. (Heb. 13:13–15)

Yes, let us go to him. Let us leave this ephemeral city and go directly to Christ. Let us contribute our own offering through him—one of gratitude and praise in recognition of who God is and what he has done.

Hebrews 13:20–21

> Now may the God of peace who brought again from the dead our Lord Jesus, the great shepherd of the sheep, by the blood of the eternal

covenant, equip you with everything good that you may do his will, working in us that which is pleasing in his sight, through Jesus Christ, to whom be glory forever and ever. Amen. (Heb. 13:20–21)

The title "God of peace" is only peaceful toward us because of the priesthood and sacrifice of "our Lord Jesus, the great shepherd of the sheep" and mediator "of the eternal covenant." Because Christ's blood atoned for our sins, God's just anger was turned away, pro- pitiated for us. Appeased and pacified because his holy justice was perfectly and eternally satisfied, he is no longer hostile and alienated; instead, he is friendly and intimate.

All this stands in stark contrast to those items often brought by misguided sinners to God in an attempt to pacify him and cause him to be come peaceful toward them: self-sacrifice, self-abasement, self-loathing, self-righteousness, self-improvement, good excuses, good works, gifts, and service. None of that can begin to change our personal standing before a holy God who is rightfully angry about even a single sin. All such attempts to please or appease God apart from Christ will fail. But the sinless life and sacrifice of Christ succeeded where we could not; and his finished work of atonement on our behalf is all we will ever need to enter and remain in rela- tionship with "the God of peace."

The hard evidence of Christ's success for us in living a perfect life and dying on our behalf consists of this: he was "brought again from the dead." Christ's actual, historical resurrection is indeed the ultimate proof that God is now a "God of peace" toward those Christ represents as the priest of his own sacrifice. Of course, God is now forever peaceful toward the Son. And because of that fact, he is peaceful toward those in Christ—the sheep for which he is the Great Shepherd. It is interesting to note that this is the only time in his letter that the author uses the shepherd metaphor. While he could have used it in many places, he saves it until the end. Perhaps it is for emphasis. Perhaps it is for comfort.

The writer then moves to reestablish a mighty truth—that progres- sive sanctification is only "by the blood of the eternal covenant," as if this fact is worth repeating one more time, lest we forget. He firmly asserts that it is only on the basis of Christ's great atonement that "the God of peace," the great resurrector of "the great shepherd of the sheep," will move to "equip [us] with everything good that [we] may do his will, working in us that which is pleasing in his sight, through Jesus Christ, to whom be glory forever and ever. Amen."

Amen and amen because this means that with Christ as our representative, we are never on our own. He does not leave us to our own devices to transform ourselves into his image by white-knuckled willpower or other expressions of foolish self-sufficiency. He will "equip us . . . to do his will." Furthermore, he will "work in us that which is pleasing in his sight" through Christ. Paul provides similar affirmation, declaring, "I am sure of this, that he who began a good work in you will bring it to completion at the day of Jesus Christ" (Phil. 1:6) and, "for it is God who works in you, both to will and to work for his good pleasure" (Phil. 2:13).

Oh how important, no, how vital, this is! We must embrace and savor this truth about the unbreakable connectedness to God first through the atonement and second to God's own further work in us. Otherwise we risk insulting both the cross of Christ and the power of the Holy Spirit by attempting to do it ourselves, on our own, by our own strength. What pride emanates from such an approach; it robs Christ of his due glory! No! No! No! To *him* be the "glory forever and ever." He deserves it and will have it. We do not deserve it, and we never will. If it were not for his offering, we would be nothing more than condemned criminals like Satan. If not for his ongoing work in us, we would never grow at all. We would never be justified, we would never be sanctified, we would never be glorified. Because Christ died once for all, in our place, as our substitute, he is our boast, our glory, and our sufficiency. He is all we have and all we need.

CHAPTER 18

1 Peter

Although the apostle Peter denied the Lord on the eve of his crucifixion, he was privileged to preach the first evangelistic sermon on the Day of Pentecost (Acts 2:14–41). It was through Peter that the door for the Gentiles to receive the gospel was opened in the home of the Roman centurion named Cornelius (see Acts 10). Peter is known as the apostle of hope the way John is known as the apostle of love. As we will see, this designation comes across in his letters, where the atonement is presented as hope-giving deliverance from both the consequences of sin and slavery to sin.

Peter presents the gospel in the light of its fulfillment of messianic prophecy (e.g., see 1 Pet. 1:10–12; 2 Pet. 1:19–21), and also in terms of his direct contact with Christ. Peter describes himself as "a witness of the sufferings of Christ" (1 Peter 5:1) and an "eyewitness of his majesty" (2 Pet. 1:16). He blended these together—fulfilled prophecy and personal testimony—in a most cohesive and poignant way when he described his firsthand experience of Christ's fulfillment of Isaiah 53:4–11:

> He committed no sin, neither was deceit found in his mouth. When
> he was reviled, he did not revile in return; when he suffered, he did

not threaten, but continued entrusting himself to him who judges justly. He himself bore our sins in his body on the tree, that we might die to sin and live to righteousness. By his wounds you have been healed. For you were straying like sheep, but have now returned to the Shepherd and Overseer of your souls. (1 Pet. 2:22–25)

So it is with unquestionable authority that the apostle Peter sets out in this epistle to strengthen the church by describing its hope in terms of the blood of Christ's great atonement.

1 Peter 1:2

According to the foreknowledge of God the Father, in the sanctification of the Spirit, for obedience to Jesus Christ and for sprinkling with his blood: May grace and peace be multiplied to you. (1 Pet. 1:2)

Peter addresses his epistle to "those who are elect" (v. 1). Certainly, as the one who created time and exists outside the boundaries of time, God the Father knew the individual identity of all of his elect before the world began. This is in precise agreement with Paul, who said, "[God the Father] chose us in [Christ] before the foundation of the world, that we should be holy and blameless before him" (Eph. 1:4).

Peter goes on to say that the elect are "in the sanctification of the Spirit" (1 Pet. 1:2). By this he refers to definitive sanctification—the separation of the elect from the rest of the people to become his own people. The expression "for obedience to Jesus Christ" refers to the obedience of faith, as we have described elsewhere. We make these assertions because of the immediate reference to "sprinkling with his blood." What Peter is telling us here is amazing: believers are "elect . . . by God the Father" to be set apart, to believe, and to be atoned for.

The expression "sprinkling with his blood" is reminiscent of the sacrificial language foreshadowed in the old covenant. It is the language of atonement, the language of transferred guilt, the language of substitution. The blood of Christ, indicative of his atoning sacrificial death, is sprinkled on behalf of those he represents.

They are connected to him by the obedience of faith, set apart by the Spirit as his own, and elect by the foreknowledge of God the Father. How much more secure can a believer be?

Incredibly, though, there is yet another anchor. This "sprinkling with his blood" is attached to a covenant, an irrevocable promise of God. Christ himself both initiated and commemorated this at the Lord's Supper, saying, "Drink of it, all of you, for this is my blood of the covenant, which is poured out for many for the forgiveness of sins" (Matt. 26:27b–28).

It is remarkable then, in light of all this blessing, that Peter would close his salutation by asking for even more by adding, "May grace and peace be multiplied to you." This reflects the fact that Peter knew that the fountain of God's grace is inexhaustible.

1 Peter 1:18–20a

> Knowing that you were ransomed from the futile ways inherited from your forefathers, not with perishable things such as silver or gold, but with the precious blood of Christ, like that of a lamb without blemish or spot. He was foreknown before the foundation of the world. (1 Pet. 1:18–20a)

Given that Jewish Christians constituted Peter's audience, it is not surprising that he alludes to old covenant imagery. Here he recalls the census which Moses took after the exodus from Egypt:

> The LORD said to Moses, "When you take the census of the people of Israel, then each shall give a *ransom* for his life to the LORD when you number them, that there be no plague among them when you number them." (Ex. 30:11–12)

Each person "twenty years old and upward" was required to pay this ransom in the amount of a "half a shekel according to the shekel of the sanctuary," a weight in silver of about half an ounce. Interestingly, this ransom is also referred to as an "offering to make atonement for your lives," thus equating the meaning of the word *ransom* with the words *offering* and *sacrifice* (Ex. 30:13–15). This passage sheds light on Peter's comparison of Christ's ransom of "precious blood" with the foreshadowed ransom of "perishable things such as silver or gold." Peter's use of the word *ransom* also reminded his readers of Christ's statement to his disciples: "The Son of Man came . . . to give his life as a ransom for many" (Matt. 20:28).

In Peter's day, the word *ransom* had a different meaning from the one we have today, as we noted earlier. Back then it was always used in connection with slaves or prisoners of war—a ransom was the price paid to deliver them from captivity to freedom. Thus a redeemed individual was a former captive who had been set free by the payment of a ransom. To ransom is to redeem. Concisely stated, Christ gave his perfect human life and his perfect sacrificial death as a ransom, that is, as a payment made by him to God on our behalf, to free us from the debt we owed to God because of our sin, thus delivering us from the consequences of sin, namely, eternal death.

While this payment began upon our redeemer's incarnation and proceeded throughout his sinless life, the final installment of our ransom was paid upon his death on the cross. Just as a slave was set free only when the ransom was accepted by the owner, likewise, in the court of heaven Christ's redeemed were set free from condemnation and punishment only when the blood of Christ was accepted by God as payment in full on their behalf.

There can be no other way with a holy God. Either he forfeits his holiness and becomes defiled by letting unredeemed sinners go free without a just payment, or an adequate ransom price is paid on our behalf by a qualified representative. Therefore, God must sacrifice his holiness or his Son. And sacrificing his holiness was never an option.

Those who make a metaphor of the ransom by asserting that the cross is merely an example to follow or an idea to emulate deny and demean the holiness of God. In addition, they degrade and devalue the historical incarnation, suffering, and death of Christ. Metaphors are metaphors. Blood is blood. Furthermore, to hold to the teachings of Christ and yet refute his numerous public claims about the significance of his bloody death is to hold to the teachings of a liar. Both of these approaches must be dismissed as repugnant and utter nonsense.

Instead, we hold to the truth revealed in God's Word, which is that a real ransom was paid to secure a real redemption. We have shown that there was an additional subjective component, the cleansing of guilt from our consciences, but that couldn't occur without the solid basis of a real and appropriate payment of a tangible ransom by a qualified redeemer. As priest of his own sacrifice, Christ was both redeemer and ransom. There is no biblical basis for unconditional, unpurchased pardon.

The words ransom and sacrifice are closely related. Both remove penalty—one with money, the other with blood. Both represent a price paid to satisfy the demands of justice and in order to redeem offenders. Thus both are forms of atonement. So it is easy to see the crossover from a money-based ransom to a blood-based ransom. And as Peter will soon explain, this blood is more costly than an infinite amount of silver or gold. Suffice it to say that Christ's substitutionary death can be viewed as both a ransom and a sacrifice. By it, as cause and effect, he accomplished his great atonement and our redemption.

In addition to redeeming us from the price we owed God because of our sin, the precious blood of Christ also ransomed us "from the futile ways inherited from our forefathers" (1 Pet. 1:18). The expression "futile ways" refers to the system of animal sacrifice that the Jewish forefathers depended upon, a system that failed to atone permanently for any kind of sin and failed to atone ever for moral sin. For us today, "futile ways" refers to anything inherited from our forefathers that leads us along a path of attempting to supply our own righteousness rather than to depend upon the perfect righteousness of Jesus Christ.

The fact that we are ransomed means that our old ways will necessarily change. We become the property of the one who redeemed us. We have a new master—Christ. We can never be the same once our lives are touched by his precious redeeming blood. Because once we are made holy by virtue of our union with the Holy One, we enter into the process of becoming in practice what we already are—holy in him.

Peter writes, "If you call on him as Father who judges impartially according to each one's deeds, conduct yourselves with fear throughout the time of your exile, knowing that you were ransomed from the futile ways inherited from your forefathers" (1 Pet. 1:17–18a). Futility. That describes everything that is not connected to Christ's great atonement: the pursuit of our own righteousness in an attempt to satisfy God's justice by our performance, manmade doctrine designed to make us feel self-sufficient or self-justified, the pursuit of a personal agenda designed to maximize pleasure and minimize pain, the overly busy lifestyle preoccupied with temporal pursuits, and the empty lifestyle lost in the purposeless passing of time. All of that fails to see and savor God as the all-surpassing treasure and fails to live in view of our dependency on him. All this is futility.

But Christ offers us redemption from all of these dead-end rabbit trails, false treasures, and broken cisterns that will never satisfy. Redemption—we desperately need it. Money can't buy it, for the redemption we need is far too costly to be obtained in return for "perishable things like silver or gold" (1 Pet. 1:18). We need a lasting redemption, an eternal redemption. God named the price. And God provided the payment in Christ. What else could ransom us if not the eternally valid substitutionary obedience and sacrificial death of Christ, whom God then raised "from the dead" and "gave . . . glory so that [our] faith and hope are in God" (1 Pet. 1:21) and not in our futile ways? Peter describes the blood of Christ as "precious" (v. 19). The value of sacrificial blood is determined by the value of the being that shed it—in this case a Person of infinite value because of who he is—none other than the God-man, Christ himself.

Peter began this epistle by stating that believers are "elect . . . according to the foreknowledge of God the Father" (1 Peter 1:1–2). Likewise, Christ himself was "foreknown before the foundation of the world." Peter's first official sermon on the Day of Pentecost indicated the same. Then and there Peter declared to the Jews:

> This Jesus, delivered up *according to the definite plan and foreknowledge of God*, you crucified and killed by the hands of lawless men. God raised him up, loosing the pangs of death, because it was not possible for him to be held by it. (Acts 2:23–24)

Here we see yet another reason the blood of Christ has infinite value. Christ and his blood were in the mind and plans of God when he created the world through Christ. No other person is like him; no other blood is like his.

1 Peter 2:24

> He himself bore our sins in his body on the tree, that we might die to sin and live to righteousness. By his wounds you have been healed. (1 Pet. 2:24)

The context of this verse shows Peter's instructions to Christian slaves who were suffering ill-treatment and injustice at the hands of their masters. Peter taught, "For to this you have been called, because Christ also suffered for you, leaving you an example, so that you might follow in his steps" (1 Pet. 2:21). But lest his readers misunderstand the purpose of Christ's suffering as one limited to simply providing an example for them to follow, he directs their attention to the ultimate reason Christ's body hung on a cross—his role as sin bearer.

"He . . . bore our sins in his body" (v. 24) conveys the imagery of our sins as a heavy load or burden applied to the body of Jesus. This imagery would have resonated with Christian slaves who knew what it was like to strain under overwhelming amounts of weight. Slaves encountered an inner struggle as well as a physical one. Likewise, the word *body* constitutes all that was encompassed by Christ's entire human personhood—both body and soul.

It was "on the tree" that Christ's sin-bearing, sacrificial death took place. All sacrifices are made by priests, and in this case, the priest was Christ himself. As the priest of his own sacrifice, Christ transferred our sin to the Lamb (himself) and carried the sin-bearing Lamb to the altar (the cross) where the Lamb was slain. Oh, what a tree, what a precious tree indeed, because it was there the precious atoning blood was shed.

And it was shed on that tree in order that "we might die to sin and live to righteousness."

When Peter states that Christ "bore our sins in his body on the tree, that we might die to sin and live to righteousness," he demonstrates that our progressive sanctification is the eventual goal or purpose for which Christ bore our sins in the atonement. The atonement purchased a path on which every true believer experiences growth in personal obedience. The process of progressing along that blood-bought path is woven into the very fabric of God's plan of redemption. It can never be separated from the other great blessings of the atonement, blessings such as justification, forgiveness, eternal life, and faith. None of these blessings stands alone. And as we will be reminded in the next section, there is one ultimate goal of all these blessings: God himself.

"By his wounds you have been healed" is a clear reference to Isaiah 53:5b. In fact, 1 Peter 2:22–25 shows how Christ fulfilled the multifaceted and detailed messianic prophesy of Isaiah 53. Peter offers this reference to prophecy as a proof that Jesus was indeed the sinless sin bearer (Isa. 53:4–6, 8–9b, 11b–12).

1 Peter 3:18

> For Christ also suffered once for sins, the righteous for the unrighteous, that he might bring us to God, being put to death in the flesh but made alive in the spirit. (1 Pet. 3:18)

The context surrounding this key verse on the atonement is a discussion of Christian suffering as a result of persecution (vv. 14, 17). But here Peter shows that the cause of Christ's suffering was not persecution but rather suffering "for sins." Christ "suffered" the punishment of our sins, which culminated in his death. It was because of our sins that Christ suffered and died. The sin that we sometimes regard so flippantly and indifferently actually sent Christ to the cross. Oh, that we might remember this the next time we contemplate giving in to temptation, and instead may we reach out to him for strength to do battle.

Once again we see that Christ did not die simply as a metaphorical example for us to follow. If he did, the expression "Christ . . . suffered . . . for sins" would be preposterous, especially in light of the fact that he had no personal sin for which he had to suffer the consequences. Instead, the meaning of the expression denotes vicarious substitution; the suffering was punishment endured as one on behalf of others.

The phrase "Christ . . . suffered once" could easily be misinterpreted. This expression does not mean that all the penal suffering of Christ was confined to the hours he was suspended on the cross. Instead, it means that there would never be a need to repeat the sacrifice again (as was the case with the Levitical animal sacrifices). Christ's single, all-sufficient atonement has everlasting validity.

Indeed, the suffering of Christ encompassed all of his debasement. It began with his incarnation, in which he lowered himself from a position of equality with God to partake of the limitations of a human body—a baby's body, no less. It encompassed his obedience to the plan and moral will of God the Father during his entire earthly life. His suffering culminated in Christ's "becoming obedient to the point of death, even death on a cross" (Phil. 2:6–8) and ended with Christ's cry of "it is finished." (John 19:30)

When Jesus cried out from the cross, "It is finished," he was making a profound claim: the work of atonement was over forever because all the punishment for all the sins of the redeemed had been fully rendered. Therefore, Christ's priestly work, where he sits on his royal, eternal throne at the right hand of the Father, is no longer an atoning work; it is an intercessory work, a work of mediation where he applies his atoning work to those he makes his own. And when he comes again in glory to reign on earth as King of kings, there will be no new cross, just a magnificent reminder of the old rugged one where he was "put to death in the flesh" when he "suffered once for sins."

In the expression "the righteous for the unrighteous" (1 Pet. 3:18) we have yet another clear, emphatic expression of vicarious substitution. The sinless Christ, the righteous, suffered and died for the unrighteous, the undeserving sinful ones he redeemed by his sin bearing. It was the innocent for the guilty, the pure for the impure, the holy for the unholy. The exchange is unmistakable; it is our sin for his righteousness.

Next Peter reveals the goal of the gospel—the very purpose behind Christ's great atonement. All the other grand and glorious aspects of the gospel are means to this end—"that he might bring us to God." There is nothing that can satisfy us more. There is no greater treasure than God himself. Likewise, there is no better way for sinners made righteous to glorify God than to see and savor him now and forever. Christ paid an infinite price—all for this! Christ brings us to God as the only one qualified to introduce us on friendly terms. He opened the door as priest of his atoning sacrifice on our behalf, and he keeps the door open through his eternal royal priesthood where he intercedes on our behalf.

As a result of his dual priesthood, Christ goes so far as to invite us to join him in calling God "our Father" (Matt. 6:9). Should we not shudder whenever we call God our father, remembering what a blood-bought privilege that is? And should we not continually leap for joy every time we are made aware of God's kind, warm, loving presence or receive anything from his holy hand other than the wrath we deserve? Even when we are disciplined by him, we should not "regard [it] lightly" or take it for granted, for it, too, is a blessing we do not deserve because it is proof of an intimate, family relationship (Heb. 12:5–13).

When Christ "brings us to God" he does it in such a way that the relationship with God lasts forever. We need never fear that God will have a change of heart toward us. Why? Because the person of "Jesus Christ is the same yesterday and today and forever" (Heb. 13:8), and likewise, his great atonement is a finished work, completed "once for all time." God himself initiated the plan, as Peter declared, saying "The God of all grace . . . has called [us] to his eternal glory in Christ" (1 Pet. 5:10). For all these reasons, our reward is sure, our "inheritance . . . is imperishable, undefiled, and unfading" (1 Pet. 1:4).

God himself is our ultimate reward. God is what makes heaven, heaven. Without God, without Christ, heaven would be as unfulfilling as this present world. In the upper room, in a prayer overheard by the disciples on the night before his death, Jesus revealed the meaning of eternal life—it is to know "the only true God and Jesus Christ whom [God] . . . sent" (John 17:3). Then, in a remarkable request, Jesus asked, "Father, I desire that they also, whom you have given me, may be with me where I am, to see my glory that you have given me because you loved me before the foundation of the world" (John 17:24). To know him is heaven; and to be with him is to see his unimaginable glory.

Thus, the picture becomes a little clearer. Throughout eternity, our finite knowledge of his infinite glory is never static; it is always expanding. And since our joy is directly proportional to our knowledge of him, our eternal joy as believers in Christ increases and increases and increases forever. All of this wonder emanates from Christ's great atonement, where he suffered once for sins.

1 Peter 4:1

> Since therefore Christ suffered in the flesh, arm yourselves with the same way of thinking, for whoever has suffered in the flesh has ceased from sin. (1 Pet. 4:1)

Peter again returns to his favorite theme—Christ's atoning death sets us apart (definitive sanctification) for the process of a life of transformation from sinfulness to sinlessness (progressive sanctification). It all starts with Christ's suffering. It must start there, because until his completed atonement is applied to us by faith, we have no spiritual life at all. Jesus clearly implied this when he said, "Leave the dead to bury their own dead, but as for you, go and proclaim the kingdom of God" (Luke 9:60). But when "according to [God's] great mercy, he . . . [causes] us to be born again to a living hope through the resurrection of Jesus Christ from the dead" (1 Pet. 1:3), a whole new life begins in which we grow more Christlike and less sinful.

Our union with Christ in his suffering and death means that we must arm ourselves. What is the weapon with which we must do so? It is a new "way of thinking." This mind weapon is also described by Paul, who writes, "Have this mind among yourselves, which is yours in Christ Jesus." Paul went on to summarize the sufferings of Christ: debasement, servanthood, lifetime obedience, and obedience "to the point of death, even death on a cross" (Phil. 2:5–8).

We, as believers, are one with Christ, and, thus, we are co-crucified with Christ. His death is our death (Gal. 2:20). So we are to embrace this thought pattern and enter into the battle with sin. This is the Christian mindset, the Christian worldview. We are to be atonement-minded as we humbly suffer and serve and obey and die to sin—all of which is connected to Christ's own death. Peter reminds of this connection when he says, "He himself bore our sins in his body on the tree, that we might die to sin and live to righteousness" (1 Pet. 2:24).

In view of this, how should we think about ourselves? Paul said, "You also must consider yourselves dead to sin and alive to God in Christ Jesus" (Rom. 6:11). This is a paradigm shift of the greatest proportions. Peter goes on to show how this applies to our day-to-day life: "Whoever has suffered in the flesh has ceased from sin" (1 Pet. 4:1). Paul made a similar statement: "For one who has died has been set free from sin" (Rom. 6:7). We must understand these life-changing statements in terms of vicarious substitution. In other words, when Christ was "put to death in the flesh" (1 Pet. 3:18), so were we. When we "died with Christ" (Rom. 6:8), we paid our last tribute to our old slave master, sin. Paul said it this way in the book of Romans: "For the death [Christ] died he died to sin, once for all" (Rom. 6:10). Therefore, by virtue of our representation in Christ's great atonement, we are already dead to sin—its guilt, its condemnation, and its penalty.

Dead people don't sin, so why do we sin if we are dead? We have died to the dominion of sin, our previous enslavement to sin as a controlling master. The statement that applies to us, then, is: dead people don't have to sin. As Paul pointed out, "We know that our old self was crucified with him in order that the body of sin might be brought to nothing, so that we would no longer be enslaved to sin" (Rom. 6:6).

A *dominion* is a kingdom. A dominion has a ruler, a king who controls his subjects. We were once in sin's kingdom, under sin's domain. But when we became united to Christ, we changed kingdoms. The Father "delivered us from the domain of darkness and transferred us to the kingdom of his beloved Son, in whom we have redemption, the forgiveness of sins" (Col. 1:13–14). Peter states it this way:

> But you are a chosen race, a royal priesthood, a holy nation, a people for [God's] own possession, that you may proclaim the excellencies of him who called you out of darkness into his marvelous light. Once you were not a people, but now you are God's people. (1 Pet. 2:9–10a)

Thus, our new kingdom has its own King. He is our new ruler. He has set us free from our old ruler so that we are free to obey him instead. We are to "live as people who are free, not using [our] freedom as a cover-up for evil, but living as servants of God" (1 Pet. 2:16). The harmony between Peter and Paul on this subject is remarkable. Paul says, "But now that you have been set free from sin and have become slaves of God, the fruit you get leads to sanctification and its end, eternal life" (Rom. 6:22).

So our death to sin in union with Christ's death to sin in the atonement is the basis for progressive sanctification. Without the cross, there would be no true transformation. By connecting Peter's thoughts in 1 Peter 4:1 and 2, it can be shown that Christ suffered in the flesh so that we can live for the rest of [our] time in the flesh no longer for human passions but for the will of God. Are you struggling to change? Go back to the cross; connect with him there, rest there. And when you get up to leave, never leave the cross or the one who suffered in the flesh.

CHAPTER 19

1 John

The author of this epistle is the apostle John, a fisherman on the Sea of Galilee, who, along with his older brother, James, became one of the original twelve disciples of Jesus Christ. He also penned the Gospel of John, in which he refers to himself not by name but as "the disciple whom Jesus loved." Moreover, he is the author of two other shorter epistles and the book of Revelation. John was intimate with the Savior, as illustrated by his posture at the Last Supper in which he is described as "leaning back against Jesus" (John 13:25). He was the youngest of the apostles, and was the last of them to die.

John does not address this epistle to any particular person or church. Instead, he takes the position of a father addressing his "little children," an expression that appears nine times. He apparently wrote this epistle after writing his Gospel, which dates to about AD 90. It also appears to have presupposed the writings of the apostle Paul since the important controversy regarding the role of the law in the life of the believer is not raised. We can assume it had been settled by the time John wrote this letter.

It is not difficult to conclude from the Scriptures that John had a different temperament and personality from Paul and Peter. Thus, he

263

provides another valuable perspective in his depiction of the atonement. He is known as the apostle of love, because he dwelt on the subject of the love of God throughout his Gospel and epistles. And yet in 1 John, he used the word *propitiation*, a term which takes into account the wrath of God, with greater frequency than Paul.

Like Peter and Paul, John is careful to connect the deity of Christ with the atonement. He refers to Jesus as God's Son twenty-two times in the five short chapters of this epistle. Also like the other apostles, John recognized the importance of atoning blood and vicarious substitution. Furthermore, in the book of Revelation, John refers to Christ as the sacrificial Lamb twenty-seven times. Throughout all his writings, John makes it plain that forgiveness comes directly from the atonement and not from personal law keeping.

John's message to us is a clear one. Concisely stated it is this: that Christ was sent into the world in order to bring sinners back into fellowship with a holy God, who is life and light and love, by removing sin through the provision of his great atonement.

1 John 1:7

> If we walk in the light, as he is in the light, we have fellowship with one another, and the blood of Jesus his Son cleanses us from all sin. (1 John 1:7)

John does not take long (merely seven short verses) to lead us to the cross. But before doing so, he sets the stage by directing our attention to the absolute holiness of God and the fact of man's sin. He does this in a profound way in which he invokes the greatest authority of all by declaring, "This is the message we have heard from him and proclaim to you, that God is light, and in him is no darkness at all" (1 John 1:5). He labels as practicing liars those who claim to be in fellowship with God and yet indulge in unholy conduct that is out of keeping with that union. Also in the context we find an absolute statement, repeated twice for emphasis, clearly pointing to the fact that every single human who ever lived, including believers, has personally sinned: "If we say we have no sin, we deceive ourselves, and the truth is not in us. . . . If we say we have not sinned, we make him a liar, and his word is not in us" (1 John 1:8, 10).

Therefore, it is an undeniable fact that believers frequently stray into the darkness of sin. John tells us that in order to have fellowship with God we must "walk in the light" (v. 7), but that is something we don't always do. All of us knowingly and unknowingly commit sins that cause interruptions in our ongoing fellowship with God. Some sins are blatant and obvious while others are subtle and hidden. But they all amount to walking in the darkness where we "fall short of the glory of God" (Rom. 3:23). Thankfully, God provides the solution in "the blood of Jesus his Son."

Because the person who bled and died is none other than the infinitely valuable Son of God, the blood of his sacrifice is all-sufficient to cleanse believers who continue to be periodically stained by sin. The title "Son" denotes the deity of Christ—Christ *is* God, with all the rights and attributes encompassed as a full-fledged eternal member of the triune Godhead—Father, Son, and Holy Spirit.

At first glance, John may appear to be saying that we have to walk constantly in perfect light before we can be cleansed, a conclusion that would ignore the context of this passage. Instead, the meaning is that when we walk in the light of the truth about the existence of our sin, the continuous application of his blood restores our fellowship with God and with each other because it cleanses our sins away. John's use of the present tense, "cleanses," indicates that as sin is committed and then brought into the light through confession, the merits of Christ's atoning sacrifice are freshly credited to us.

The word *cleanses* here is consistent with the use of the term in Hebrews. It cannot refer to the gradual reduction of the ongoing activity of sin in the life of the believer. Instead, this is a cleansing by sacrificial blood resulting in forgiveness of sin and imputed righteousness. John's use of the quantifier "all" makes this clear. In progressive sanctification we are never experientially cleansed from all sin. However, in definitive sanctification we are permanently, completely, and eternally cleansed from all the guilt, all the condemnation, and all the penalty of all our sins—past, present, and future—because of our union with Christ in his eternally valid substitutionary atonement.

John amplifies this conclusion in verse 9 by referring to the justice of God, to his faithfulness to his covenant promises, and to his act of forgiveness—all expressions about the cleansing of definitive sanctification. To further connect the meaning of verses 7 and 9, John repeats the word "all," stating that he cleanses us "from all unrighteousness." This meaning is consistent whenever atoning blood is mentioned in connection with the term *cleanse*. This was true even for the old covenant animal sacrifices on the annual Day of Atonement, as Moses indicated when he says, "For on this day shall atonement be made for you to cleanse you. You shall be clean before the LORD from all your sins" (Lev. 16:30).

When John says, "the blood of Jesus his Son cleanses us from all sin," he is declaring the amazing truth that those represented by Christ are already seen by God as holy and pure. They are considered to have sinlessness equal to the sinlessness of their representative, the Son of God. And they are restored to fellowship with God and one another. God welcomes them with open arms because of Christ, their sinless, sin-bearing representative. They can say along with John, "Indeed our fellowship is with the Father and with his Son Jesus Christ" (v. 3).

So whenever believers sin, they need only return to the cross and remind themselves of what God already affirms—that before his holy throne, their record is clean; it is expunged as though they never committed a single sin!

1 John 2:1–2

> My little children, I am writing these things to you so that you may not sin. But if anyone does sin, we have an advocate with the Father, Jesus Christ the righteous. He is the propitiation for our sins, and not for ours only but also for the sins of the whole world. (1 John 2:1–2)

The apostle is here taking into account the fact that sin does occur in the day-to-day life of believers. Here again John directs his readers not to a meritorious, man-centered, works-righteousness solution for sin, of which there is none, but rather to God's only true provision for them—their "advocate with the Father, Jesus Christ the righteous." An advocate is someone who presents a legal argument on behalf of and for the benefit of another. Jesus is the advocate of everyone he represents. He is their mediator before the heavenly court of God. He does this by making a judicial claim: his great atonement applies in due force on behalf of all the redeemed sinners he represents. Thus, the past and present ministries of the person of Christ combine to bring massive assurance of salvation to yet-sinful believers.

Christ is qualified to be our advocate before a holy God for two reasons. First, it is because he is "Jesus Christ the righteous" (v. 1). He is both personally and representatively sinless. Second, because in the atonement he himself "is the propitiation for our sins" (v. 2). This passage contains yet another biblical expression of the double imputation seen in the Great Exchange: the wrath owing to our sin is charged to him, and his perfect righteousness is credited to us. This has everything in common with our overarching theme verse for this book: "For our sake he made him to be sin who knew no sin, so that in him we might become the righteousness of God" (2 Cor. 5:21).

Wherever Scripture speaks of Christ's redeeming work, it almost always also speaks of the sinlessness of Christ, not simply as a prerequisite for the atonement but as an essential element of it. Furthermore, only a perfectly righteous one could be the propitiation for our sins. If Christ had sinned even once, God's justice would eternally subject Christ to infinite wrath for that sin. So, in that case, Christ could not propitiate God's wrath toward our sins because he would never be able to first absorb God's wrath toward his own sin. Thankfully for us, no one can justly accuse Jesus Christ of sin—not Pilate (John 19:4), not the intimate and beloved disciple-apostle John (1 John 3:5b), and not God himself (2 Pet. 1:17–18).

In order to come fully to terms with the biblical reality of the wrath of God, we must recognize that it involves more than just punishment; it also involves God's anger, that is, his displeasure expressed as a turbulent emotion. Can the God of love also hate?

Yes. In just one of many examples we can use to illustrate this point, consider God's response when the fallen nation Israel attempted to cover up their sin with ceremonial ritual:

> I hate, I despise your feasts,
>   and I take no delight in your solemn assemblies.
> Even though you offer me your burnt offerings and grain
>   offerings,
>   I will not accept them;
> and the peace offerings of your fattened animals,
>   I will not look upon them.
> Take away from me the noise of your songs;
>   to the melody of your harps I will not listen.
> But let justice roll down like waters,
>   and righteousness like an ever-flowing stream. (Amos
>   5:21–24)

Can you feel his emotion, the vehemence of his repulsion and loathing? Jesus also experienced anger (Mark 3:5; John 2:15–17). And we get prophetic insight into the unfolding of the wrath of Father and Son in another of John's writings, where those who are the object of his anger call out to the mountains and rocks saying:

> Fall on us and hide us from the face of him who is seated on the throne, and from the wrath of the Lamb, for the great day of their wrath has come, and who can stand? (Rev. 6:16–17)

Make no mistake: this is not mythology. The sin of a real creature is visited by the wrath of a real and holy Creator. If we want to deeply understand this truth, we need look no further than the wrath God poured out on his Son, our wrath-bearing substitute. This, too, is not mythology; it actually happened. The events of the passion of the Christ depict real wrath toward real sin—ours. And they depict real propitiation as well. It was severe. It was ultimate. There was excruciating suffering. There was blood and there was death. Worse, there was unbearable separation from the Father. Those elements constituted the only means possible for Christ to deplete God's wrath toward our sin. No excuses will be accepted if we fail to acquire protection under the invulnerable shield of Christ's atoning sacrifice and righteousness. The Bible declares that all men are by nature "children of wrath" (Eph. 2:3). Should we not tremble? And should we not savor as infinitely precious treasure the good news that "Jesus Christ the righteous . . . is the propitiation for our sins"?

How many millions from every tribe, tongue, and nation are united to Christ? Only God knows. And yet, there are definitely millions for whom Christ's atonement does not propitiate, because they do not trust in the sacrifice and righteousness of Christ alone to atone for their sins before a holy and just God.

1 John 4:9–10

> In this the love of God was made manifest among us, that God sent his only Son into the world, so that we might live through him. In this is love, not that we have loved God but that he loved us and sent his Son to be the propitiation for our sins. (1 John 4:9–10)

Here John leads his readers back to the source of the atonement and thus provides a glimpse into the very heart of God—the divine element of love. In his Gospel, John had penned the quotation from Jesus that is perhaps today's most well-known Bible verse, John 3:16. And just as that oft-quoted verse places God's great act of love into the context of condemnation and judgment (John 3:16–19), this passage does likewise—it connects the sending of God's Son with the propitiation of God's wrath toward our sins.

Earlier in the epistle John stated that "God is light" (1 John 1:5), which is a concise way to depict his holiness as part of his essential nature. John now doubly states that "God is love" (1 John 4:8, 16), a concise way to depict the essence and nature and identity of God in his compassion, kindness, and mercy. By saying that God is love, John does not merely present a God who is full of love or a God who has loving intentions; instead, love is what God is. In the same way that holiness is what God is, love is what he is. Furthermore, he is light, and he is love at the same time. These are not attributes he switches on and off. When understood in its full biblical context, it becomes clear that these two massive aspects of God, holiness and love, are not incompatible. Indeed, through the atonement, they are interwoven in such a way as to pale any other expression of beauty ever known or imagined by mankind.

Transcendentalists, New Age spiritualists, and moralists, among others, seek to present a righteousness of their own by making love their god. When love stands alone as a god, it is a mere abstraction, and a relative one at that. We must also be careful not to limit the meaning of "God is love" by thinking of it exclusively in terms of our human experience. God's love is more than affection, warmth, caring, and kindness. When a sinner demonstrates an act of love, it does not compare to God's act of love. Even if a sinner takes a bullet for an absolute enemy, that act of love falls far short—it atones for no one.

Likewise, our use of the phrase "I love you" is at best a mere shadow of the expressions of God's love spoken to us in his Word and during prayer. We may possess love for another, but God *is* love. Love is not merely an attribute of God; rather, love is a fundamental element of his very being. This is not true of any human because of sin. Consequently, in a wondrous paradox, it is precisely because God is holy and sinless that he is love. And therefore, he sent his Son to be the propitiation for our sins.

God's love is not an amorphous sentiment. God's love is an active initiative. God *is* something—love, so he *does* something—love. The epicenter of his act of love is the sending of his Son to be the propitiation for our sins. That deed of his constituted the ultimate act of love. It overcame the single obstacle we faced, an overwhelming obstacle at that—God's holiness and the resulting wrath of God against our sin.

"In this is love, not that we have loved God but that he loved us" (1 John 4:10). Therefore, God did not provide the propitiation for us out of gratitude for our love for him. Besides, as sinners we have utterly failed to love him, because to love him is to obey him (John 14:15), and we have not obeyed. God was not compelled by us to send the Son. Sinners are not in a position to bargain with God. At best, we are merely in a position to beg. And the one thing for which we should beg, God the Father and God the Son have already provided by their own unilateral action. They acted not as a response to anything we do or say, but because of who God is—love. They took all the initiative to provide our propitiation, because it was their own will to express their love in this way in view of God's holiness and our sin.

The second aspect of our living "through him" (1 John 4:9) is our ongoing spiritual and eternal life, the life we carry forward once we are born again. It is an abundant life. John's Gospel records Jesus saying, "I came that they may have life and have it abundantly" (John 10:10b). It is an eternal life: "God gave us eternal life, and this life is in his Son" (1 John 5:11b). It is a life of transformation from futile to fruitful:

> Abide in me, and I in you. As the branch cannot bear fruit by itself, unless it abides in the vine, neither can you, unless you abide in me. I am the vine; you are the branches. Whoever abides in me and I in him, he it is that bears much fruit, for apart from me you can do nothing. (John 15:4–5)

All these blessings are given to us as a result of our union with Christ, a union which is absolutely rooted in and dependent upon Christ's great atonement, apart from which we would remain no more than sinners under guilt, condemnation, and eternal death.

The greatest blessing of the gospel is God—our personal connection with Father, Son, and Holy Spirit in all their glory. Seeing and savoring God brings us true satisfaction, because God is God. Incomparable in all his perfections, the God of immeasurable glory is ours, and we are his in Christ. What blessing in heaven or earth could ever rival that?

How did all this happen for us? It happened because of the atonement, the result of God's great love in action, which, in turn, happened because God is love.

CHAPTER 20

Revelation

The book of Revelation, like 1 John, was authored by the apostle John. It contains John's account of the remarkable firsthand experience he had with Christ during his exile to the island of Patmos at the close of the first century. While it provides a prophetic outline that dramatically displays the ultimate and eternal dominion of Christ over all heaven and earth, John is careful to connect Christ's triumphant reign directly to his atonement. John testifies that he "saw a Lamb standing, as though it had been slain" (Rev. 5:6). This is the first of twenty-nine references to Christ as Lamb, and thus it is clear that every time he uses this term he intends to call our attention to the spotless sacrificial Lamb, the fulfillment of foreshadows, the Lamb of God that bled and died once for all time for the sins of all his own. By his persistent emphasis on Christ as Lamb in the midst of declaring his victorious and glorious reign, John aims to demonstrate that Christ's cross is the foundation of his throne. In fact, in the last chapter of Revelation, the last chapter of the Bible, John twice specifically connects the symbols of the lamb and the throne (Rev. 22:1, 3).

John's emphasis of Christ as the Lamb is not surprising. In his Gospel, John recorded John the Baptist's use of the term (John

1:29, 36). As well, John was taught the meaning of Christ's blood and death as our sin sacrifice by Jesus himself. And he personally witnessed the cross.

In Revelation, John tells us that the Lamb is the one who opens the seals that unlock our glorious future in him (Rev. 6:1). He tells us, "The Lamb in the midst of the throne will be [our] shepherd, and he will guide [us] to springs of living water . . ." (Rev. 7:17). He tells us that it is "by the blood of the Lamb" that we have conquered our accuser, Satan (Rev. 12:11–12). He tells us our names were written "before the foundation of the world" in an amazing book, namely, the "book of life of the Lamb that was slain" (Rev. 13:8). And he tells us that the Lamb is the ultimate conqueror (Rev. 17:14).

In a startling display of prophetic wonder, John records the way the angel connected the Lamb and the church:

"Come, I will show you the Bride, the wife of the Lamb." And he carried me away in the Spirit to a great, high mountain, and showed me the holy city Jerusalem coming down out of heaven from God, having the glory of God, its radiance like a most rare jewel, like a jasper, clear as crystal. (Rev. 21:9b–11)

This holy city, the bride, the New Jerusalem, will have no temple, "for its temple is the Lord God the Almighty and the Lamb" (Rev. 21:22b). It will have "no need of sun or moon to shine on it, for the glory of God gives it light, and its lamp is the Lamb" (Rev. 21:23).

The book of Revelation describes unimaginable glory. It displays the Lamb that was slain as the most glorious person in the universe, and his sacrificial death as the blazing center of his glory.

Revelation 1:5b–6

To [Jesus Christ] who loves us and has freed us from our sins by his blood and made us a kingdom, priests to his God and Father, to him be glory and dominion forever and ever. Amen. (Rev. 1:5b–6)

Early in the book of Revelation, John, the apostle of love, points to Christ's love for us, that is, for those who comprise the church. He then immediately points to his blood as the evidence of that love. This was not mere sentimental love—it was love in action. His love led to shed blood, and his shed blood led to his sacrificial atoning death. By this death, we are freed from our sins. At the moment we become united to Christ by faith, we are permanently released from the guilt, condemnation, and judgment we rightly deserve as sinners.

But, astonishingly, there is yet more, as John proceeds to announce: "Jesus Christ has made us a kingdom, priests to his God and Father" (Rev. 1:6). This statement is reminiscent of the one God told the nation Israel through Moses: "Now therefore, if you will indeed obey my voice and keep my covenant, you shall be my treasured possession among all peoples, for all the earth is mine; and you shall be to me a kingdom of priests and a holy nation." (Ex. 19:5–6). Jesus Christ fulfills these old covenant foreshadows. He perfectly obeyed God's voice on our behalf. We can only imagine exactly what this may mean for us in our future, in an eternity spent with God!

Can it really be that John referred to us when he writes, "They will reign forever and ever" (Rev. 22:5)? Amazingly enough, this is what he meant. He quotes Jesus as saying, "The one who conquers, I will grant him to sit with me on my throne, as I also conquered and sat down with my Father on his throne. He who has an ear, let him hear what the Spirit says to the churches" (Rev. 3:21–22). Do we in today's churches have ears to hear this? We should. For in him we conquer because he conquered our sin and our death. Jesus told the disciples:

> "When the Son of Man comes in his glory, and all the angels with him, then he will sit on his glorious throne. . . . Then [King Jesus] will say to those on his right, 'Come, you who are blessed by my Father, inherit the kingdom prepared for you from the foundation of the world.'" (Matt. 25:31, 34)

Those in Christ share in all that is his. His reign is our reign. Did he not say we would sit with him on his glorious throne? Did he not say his kingdom is our inheritance? And what is the best part of sitting with him on that throne? It is him, just being with him. This is exactly what Jesus prayed for before going to the cross when he asked, "Father, I desire that they also, whom you have given me, may be with me where I am, to see my glory that you have given me because you loved me before the foundation of the world" (John 17:24).

May we never forget for a fraction of a moment that all of this was purchased for us by the blood of Christ's great atonement! May we exclaim along with John, "To him be glory and dominion forever and ever. Amen."

Revelation 5:9–10

And they sang a new song, saying,

> "Worthy are you to take the scroll
>   and to open its seals,
> for you were slain, and by your blood you ransomed people
>   for God
>   from every tribe and language and people and nation,
> and you have made them a kingdom and priests to our God,
>   and they shall reign on the earth." (Rev. 5:9–10)

John reports that in heaven he saw a scroll "in the right hand of him who was seated on the throne . . . sealed with seven seals." And a "strong angel" proclaimed with a loud voice, "Who is worthy to open the scroll and break its seals?" The scroll signifies the unfolding of the future, and John wept because "no one in heaven or on earth or under the earth was able to open the scroll or to look into it" (vv. 1–4).

But then one of the heavenly elders announced, "Weep no more; behold, the Lion of the tribe of Judah, the Root of David, has conquered, so that he can open the scroll and its seven seals" (v. 5). The next statement is astonishing. John sees Jesus, the Lion, the mighty conqueror, and describes what he sees: "I saw a Lamb standing, as though it had been slain." This slain-looking Lamb "took the scroll from the right hand of [God]" and then the most magnificent creatures in all the universe fell down and worshiped the Lamb and "sang a new song, saying, 'Worthy are you to take the scroll and to open its seals, for you were slain, and by your blood you ransomed people for God from every tribe and language and people and nation'" (Rev. 5:1–9).

What made Christ worthy of this grand celestial honor? Was it his inexorable, uncontainable power? No, though he certainly has that power. Instead, it was the fact that the ultimate glory of God had been displayed in his lamb-like, slain body by the blood through which atonement for the sins of the redeemed was made. Therefore, wonder, love, and gratitude for Christ's great atonement are now and always will be the focus of all heavenly worship, as we recall the pit from which we were rescued and the glory to which we were saved. Therefore, no redeemed sinner in heaven will cease, even for a moment, to marvel at what Christ did on the cross. And that is as it should be, for apart from his finished work of obedience there, none of us would be worthy to be found in heaven in the first place. We would get only what we deserved, eternal separation from the glorious Lamb and God the Father.

As history will attest, the blood of the mighty, slain Lamb has had an impact felt around the globe for two thousand years. Starting with the Day of Pentecost through the present day, the life-changing and eternal benefits of his atoning sacrifice have been shared by a vast array of people. Heaven will be populated by the most diverse collection of individuals ever assembled. And every one of them will be there for the same reason—they were ransomed by the same blood of the Lamb's atoning sacrifice.

He unites redeemed believers who might otherwise be at odds because of differences in race and nationality. He bridges language and gender barriers. Jesus ransomed this diverse group of people for God. When he ransomed them, he did not bestow on them individual freedom or independence to do as they pleased. Like the redeemed slaves of ancient times, they were ransomed away from their old owner into the service of their new owner. They now all have the same owner—God. They are all, each and every one no matter their differences, his blood-bought, rightful property, and thus they are irreversibly united together.

They are adopted into the common family to which they all belong—God's. They are brothers and sisters. They may call the awesome Lamb their own brother (Matt. 12:48; Heb. 2:11). And they may call Jesus' Father their own Father. "The one who conquers will have this heritage, and I will be his God and he will be my son" (Rev. 21:7).

The Bible uses two more wondrous images to describe the union of believers that are likewise united to Christ: a single body with Christ as the head and a single bride with Christ as the husband. Oneness like this between people of unprecedented diversity is unheard of in the world. And it is made possible only because of the one Christ, the Lamb that was slain and has paid the ransom for all—in blood. Therefore, all of heaven with one voice calls him worthy!

John writes, "They shall reign on the earth" (Rev. 5:10). What are we to make of that? Can it be that this, too, is an expression of our union? Christ's glory and our reign are one and the same. We reign through him, and he reigns through us. His glory is our glory, and our glory is his glory. Yet all the glory is his, including our glory. All the dominion is his, including our dominion. Were this not in the Bible, it would be inconceivable. To be sure, were it not for the all-sufficient sacrifice and transferable righteousness of Christ, it would be impossible. It is no wonder all creatures of heaven and all the redeemed in heaven and earth will cry out with one voice, "Worthy!"

> Then I looked, and I heard around the throne and the living creatures and the elders the voice of many angels, numbering myriads of myriads and thousands of thousands, saying with a loud voice, "Worthy is the Lamb who was slain, to receive power and wealth and wisdom and might and honor and glory and blessing!" And I heard every creature in heaven and on earth and under the earth and in the sea, and all that is in them, saying, "To him who sits on the throne and to the Lamb be blessing and honor and glory and might forever and ever!" (Rev. 5:11–13)

Yes, glory to "the Lamb who was slain"! Glory in heaven, and glory from all his redeemed. Glory to the sinless one, who for our sake was made to be sin. Glory to Christ; in him, we become the righteousness of God. Glory to him for the Great Exchange: our sin for his righteousness!

Conclusion

Our book, *The Great Exchange: Our Sin for His Righteousness*, has come to an end, but Jesus Christ will never end, and neither will the validity of his finished work of substitutionary atonement on our behalf. We exceedingly rejoice that as redeemed sinners, we have changed places with him forever. Our holy, triune God not only endorses substitutionary atonement, he initiated, executed, and secures it forever. In fact, he devised it before the world began as the ultimate display of his glorious grace whereby instead of getting the curse we deserve, we get God's blessing in its place.

God's plan of substitutionary atonement, our redemption through Christ's blood, is unfolded in the message of the good news on behalf of sinners. It is a message that has stood the test of time thus far, and it will stand on the last day and forevermore, because it is God's own message and God's own plan sealed by his own Son and Spirit. Furthermore, it was by his sovereign authority that Jesus Christ paid the penalty for our sins with the perfect sacrifice and cloaked us with his own perfect righteousness. God's intended purpose for the gospel cannot be suppressed or thwarted because it is all God's own, and he is God.

The Good News of the Gospel: A Review

Marvel at this Great Exchange one last time with us before we close this book.

279

- *We are sinners before a holy God.* We are doubly defiled. First, we are born with a sinful nature like everyone descended from Adam, and, second, we personally commit sin every time we break one of God's commandments. God is holy and therefore his justice must be served. To overlook his justice would be to subvert his holiness, and that is simply not a possibility. Thus, as guilty sinners, we stand condemned, under God's curse, subject to his wrath, and destined to receive the inevitable penalty required by God's law—the punishment of eternal death. Furthermore, there is no hope of redeeming ourselves because there is nothing we can do to make ourselves undefiled or to erase as much as a single sin. In the face of our dire condition as sinners, God planned and acted unilaterally to redeem all those united to Christ by the gospel of grace. Instead of getting what we deserved, we get this good news in its place.

- *God charged our sin to the sinless Christ.* Our sin, along with its condemnation, penalty, curse, and shame is no longer charged to us but to our sin-bearing substitute. The entire wrath of God that we deserve was duly spent, but it was spent on Christ. None of the punishment we deserve from God for our sin is left for us to bear because he bore it all.

- *God credits us with Christ's sinlessness.* Jesus Christ lived a sinless life in a human body, and his obedience is counted as our obedience. In other words, he obeyed in our place and his perfect righteousness is credited to us. Therefore, in God's holy eyes we are already as holy as Christ himself.

- *God's law is doubly satisfied on our behalf.* We who are represented by Jesus Christ in his substitutionary atonement have met the demands of the law in two ways. First, the penalty for our sin required by the law was paid in full by the perfect sacrificial death of our sin bearer. Second, the Sinless One supplied us with the perfect righteousness required by the law, a righteousness we desperately needed in order to be accepted by God. Thus, we are declared not guilty and counted righteous, as though we had never sinned, and as though we had personally performed all of Christ's obedience.

- *We share in our sin-bearing substitute's reward.* As our substitute, Christ lived the way we should have lived—obediently—and received what we deserved—death. In our union with Christ, redeemed sinners received what only he deserved—God himself, including his acceptance, favor, and blessing whereby he welcomes us into his family and forever treats us as his own adopted sons and daughters.

The single source for all of this good news can be traced directly to the cross, the culmination of the substitutionary atonement and the fulcrum of the Great Exchange.

The Indescribable Glory of the Gospel

Our meditations on the cross while writing this book have led to many moments of self-forgetfulness as we get fresh glimpses in Scripture of the infinite value of Christ crucified for our sins, and as we savor the insurmountable weight of the truth and wonder and glory of the gospel. Our intent was to share this with you in hopes that you, too, would join us in seeing and savoring Christ and his cross more and more.

However, we freely acknowledge that our endeavor to portray the central event of all time, and its application to sinners, is at best deficient and incomplete. This is because both of us are inadequate sinners, holding "this treasure in jars of clay" (2 Cor. 4:7), in frail and fallible human minds and bodies incapable of suitably conveying the all-surpassing glory and honor God deserves in the gospel.

> For my thoughts are not your thoughts,
>   neither are your ways my ways, declares the LORD.
> For as the heavens are higher than the earth,
>   so are my ways higher than your ways
>   and my thoughts than your thoughts. (Isa. 55:8–9)

Another reason our descriptions fall short is the limitation of language itself. There are no superlatives adequate to accurately describe the glory of God revealed in the gospel. God, as the creator of language, is infinitely above language. Consequently, our words and phrases and paragraphs fall short of the mark. Consider the word *infinite*. Even that word is inadequate to describe God because God is beyond infinite since he created infinity.

> You have multiplied, O Lord my God,
>   your wondrous deeds and your thoughts toward us;
>   none can compare with you!
> I will proclaim and tell of them,
>   *yet they are more than can be told.* (Ps. 40:5)

Only God's Word and the person of Christ are real and true and infallible; it is there we must pursue mankind's grandest endeavor—attempting to plumb the unfathomable depths of the gospel. This is precisely why there are over one thousand references to Scripture referenced in this book. And this is why the focus of this book is Christ—who he is, what he did, what he's doing, and what he will do.

The Glorious God-centeredness of the Gospel

The Bible tells us, "In the beginning . . . God said, 'Let there be light,' and there was light" (Gen. 1:1–3). Similarly, it is God who said, "Let light shine out of darkness," and then caused that light to shine "in our hearts to give the light of the knowledge of the glory of God in the face of Jesus Christ" (2 Cor. 4:6). And exactly what is this light? It is "the light of the gospel of the glory of Christ, who is the image of God" (2 Cor. 4:4). God created the gospel, and he causes the truth of the gospel to be seen by sinners. The gospel, therefore, is God-centered in its origin and application to individual sinners.

In addition, the gospel is where the glory of God and Christ is revealed by God and seen by enlightened sinners. When we are enabled to behold this awesome glory in Christ in the gospel, we gladly forget ourselves. We are happy to feel inconsequential, and we are thrilled to magnify him.

Just as God created physical light and causes it to shine without the assistance of man, the light of the gospel and its resultant glory emanates from God alone. Redeemed sinners are merely the recipients, the beneficiaries. The gospel is ours only because God gave the Son as our sin bearer and then awakened us to our sin and our need for a qualified sin bearer, the treasure of all time, Christ crucified for us. "We have this treasure in jars of clay, to show that the surpassing power belongs to God and not to us" (2 Cor. 4:7).

To what can the goodness of the promises and assurances of the gospel be compared? Is it like the news that a one-hundred-million-dollar lottery ticket is in your pocket? Hardly. Or is it like a guarantee that you will live a hundred years in health, wealth, safety, security, comfort, and prosperity? No, because a hundred years of the good life is no more than "a mist that appears for a little time and then vanishes" (James 4:14). What is the best news you can imagine as a gift from the hand of an all-powerful God? Would it be an absolute assurance that your family will be happy and enjoyable at every turn with husband, wife, children, brothers, sisters, parents, grandparents? Even this cannot be the ultimate good news, because all those lives must come to an end; all must depart this world alone and face judgment alone (Heb. 9:27), not to mention the fact that no true happiness can be found apart from the riches of Christ. It will all be futile vanity—a chasing after the wind.

What Makes the Good News Good?

There are many, many blessings of the gospel. They are all gifts, and they are all purchased for us by the blood of Christ. We are given complete forgiveness and a clean conscience. We are given deliverance from both Satan's dominion and our previous slavery to sin. We are given hope in the midst of suffering. We are given freedom from the fear of death. We are given access to the throne of grace and to the strengthening power of the Holy Spirit. We are given eternal life in heaven where we receive all that God can give of himself for our ever-increasing enjoyment. There, our knowledge of God will continually expand and, therefore, so will our joy. What could possibly be better than all this good news?

Incredibly, there is more. The best, highest good news of the gospel is that we have God himself; there is no other blessing higher or better or more costly than that. Just think of it: hell-deserving sinners safely in the very presence of an infinitely holy God. And more than safe— welcomed—and more than welcomed—cherished by the most amazing, awesome, creative, fascinating, satisfying, desirable, and delightful being in the universe. His raw power is inconceivable, as demonstrated in his effortless creation of the universe and life. His capacity to love us is immeasurable, as demonstrated at the cross. We have him—right now and forevermore. There is no greater reward or prize imaginable than God.

Our Initial Response to the Gospel

First we must hear the gospel, be awakened to it by God himself and become united to Christ by believing the gospel. In so doing we must abandon, renounce, and utterly forsake any reliance on our own goodness and rely on his alone, "for Christ is the end of the law for righteousness to everyone who believes" (Rom. 10:4). We must strike the death blow to the lie that we are acceptable to God because our good deeds outweigh our bad deeds. We truly believe only when we repent of all self-sufficiency and place all our dependency for our salvation and life in Christ alone.

There are no exceptions; all must come to him this way. Paul goes on to say, "There is no distinction between Jew and Greek; the same Lord is Lord of all, bestowing his riches on all who call on him. For "everyone who calls on the name of the Lord will be saved" (Rom. 10:12–13). Even the faith by which we become united to Christ has its source in the gospel, because "faith comes from hearing, and hearing through the word of Christ" (Rom. 10:17). What is "the word of Christ" if not the gospel?

Our Ongoing Response to the Gospel

Once we have become united to Christ by faith, the gospel continues to impact every aspect of our day-to-day lives. As we describe our response to this impact, it is essential that we keep foremost in our minds and hearts that none of this activity is to be pursued with the intent of earning God's blessings or satisfying God's justice by our own personal sacrifice, merit, or righteousness.

Instead, our pursuits become motivated by overwhelming gratitude for the blessings and acceptance bought by the sacrifice and righteousness of our sinless sin bearer. We are overwhelmed with gratitude because we remain painfully aware that in and of ourselves we are merely bankrupt sinners who are desperately dependent on Christ's finished work of sin bearing. We are overwhelmed with gratitude every time we look God in the eye in prayer or in worship or in fellowship over his Word or with other believers, because we remember that all this is possible only under the banner of Christ's substitutionary atonement. Therefore, every aspect of our response to this grace is motivated by one thing only—to make a joyful demonstration of our gratitude for Christ's substitutionary atonement.

Having said all that, we now offer practical venues in which "we all, with unveiled face, beholding the glory of the Lord, are being transformed into the same image from one degree of glory to another. For this comes from the Lord who is the Spirit" (2 Cor. 3:18):

- Through the gospel, we are to grow in seeing and savoring God. We pursue our own satisfaction and fulfillment and joy in him as we delight in him more and more and desire him above all else. In so doing, we automatically magnify God's glory since we are in essence declaring him infinitely preferable to all other treasures.

- Through the gospel we are to pursue a path of personal obedience. Jesus said, "If you love me, you will keep my commandments" (John 14:15). John said, "We love because he first loved us" (1 John 4:19). Our obedience, then, is an expression of our gratitude designed to bring him glory by calling attention to his love.

- Through the gospel we are to pursue a path of transformation, which includes serving, giving, good works, and the practice of the spiritual disciplines. When these pursuits are rooted in gratitude, God gets the glory, and we get the joy!

- Through the gospel we are to seek to live all of life as an expression of worship in which everything we do, say, and think becomes an offering, a sacrifice of praise. This involves the direct, undiluted declaration of his glory.

- Through the gospel, when our faith falters and we don't desire him, obey him, or worship him as we should, we are to turn to the cross and seek repentance (2 Tim. 2:25) and grace to help in time of need (Heb. 4:13–16). Even this brings glory to God, because it is an expression of our dependency on him and his sufficiency for us.

Here we must emphasize that in all of these pursuits we are totally dependent on God's enabling power. Our ability to grow and transform and perform good works is completely God-centered. We are incapable of any of this apart from the strength and wisdom and grace he provides. This is yet another reason we must insist on transferring all the glory to God for any and all results. In sum, our ongoing response to the good news should consist of gratitude-driven, God-dependent, cross-saturated, humble, joyful attitudes and actions that aim to magnify God's glory and grace.

Loving the Cross

If you are a redeemed sinner, one represented by Christ in his great substitutionary atonement, and if you have understood the biblical passages unpacked in this book, we suspect that, like us, you love the cross. You cannot help loving the cross. In fact, you love it to the point of distraction.

We love the cross this way because there we see the supreme display of the beauty of Christ. There, at the intersection of God's impeccable holiness and perfect love, we observe the glory of God's grace unfold and erupt into a universe-sized kaleidoscope of joy. The joy itself is God himself. He is no longer a God far off but rather a God brought near, because the sin that separated us from him has been borne away by Christ crucified, and we are made holy by Christ's righteousness. This is the Great Exchange, and it culminated at the cross we love. To God be all glory, and honor, and praise. Amen!

An Outline of the Doctrine of the Atonement

No man can ever plumb the full depth of the meaning of the cross. The never-ending riches purchased by Christ's great atonement cannot be enumerated. Therefore, any attempt to put this greatest of all doctrines into outline form will be oversimplified and inadequate. Nevertheless, no subject merits our undivided attention more. So we humbly pursue it, even with desperation and passion, and in that spirit, this outline is offered:

1. The Assumptions Underlying the Atonement
   a. Atonement was necessary because of man's sin.
   b. God's justice, including his wrath against sinners, and God's love for sinners co-exist in perfect harmony at the cross.
   c. The sacrifice must be sinless, and therefore must be God.
   d. The sin bearer must be a man, in order to provide for the possibility of substitutionary death, since God cannot die.

2. The Prerequisites for the Atonement
   a. Christ's *active obedience*: he gave perfect obedience to the moral will of God on behalf of the redeemed.
   b. Christ's *passive obedience*: he endured suffering for the penalty of the broken law on behalf of the redeemed.
3. The Results of the Atonement
   a. Sinners gain freedom from dependence on keeping the law and participating in ceremonies.
   b. Sinners gain a position of acceptance and favor before God including: righteousness, redemption, forgiveness, justification, and reconciliation.
   c. Sinners gain a new relationship to the triune God:
      i. to the Father, as his adopted children;
      ii. to Christ, as his blood-bought property;
      iii. to the Holy Spirit, as his temple.
   d. Sinners gain the privilege of approaching a holy God in worship.
   e. Sinners gain the capacity for experiencing a transformed life.
   f. Sinners gain the ability to be motivated by gratitude for the cross.
   g. Sinners gain a new relationship to men of all nations.
   h. Sinners gain a new relationship to angelic beings.
   i. Sinners gain victory over Satan, the world, and death.
   j. Sinners gain the ability to no longer be mastered by sin.

Notes

Foreword

1. J. I. Packer, *Knowing God* (Downers Grove, IL: InterVarsity, 1973), 182.

2. They have been republished in two fine volumes by The Banner of Truth Trust, Edinburgh and Carlisle, PA.

3. From the hymn "Man of Sorrows" by Philip P. Bliss (1838–1876):

Preface

1. George Smeaton, *The Apostles' Doctrine of the Atonement* (Edinburgh: Banner of Truth, 1991; orig. 1870).

Introduction

1. George Smeaton, *Christ's Doctrine of the Atonement* (Edinburgh: Banner of Truth, 1991; orig. 1870).

Chapter 6

1. Roland H. Bainton, *Here I Stand: A Life of Martin Luther* (Nashville: Abingdon Press, 1950), 49.